To the Line of Fire

NUMBER ELEVEN

C. A. Brannen Series

To the Line of Fire

Mexican Texans and World War I

José A. Ramírez

Texas A&M
UNIVERSITY
PRESS
College Station

FIRST EDITION

This paper meets the requirements of
ANSI/NISO Z39.48-1992 (Permanence of Paper).
Binding materials have been chosen for durability.

Library of Congress Cataloging-in-Publication Data

Ramírez, José A., 1975–
To the line of fire! : Mexican Texans and World War I / José A. Ramírez. — 1st ed.
p. cm. — (C. A. Brannen series ; no. 11)
Includes bibliographical references and index.
ISBN-13: 978-1-60344-136-0 (cloth : alk. paper)
ISBN-10: 1-60344-136-0 (cloth : alk. paper)
1. World War, 1914–1918—Participation, Mexican American. 2. Mexican American soldiers—Texas—History—20th century. 3. Hispanic American veterans—Texas—History—20th century. 4. Mexican Americans—Texas—History—20th century. 5. Mexican Americans—Civil rights—Texas—History—20th century. I. Title. II. Series: C. A. Brannen series ; no. 11.
F395.M5R36 2009
940.4'127308968720764—dc22
2009006180

To Carmen

Contents

List of Illustrations

Illustrations appear in a gallery following p. 74.

Acknowledgments

It is with great pleasure that I recognize those who contributed to the completion of this book. My research was funded almost entirely by the William P. Clements Department of History and Center for Southwest Studies at Southern Methodist University, for whose doctoral program in history this study originally served as my dissertation. I am especially grateful to the members of my dissertation committee—Drs. John R. Chávez, Benjamin Heber Johnson, Jerry D. Thompson, and David J. Weber. In his role as advisor, Dr. Chávez guided this project throughout its duration, and I thank him for his patience and wise counsel. Also helpful were Drs. Edward F. Countryman, S. Lynne Stokes, Roberto R. Heredia, Linda Vance, and Emilio Zamora, as well as Fred Morales of El Paso, Col. Thomas Brown of Laredo, Kathryn Kenefick of the Center for American History, Mitch Yockelson of the National Archives II, and Mary Lenn Dixon and Thom Lemmons at Texas A&M University Press. In one way or another, these individuals, along with the history faculty and graduate students at SMU, allowed this book to come into being. Finally, the members of my family—especially my wife Carmen, daughter Abby, and parents Juan José and San Juanita Ramírez—merit the most appreciation for their love and support. *Mil gracias a todos.*

Introduction

During the summer of 1917, less than two months after Pres. Woodrow Wilson asked Congress to declare war against Germany, José de la Luz Saenz, a twenty-nine-year-old schoolteacher and father of three from Dittlinger, Texas, a small company town in southeastern Comal County, joined ten million other Americans in registering for the first military draft in the United States since the Civil War. Passionate and idealistic, with dark skin and Indian features, Saenz had spent the last several years campaigning against school segregation in Central and South Texas, inculcating cultural pride into his Mexican and Mexican American students at every opportunity. When he was later inducted into the army, he eschewed the military deferment that his wife and young family might have secured for him, regarding military service as a chance to prove his loyalty to his country. Besides, he reasoned, the military contributions of Tejanos to the Great War (as World War I was more commonly known initially) would provide them with leverage for a future civil rights campaign at home. "Let us demonstrate once and for all that we are worthy of fighting for [human] rights," he wrote to his ethnic counterparts, glorifying the overseas mission of the American military in much the same manner as President Wilson, "so that in the future we may be accorded those same rights."[1]

Saenz was one of thousands of men from the Tejano community inducted into the American military during World War I. But not all of these inductees were as upfront about their ancestry as the Dittlinger resident. One such individual was David Cantú Barkley. Born in Laredo, Texas, in 1899 to Josef Barkley, a career army man, and Antonia Cantú, a South Texan of Mexican descent, Barkley acknowledged only his Anglo roots when he enlisted as a private in the army. Fearful that the military might treat him and other soldiers of Mexican ancestry like African American servicemen, whom most officials considered inferior and often assigned to labor battalions instead of combat units, the light-skinned Tejano took every precaution to conceal his heritage in order to serve on the front lines—which he eventually did. Ever distrustful of his superiors, he even warned his mother about using her Spanish surname in their correspondence. "Please don't use the name," he reportedly asked her in one letter.

"Just tell them it's Barkley." With such careful measures, he succeeded in keeping his secret from the military even beyond his dying day, which came on November 9, 1918, a mere forty-eight hours before the signing of the armistice that signaled the end of the war.[2]

I

The wartime experiences of Saenz and Barkley, as well as those of other servicemen of Mexican descent, remain neglected subjects of investigation. That this is so ninety-one years after the close of the war merits consideration. After all, few other topics in the field of American history have generated as large a body of literature as World War I. In fact, the sheer number of books on diplomacy, the military, domestic dissent, aftermath, and other aspects of the war makes it almost impossible to write a comprehensive essay on its historiography. This task has become even less enviable with the recent outpouring of works on the significant but previously ignored roles of minorities and women in the war.[3]

Why, then, have historians ignored the World War I experiences of Mexican-origin individuals? On the one hand, one reason is that most Chicano historians, many of whom objected to the Vietnam War and its disproportionately high Mexican American casualties, have seemingly avoided military topics on the whole.[4] (That said, Chicano history is a relatively young field of study, and there is, of course, the possibility that its few practitioners have simply devoted themselves to other subjects.) Military historians, on the other hand, have probably neglected the topic because of the nature of the sources on Mexican Americans in World War I. The American government did not recognize Mexican Americans as a distinct ethnic or racial group before, during, or immediately after the war. Consequently, the military kept no records of Mexican Americans—whom it categorized as "white"—similar to the documents on African Americans and American Indians. The lack of readily available information on, among other things, the total number of Mexican American servicemen, draft registrants, and casualties has likely kept scholars from attempting any in-depth studies on Mexican-descent soldiers in World War I.[5]

This book is the first extensive treatment of this long-neglected topic. With its exclusive focus on Texas—which, as the state with the largest Mexican population during the 1910s, offers a unique glimpse into the wartime experiences of Mexicans and Mexican Americans—it circumvents some of the problems of the sources, primarily the difficulty of compiling nationwide statistics and information on the aforementioned subjects. It also takes a new military history approach.[6] Instead of generals and their battle plans—the conventional fare of military historians—it examines in the broadest possible manner how World War I affected and changed the Tejano community, and how these developments, in turn, affected and changed America. Like other new military history studies, it posits that because wars do more than just pit human beings against one another in battle, their proper study necessitates a larger and more far-reaching perspective. This means that, in the pages that follow, the home front in Texas appears just as prominently as the battlefields of France; servicemen and civilians—Tejanos and Tejanas—all receive coverage.[7]

In essence, therefore, the study has a twofold purpose: first, to provide with as much fullness as possible an account of the Tejano community during World War I, and, second, to emphasize the importance of the events described therein to history. Through the use of a wide range of published and unpublished sources relating to Mexicans and Mexican Americans, in addition to historical comparisons with the wartime experiences of other racial and ethnic minorities like African Americans and American Indians, the portrait that emerges reveals a relationship between the Tejano community and the U.S. government that was intricate to say the least. It also shows that the war would have implications that extended far beyond the period of belligerency, providing a major catalyst for positive change in the realm of civil rights.

II

It should surprise no one that the Tejano community also felt the tremors of World War I, as this momentous conflict damaged more of the world than any previous war in history. Its consequences were indeed staggering. Nearly ten million men lost their lives in the war. Germany, Russia, France, and Austria-Hungary all lost over a million men. Even the United States, a latecomer to the war, lost 114,000 of its most able-bodied sons.[8] The German, Austro-Hungarian, Ottoman, and Russian empires fell, and, for many countries, so did the Enlightenment culture of the prewar years. In the aftermath of the war, totalitarianism took hold in Russia, Italy, Germany, and Spain, and this, along with newer and more efficient versions of World War I weapons, unleashed the even greater horrors of World War II, turning the twentieth century into the most sanguinary ever.[9] Few re mained unaffected by this catastrophe; the Tejano community was no exception.

Chapter 1 examines the period just prior to the American declaration of war against Germany. As the chapter shows, World War I arrived during one of the most chaotic eras in Tejano history. Like much of Europe, Mexico was suffering from the ravages of warfare. The Mexican Revolution brought thousands of refugees to Texas, revitalizing the Tejano community, but with this benefit also came problems. The political upheaval in Mexico, the intrigue and violence of which sometimes reached American soil, strained U.S.-Mexican diplomatic relations. The participation of some Tejanos—driven by a recent surge in anti-Mexican prejudice—in an irredentist movement known as the Plan of San Diego Rebellion in the Lower Rio Grande Valley only made matters worse. By the time the United States joined the fight overseas on the side of the Allies, the Tejano community was uniquely prepared for the turbulence and flux of wartime life.

This community's answer to the country's call to arms is the subject of the next chapter. Predictably, given their diversity and large numbers, Tejanos were not unified in their response. Thousands of them either volunteered for military service or submitted willingly to the draft. But the Tejano community was not without its share of draft resisters. In most cases, opposition to the draft took the form of flight. During the war, Mexican citizens—as well as some Mexican Americans—fled south of the border in droves. This Mexican Exodus, as it became known, sent panic throughout much of the state, where many principle industries relied heavily on Mexican labor. The chapter discusses the efforts to curtail the exodus and the lasting effect this episode had on the image of the Mexican in Texas.

In order to fully understand how the war affected the Mexican people of Texas, it is necessary to explore more in depth their relationship with the American government (as is done in chapters 3 and 5), which was uneven in nature. Chapter 3 focuses on its darker side. During the tension-filled days of the war, basically anyone was a potential subversive to American authorities. But due to Mexico's deteriorating bonds with the United States and its burgeoning friendship with Germany, to say nothing of the infamous Zimmermann note, persons of Mexican descent came under particular suspicion. The U.S. intelligence community kept a close watch on Tejanos and Tejanas, fearful that German-Mexican collusion could undermine the American war effort from within.

Ironically, as chapter 4 explains, these targets of surveillance were more often than not lending their full support to the war cause. They organized Loyalty Day parades, contributed to the Red Cross, and purchased war bonds and thrift stamps. The artistically inclined, meantime, employed patriotic themes in their works, which included everything from songs to political cartoons. And all the while most of the Spanish-language press in the state maintained a steady drumbeat of prowar advocacy. Of course, not everyone rallied around the flag, but on balance the Tejano community built an admirable record of service on the home front.

The next chapter describes how the military dealt with Tejano recruits during basic training. Unlike African Americans, Mexican-descent servicemen were not segregated in the ranks, which allowed them to interact with troops of varied backgrounds and to take full advantage of the recent changes in the army. During the war, the military was concerned with turning out not only good soldiers but also men of character whom it could later count on to be productive civilians. As a result, Tejanos received instruction in topics as diverse as weapons use and morality. The War Department's adoption of many of the scientific management ideas of progressive reformers, which led it to regard low troop morale as a threat to efficiency, translated into English classes and other special training for non-English speakers, religious services for non-Protestants, and rules forbidding discrimination against immigrant troops. Not surprisingly, the military's latest innovations made for a largely positive training camp for Tejanos.

With the completion of training, most of these troops were off to the western front. There, as chapter 6 illustrates, they helped tip the scales in favor of the Allies. In locations such as the St. Mihiel salient, the Meuse River, and the Argonne forest, they experienced firsthand the horrors of modern warfare, with its machine guns that mowed men down by the thousands and poison gas that made nausea on the battlefield ubiquitous. Most Tejano soldiers served in quiet dignity, but some earned awards for valor from the American military and its European partners. As during training camp, the provincialism of many of these men, more than a few of whom were farm workers and ranchers with little formal education and weak English-language skills, faded during their time abroad.

Following the end of the war, they returned to a hero's welcome. Parades and celebrations followed them from their disembarkation points all the way to their homes in Texas. A few even received preferential treatment from employers in the job market. Now war-hardened veterans, they were less apt to tolerate the poverty and discrimination that continued to plague the Tejano community. For many, social activism would preoccupy their postwar days. Tejano veterans were among the founders and leading forces behind such civic groups as the Order of the Sons of America, the Sons of Texas, the Order of the Knights of America, and the League of Latin American Citizens, which they would later help merge into the League of United Latin American Citizens (LULAC), the oldest surviving Hispanic civil rights organization in the country. Through this civil rights work, chapter 7 demonstrates, these veterans changed the country's social and political landscape forever.

III

It has been over nine decades since Saenz and Barkley signed up for military duty. Despite their relative obscurity, both wound up leaving their mark on Mexican American history. Saenz's diary, which was published along with several additional pieces as *Los México-Americanos en la Gran Guerra: Y Su Contingente en Pro de la Democracia, la Humanidad, y la Justicia* in 1933, is the only extant personal account of a Mexican American doughboy.[10] Saenz would also go on to become a major figure in the Mexican American civil rights movement after the end of the war. Meanwhile, Barkley, who died while on a reconnaissance mission near Pouilly-sur-Meuse in France, was one of only four World War I servicemen from Texas—and, from what we know, the first Mexican American—to receive the Congressional Medal of Honor, the highest award for valor of the United States Armed Forces. Barkley's Mexican origins remained hidden until the late 1980s, when a grandnephew finally divulged the truth about his ancestor to the public. In an ironic twist, given the young Tejano's motive for passing as an Anglo-American, the revelation initiated a series of events that led to a 1989 ceremony at the San Antonio National Cemetery—Barkley's final resting place—honoring the World War I hero as a member of the select group of Hispanic Medal of Honor recipients.[11]

To a large extent, the contrast between these two very different men—recurring characters in this study—reflects the multifarious nature of the Tejano community's World War I experience. The Mexican people of Texas responded diversely to the war and, as it turns out, received inconsistent treatment from the American government, whose military dealt fairly with them even as the intelligence community cast a suspicious eye in their direction.[12] By the time the belligerent powers agreed to a ceasefire, Tejanos and Tejanas had emerged from the crucible of war a people more capable of coping with the inequalities prevalent in American society. This is their story.

A final note to the reader: This book employs the term "Tejano" (and its female equivalent, "Tejana") to describe any Texas resident of Mexican extraction—regardless of nationality—although, when necessary, it identifies the citizenship of certain individuals or groups. By extension, the term "Tejano community" refers to the entire Mexican-descent population in Texas, including non-U.S. citizens.

To the Line of Fire

CHAPTER ONE

Prelude

WHAT WAS HAPPENING IN THE TEJANO COMMUNITY DURing World War I? Any study that proposes to answer this question must deal not only with the period of American involvement in the war but also with the thirty-three months that preceded it. From the beginning of the war on June 28, 1914, to April 6, 1917, when the United States finally joined the fray, the Tejano community was in the midst of change and instability unlike any since the days of the Texas Revolution of 1836 and the U.S.-Mexican War of 1846–48. As economic transformation heightened anti-Mexican prejudice in South Texas, the Mexican Revolution was sending refugees, intrigue, and violence across the border. The result was that by the time of the American declaration of war against Germany, Tejanos and Tejanas were as ready as anyone else for the wartime upheaval that lay ahead. Until then, however, local concerns took precedence over foreign ones, even when it came to the largest and most destructive war the world had ever known.

I

As mentioned already, Mexican affairs were largely responsible for ushering in this turbulent new era in Tejano history. Besides triggering the first great wave of Mexican immigration to the United States, convulsions from south of the border put the Tejano community in an awkward position by exacerbating diplomatic relations between the United States and Mexico.

The policies of Porfirio Díaz lay at the heart of these developments. The former general had set about modernizing and pacifying his war-torn country shortly after assuming the Mexican presidency in 1876. Díaz suppressed one revolt after another and, largely through his cooperation with American and other foreign capitalists, produced economic and industrial growth unprecedented in the history of Mexico. As investment poured in from the United States and abroad, railroads and manufacturing plants sprang up all across the country, and the Díaz government oversaw the creation of an agricultural sector capable of raising surplus crops for export abroad.[1]

Nevertheless, the transformation had its downside. The growing influence of U.S. corporate capitalism south of the border, according to scholars Gilbert G. González and Raul A. Fernández, eventually relegated Mexico to the status of "economic colony," with unsettling results for the masses. As the profits of the changing economy mainly went to foreign capitalists and a select group of the richest Mexicans, peasants derived little, if any, benefit from their country's new wealth and actually saw their standard of living plummet. In many cases, this was the result of new land laws that required them to prove ownership of their communal landholdings through legal title, a blatant attempt by Díaz to confiscate "inefficient" village lands for his agricultural and colonizing projects. Without the means to support themselves, landless peasants were forced to seek seasonal migrant work, toil in unimaginably harsh conditions on sprawling haciendas, or immigrate in search of higher wages to the United States, where they were integrated mostly as unskilled laborers into the agricultural and industrial sectors of the American economy.[2]

The events of the 1910s provided even more incentive for Mexicans to flee northward. By then, the Díaz presidency, with its sham elections, intimidation tactics, and occasional use of force to bludgeon critics into submission, had transmuted into a brutal dictatorship. When, in late 1910, a wealthy but democratically inclined landowner named Francisco Madero issued a manifesto calling for a mass uprising against the government, commoners and idealistic aristocrats alike responded with the force of thirty years' worth of pent-up resentment. In a little over two years, Mexico saw Díaz escape to Europe in exile, a properly elected Madero lose the presidency in a coup led by Victoriano Huerta, one of his former generals, and the Mexican Revolution, as this conflagration would come to be known, degenerate into factional warfare.[3]

Initiated during the Díaz presidency, one of the most astonishing demographic shifts of the twentieth century came to pass. By 1930, when the final, lingering effects of the revolution at last faded away, Mexico had lost close to 1.5 million people—roughly 10 percent of its population—to the United States.[4] Desperate to escape the ravages of warfare and, in many cases poverty and political persecution, most of these refugees arrived in the American Southwest. In Texas, the Mexico-born population increased from approximately 125,000 to 252,000 from 1910 to 1920. By the latter year, Mexican immigrants actually outnumbered native-born Tejanos in each of the state's major ethnic Mexican settlement areas except Laredo, where these immigrants were 50 percent of the population, and Corpus Christi, where they made up 35 percent. In El Paso, immigrants composed an incredible 73 percent of the ethnic Mexican population.[5]

Besides engorging it, the new arrivals reinvigorated the Tejano community. Although their numbers paled compared to those of their less fortunate counterparts, many members of the middle and upper classes also found their way into Texas, and with them came new restaurants, grocery stores, pharmacies, and businesses of other sorts. Meanwhile, newcomers of all backgrounds provided Tejano enclaves with a fresh infusion of customs and folklore from the traditional homeland. The Spanish language itself found new life in Texas not only orally but also through the writings of exiled authors, intellectuals, and journalists. Some of these individuals thought of the United States as only a stopover, as with Ricardo Flores Magón, editor of the anarchist newspaper *Regeneración,* who campaigned actively from San Antonio—and then later from Los Angeles—for the total reformation of Mexican society. Others came to stay. For example, Nicasio Idar, whose *La Crónica* rivaled Flores Magón's paper in readership throughout the Southwest, settled permanently in Laredo and concerned himself primarily with the edification of his fellow Tejanos. Their differences notwithstanding, both men, like their transplanted compatriots, significantly enhanced the Mexican presence in Texas.[6]

Of course, the revolution also had its deleterious effects on the state, particularly in that the violence and banditry it spawned often spilled across the border. In February 1916, Secretary of State Robert Lansing reported to the Senate that twenty American civilians and sixteen servicemen had died at the hands of Mexican bandits in U.S. territory from 1913 to 1915.[7] Many of these Americans had either lived or served militarily along the border in Texas. Not surprisingly, state officials had raised cries of alarms years prior to the issuance of Secretary Lansing's report. As early as 1911, Gov. Oscar Colquitt had expressed his concerns to Pres. William H. Taft after stray bullets from a firefight in Ciudad Juárez killed several El Paso residents.[8] Then, in early 1914, he requested permission from the Wilson administration to allow Texas Rangers to pursue a group of Mexicans who had allegedly kidnapped and murdered a Tejano rancher named Clemente Vergara. After the White House had denied his request, Colquitt excoriated the president for his "namby-pamby" handling of Mexican affairs. For years, he argued, "bandits and marauders" from Mexico had invaded Texas soil and committed depredations of all sorts against Americans and their property.[9] A year later, members of the Texas House of Representatives made the same observation in a resolution requesting aid for more federal troops to patrol the border. "Particularly since the factional war in Mexico," they declared, "straggling bands of Mexicans have been crossing the Rio Grande river [*sic*] into Texas for the purposes of plundering the citizens of this State." During these raids, they continued, "American citizens are being ruthlessly taken by these murderous outlaws."[10]

To the further chagrin of U.S. officials, Texas had become a hotbed of clandestine activity, much of which violated American neutrality laws. From the areas on the U.S. side of the border, refugees lent support to a wide array of political and military leaders in Mexico. Madero himself had plotted the overthrow of the Díaz government as an exile in San Antonio.[11] With arms and ammunition now prized in revolutionary Mexico, unscrupulous American soldiers sometimes profited by stealing machine guns from military armories and selling them across the Rio Grande. Meanwhile, a few Texas Rangers were known to trade arms for cattle with revolutionary factions. Gunrunning became a thriving business, with more than a few members of the Tejano community—in many cases the most desperate and underprivileged—joining the smuggling rings that soon prevailed along the border.[12]

By the mid-1910s, U.S.-Mexican diplomatic relations, once so harmonious due to Díaz's encouragement of American investment in Mexico, had reached their lowest point in a half-century. A particular point of contention was that the revolution imperiled the lives and property of Americans not only in the United States but also in Mexico. The anti-Americanism of most revolutionaries—in many cases peons resentful of the privileges Díaz had granted foreign capitalists—made such dangers all the more acute. One American who fell into the hands of a rival faction in Coahuila was allegedly burned at the stake. A different account told of another captive having his American passport pinned to his chest and fired at as a target.[13] The defacement of the U.S. flag that accompanied the murder of John B. McManus in Mexico City—in addition to other similar deeds—confirmed to authorities that these incidents represented deliberate targeting of Americans, not random acts of violence.[14] By the end of 1915, according to one report, a total of 123 Americans had lost their lives in Mexico since the start of the revolution.[15]

As such incidents mounted, President Wilson and many other Americans condemned their neighbors to the south. The idealistic Wilson even refused to grant Huerta official recognition as president of Mexico following the overthrow of Madero, and then worked to bring down the former general. In April 1914, the White House pointed to the mistaken arrest of several American sailors and their commanding officer by Huerta's troops in Tampico, using what should have been a relatively minor incident as an excuse to intervene in Mexican affairs. The sailors' commander demanded a formal apology and a twenty-one-gun salute to the U.S. flag despite the immediate release of the prisoners. In response to Huerta's refusal, Wilson ordered American troops to occupy the port of Veracruz, where Mexican soldiers resisted fiercely for two days. In the end, the downfall of Huerta that Wilson so badly wanted transpired, but the seizure of Veracruz and its bloody aftermath only increased the bitterness between the United States and Mexico.[16]

II

While the fighting raged south of the border, Texas was undergoing a revolution of its very own. With the arrival of the railroad, commercial farming, or agribusiness, replaced ranching as the major industry in many parts of the state—including those with large Mexican populations. The switch altered more than just the economy, influencing how Anglos and Tejanos would interact for many years to come.

The iron rail had first arrived in Texas prior to the Civil War, but railroad construction exploded in the late nineteenth century. Faster, cheaper, and more reliable than wagon freighting, the railroad signaled progress and prosperity to most Texans. Farmers and mine owners seeking previously inaccessible markets for their raw materials undertook a vigorous campaign to lure railroad companies into their state, knowing that this new invention could link even the crudest backwater with major commercial centers worldwide. Some towns offered cash bonuses, while other cities and counties relied primarily on land grants to acquire rail lines. The state eventually handed over approximately thirty-two million acres of public land—an area about the size of Alabama—to the railroad companies. By 1904, Texas boasted ten thousand miles of track.[17]

Some wound up in traditionally Mexican towns. Of these, San Antonio was the first recipient of a rail line, with the Southern Pacific reaching it in 1875. Laredo saw the arrival of the Texas-Mexican Railway and the International and Great Northern in 1881, by which time El Paso had received no less than four railroads—the Southern Pacific, the Atchison, Topeka, and Santa Fe; the Texas and Pacific; and the Galveston, Harrisburg, and San Antonio. Business boomed in each of these towns, and their infrastructures expanded. Most impressively, El Paso went from an isolated West Texas village consisting mostly of a few Tejanos and even fewer Anglos into a hub of railroad, mining, and ranching activity.[18]

Amid this flurry of railroad construction, agribusiness proliferated throughout the state. The days of subsistence farming, wherein crops were raised for personal consumption and sold at market only occasionally, were gradually coming to an end. And so were those of the legendary cowboy, as overgrazing, overproduction, droughts, quarantine laws in the North, and the closing of the cattle trails had taken a deadly toll on the ranching industry. To keep afloat, desperate ranchers often found it necessary to sell off portions of their landholdings. Enterprising farmers from the Midwest and the South pounced on huge tracts of these lands, convinced that the latest irrigation systems and dry farming techniques, as well as the new rail lines in the state, now made intensive farming possible even in the hottest parts of Texas. By 1880, Texans were producing a cotton crop valued at $39 million, and, by the early twentieth century, bumper crops of citrus fruits were making commercial farmers in South Texas a tidy fortune.[19]

The combination of the railroad and the agricultural revolution led to the first great influx of Anglo Americans into Tejano strongholds. In the Lower Rio Grande Valley in South Texas, for example, entire towns with predominantly Anglo populations sprouted overnight. "As if by magic," marveled *La Crónica* on April 9, 1910, "the towns of Mercedes, San Benito, Chapin, Raymondsville, San Juan, Mission and other places have risen in the lower Rio Grande."[20] In 1915, the *Houston Chronicle* also made a note of this transformation, arguing that the recent arrivals' introduction of waterworks, ice plants, electricity, and other elements of "civilized life" into South Texas had made the region "one of the most progressive sections of Texas, and this, too, despite the handicap of a large and ignorant Mexican population."[21]

In time, the politics of the region made the newcomers resent the Mexican population. The newcomers sought publicly financed roads, irrigation projects, and other improvements necessary for intensive farming, but faced steadfast opposition from political bosses and ranching interests, who opposed any measures that would raise taxes for ventures that offered them little direct benefit. As the wrangling intensified, disgruntled farmers denounced political machines and their largely Mexican American electorate, saving their most heated vitriol for the Tejanos who, in their view, served as "ignorant tools in the hands of bosses."[22] Lacking any real understanding of the history or political motivations of these Mexican voters, the Anglo newcomers concluded that the willingness of Tejanos to "attach themselves to any one who may have shown them a kindness" made them a "political menace" that needed containment.[23] Eventually, their wealth and numbers translated into greater influence in the political arena, giving the recent arrivals the means necessary to enact poll taxes, "white primaries," and other discriminatory voting laws. In the process, they effectively disenfranchised Tejanos and secured their place atop the political hierarchy of the state.[24]

The anti-Mexican sentiment engendered by the politics of the region soon carried over into other aspects of society. Between 1907 and 1912, to cite one example, Texas Rangers and other law officers in Cameron and Hidalgo counties killed sixteen Mexicans, whom they invariably accused of resisting arrest; Tejanos, for their part, blamed the officers themselves and argued that the deaths were the result of recklessness and bigotry. Not as sensational but no less cruel was the segregation Mexicans now faced in restaurants, picture shows, and other public places, which increasingly reserved admittance for "whites only." Even the Mexican elite—ever prideful of its "Spanish" lineage—was not spared this indignity. To the newcomers, a Mexican—no matter how wealthy or well-connected—was still a Mexican and thus subject to the same treatment as his less prosperous counterparts. Not surprisingly, the new order embittered many of these privileged Tejanos, accustomed as they were to receiving at least some credit for their European roots from the Anglos of the region. "Since the coming of the 'white trash' from the north and middle west we felt the change," noted one. "They made us feel for the first time that we were Mexicans and that they considered themselves our superiors."[25]

Those old enough to remember the upheaval following the Texas Revolution and the U.S.-Mexican War would have found it impossible to miss its similarity to current events. After all, besides losing social and political status, Tejanos again faced the threat of dispossession. The problems that plagued their community in the past resurfaced. For one thing, property disputes with farmers often resulted in long, drawn-out court cases, meaning that, even when Tejanos won their legal battles, they were usually compelled to part with at least some portions of their landholdings to defray their legal bills. In other cases, the newcomers simply forced landowners off their property, but, more often than not, it was the changes in the local economy that proved the most harmful to Tejanos. With property values skyrocketing because of the new rail lines, taxes turned into an insurmountable financial burden for many, leading to widespread foreclosures and even more sell-offs.[26]

To some extent, the repercussions of these Tejanos' dispossession also coincided with those of their forebears. Many of them, for example, wound up working for the same individuals responsible for their financial difficulties. Yet, whereas the old-timers had simply transferred their duties and skills as *vaqueros* (cowboys) from their own ranches onto those of their new employers, they more often than not found themselves in the unfamiliar—and detested—role of farm laborers. Low-paying, repetitive, and backbreaking, farm work required hour upon hour of hoeing and picking crops. And since one's meager wages depended on the total harvest, pacing oneself was a luxury that few could ever afford. Gone were the days when *vaqueros* and ranch hands could take pride in their horsemanship and stock-handling skills, or, at the very least, when multiple tasks reduced boredom on the job. Now many Tejanos were forced to work in whatever jobs were available, and for people who, in many cases, considered them little more than a source of cheap labor.[27]

III

It was at this time, when deteriorating race relations and foreign and domestic instability were wreaking havoc with their daily lives, that some Tejanos grew restless enough to lend their support to a separatist and irredentist movement known as the Plan of San Diego Rebellion. As a result, the Lower Rio Grande Valley soon became the stage for one of the bloodiest episodes of racial violence in American history.

A revolutionary manifesto of unknown authorship datelined in the small Texas town of San Diego in Duval County, the "Plan of San Diego" called for an all-out war against the United States. As part of its provisions, a "Liberating Army for Races and Peoples" composed of Mexicans, blacks, and Japanese were to execute all Anglo males over the age of sixteen in order to reclaim Texas, New Mexico, Arizona, Colorado, and California, which the plan alleged had been "robbed in a most perfidious manner by North American imperialism." After securing the Southwest for Mexican Americans, Asians would be liberated, the ancestral homelands of the American Indians would be returned, and six states contiguous to the region would be taken to serve as an independent republic for blacks.[28]

Either out of fear of reprisals or concern that Mexican Americans would renege on their promises, few blacks and Japanese actually participated in the rebellion, but the rhetoric and apolitical nature of the revolt made it especially attractive to many Tejanos. At a time when the factional warfare of the revolution had created deep fissures among Mexicans on both sides of the border, the plan invited all Mexicans, regardless of political allegiance or citizenship, to unite behind a common cause. Mexicans and Mexican Americans alike could forget their differences and instead focus on avenging "Yankee tyranny." What was more, despite the ostensible goal of territorial reclamation, the movement eventually became more of a fight against Anglo oppression and a reaffirmation of the dignity of the Mexican people. "Enough of tolerance!" insisted the rebels in a subsequent manifesto known as the "¡Ya Basta!" handbill. "Enough of suffering insults and contempt! We are men, conscious of our acts, and who know how to think as well as they, the 'Gringos,' and who can and will be free; and we are sufficiently well educated and strong enough to elect our own governors, and we will do so."[29]

In the end, of course, the rebels failed in their objectives, but, for several months in the summer and fall of 1915, their actions paralyzed the Valley. The approximately one thousand to three thousand Mexican and Mexican Americans who pledged to the Plan of San Diego, usually organized in paramilitary companies of twenty-five to a hundred men on horseback, destroyed railroad bridges and tracks, killed farmers and their families, and clashed with local posses before making their getaway across the Rio Grande. In many ways, their raids were similar to those that had plagued the border since the start of the revolution, except for the deliberate targeting of farmers and the railroads, the bane of Tejanos in the early twentieth century. From early July to late October in 1915, and then again briefly in June of the following year, the rebels, known among Tejanos as the *sediciosos* (seditionists), destroyed property worth thousands of dollars, shattered the regional economy, and killed or wounded about sixty Anglos.[30]

The racial violence and the discovery of the plan sent shock waves throughout the state. Rep. John Nance "Cactus Jack" Garner, the witty and colorful congressman and future vice president from the South Texas town of Uvalde, was dead serious in his call for a declaration of martial law.[31] No less rattled, the new governor of the state, James "Farmer Jim" Ferguson, quickly fired off requests for more American troops along the border. "I am daily receiving information of acts of theft, robbery and murder all along our border," Ferguson informed President Wilson in an unsuccessful appeal for an increased Texas Ranger force. "It has been only a few weeks since two of our rangers and one of your river guards were killed by Mexican bandits in the line of action on our territory."[32] Terror struck the farmers of the region. A few days following the first attacks, many of them left the rural areas for nearby towns, where they felt there was security in numbers. There, they organized home guards and patrolled their areas nightly. By August, though, their inability to curtail the raids led many to quit the Valley. Some fled north to Corpus Christi at the mouth of the Nueces River, whereas others left the Lone Star State altogether, opting instead to return to their native soil in the North and Midwest.[33]

To some extent, though, the fears were overblown. Despite the enormous property damage and disruption of day-to-day life that the *sediciosos* caused, the human cost they inflicted on their enemies was hardly staggering. Ultimately, and lamentably, their quixotic mission wound up triggering a terrible wave of violence against persons of Mexican descent, with Anglo panic translating into a murderous backlash by Rangers, local officers, and civilians whose death toll far exceeded anything the rebellion had theretofore wrought.

The killings commenced a few days after the first Plan of San Diego raids. On July 24, in the small town of Mercedes, sheriff's deputies shot two suspected raiders for "resisting arrest," the traditional standby for trigger-happy law officers. Less than a week later, outside of nearby San Benito, armed men lynched another Tejano, in this case seizing the suspect by force from two Texas Rangers who were transporting him to a Brownsville jail to await trial. When neither incident elicited criminal charges for the murderers or disciplinary action for the Rangers, vigilantes crawled out of the proverbial woodwork.[34] They were bolstered in their enterprise by English-language papers, such as the *San Antonio Express,* which decried the use of "half-way methods" to pacify the border,[35] as well as the *Lyford Courant,* which actually went so far as describing lynch law as "never a pleasant thing to contemplate" but "sometimes the only means of administrating justice."[36] By September, the *Express* was reporting that "the finding of dead bodies of Mexicans, suspected for various reasons of being connected with the troubles, has reached a point that where it creates little or no interest."[37]

In reality, no one of Mexican ethnicity, regardless of whether or not he or she was a real suspect, was safe from the backlash. Relatives of suspects, persons whose names sounded similar to known raiders, and even those who simply lived near the site of raids all fell to assassins' bullets or mob rule. Although officials reported only about one hundred Tejano deaths, the discovery of buried skeletons with bullet holes in their skulls years later suggests that some scholars' estimates of a number in the vicinity of five thousand is more accurate.[38]

As a result of these atrocities, many Tejanos were torn about the Plan of San Diego. Whereas some took pleasure in seeing Anglos suffer for a change, they nonetheless lamented that it was the innocent and defenseless members of the Tejano community who bore the brunt of the gringos' retribution. Interestingly, some actually attempted to absolve Mexican Americans of any participation in the rebellion and laid the blame for the violence entirely on "true-born" Mexicans, as in the following *corrido* (folk ballad) called "Los Sediciosos" (The Seditionists):

In this place called Norias, it really got hot for them;
  A great many bullets rained down on those cursed *rinches* [Texas Rangers]

Now the fuse is lit by the true-born Mexicans,
  And it will be the Texas-Mexicans who will have to pay the price.

Now the fuse is lit, in blue and red,
  And it will be those on this side who will have to pay the price

Now the fuse is lit, very nice and red,
  And it will be those of us who are blameless who will have to pay the price.[39]

Understanding their vulnerability, many Tejanos aimed to cooperate with Anglos. The residents of the small, predominantly Mexican hamlet of San José, for example, appealed for protection from the U.S. Army on the basis that they were "good Mexicans," thus distancing themselves from adherents of the Plan of San Diego. Similarly, in San Benito, about one hundred Tejanos voluntarily turned over their arms and ammunition to local officials, an extraordinary move considering that they were leaving themselves virtually defenseless at a time when innocent Mexicans were often targets of vigilante violence. The townsfolk were issued receipts for their rifles, shotguns, and pistols, which were to be stored in a bank until the troubles subsided.[40]

Others simply fled. On September 11, 1915, a little over two months after the first Plan of San Diego raids, the *San Antonio Express* reported that Mexican families were moving south of the border in droves, an act that, given the upheaval in Mexico, suggested the desperation of the refugees. Automobile passengers driving into Brownsville, it noted, told of spotting as many as nine moving families within an hour's ride.[41] With them, they took "their horses, mules, wagons, household furniture, farming implements, chickens, cows, and, in fact, all their effects which could be moved,"[42] though out of necessity leaving behind their lands, houses, and even untended crops. Eventually, the exodus left entire areas of the region depopulated, causing a severe labor shortage and leading some farmers to call for the importation of African American workers from East Texas and outside of the state. During September and October, over seven thousand Mexicans and Mexican Americans evacuated Cameron and Hidalgo counties—a number amounting to about half of the ethnic Mexican population of both counties.[43]

IV

Events in Mexico finally led to the end of the rebellion and its even gorier reprisals. But the turmoil along the U.S.-Mexico border was by no means over. As it happened, one form of unrest was simply replaced by another.

Since his overthrow of Madero, Huerta had been besieged by challengers from every part of the country. The most serious threat came from the so-called Constitutionalist Army, a coalition of northern forces under the leadership of Venustiano Carranza, the governor of Coahuila. After Huerta's own downfall, the revolution entered its most chaotic period, as the Constitutionalist Army splintered among the followers of Carranza and the *Villistas,* who supported Francisco "Pancho" Villa, a rebel leader from Chihuahua. With designs on the Mexican presidency, Villa courted the Wilson administration, even refusing to utter a single word of criticism publicly against its actions in Veracruz. The United States, for its part, initially supported him against Carranza, with the press depicting the Chihuahua native as the heroic, horse-riding leader of the downtrodden masses. Eventually, though, the White House was forced to switch sides after the *Villistas'* disastrous defeat by Carranza's forces at the battle of Celaya in April 1915. On October 19 of that year, with Villa seeming less and less likely to ever regain his former strength, Wilson swallowed his pride and recognized Carranza, the only leader who appeared capable of uniting Mexico and finally bringing peace to the beleaguered country. In return, Carranza obliged the White House's request to crack down on the *sediciosos,* who had always used the northern state of Tamaulipas as a refuge and staging ground for their attacks. With so many Tejanos having left the Valley to avoid its rampant vigilantism—thus depriving the rebels of another means of shelter and support—and with Constitutionalist regulars on their tracks, the rebels were essentially contained by late in the fall. The backlash petered out shortly thereafter as well, and, save for one last, unsuccessful rebel uprising in June 1916, the race war in the Valley had finally ended.[44]

Soon, though, other parts of the border fell into turmoil. Enraged by his betrayal at the hands of the American government, Villa vowed revenge. On January 10, 1916, his forces, under the command of Col. Pablo López, took action. After stopping a train of the Mexican North Railway Company near Santa Ysabel, Chihuahua, 240 miles south of El Paso, López ordered sixteen American passengers off the train and promptly had them executed.[45] A few weeks later, on March 7, Villa himself led an army of five hundred soldiers in an attack on Columbus, New Mexico, a small town sixty miles west of El Paso. Once the smoke had cleared, seventeen Americans, mostly civilians, lay dead. It had been the first attack by a foreign army on American soil in over a hundred years.[46]

Villa's actions sparked a wave of outrage among the American public. Although only one of the numerous Mexican raids into American soil since the start of the revolution, the attack on Columbus was deemed especially outrageous because it was comparatively large and led personally by an important Mexican leader.[47] "Villa must be suppressed," declared the *New York Times*. "His villainous activities must be stopped for all time, and we must do it."[48] Its cross-town counterparts were no less irate. "Nothing less than Villa's life can atone for the outrage at Columbus, N.M.," blustered the *World*. "Every drop of American blood shed at Columbus is on his hands." The *Tribune,* meanwhile, blamed Wilson almost as much as Villa for the attack. "The administration," it argued, "has evaded a duty to Americanism long enough. If our flag, our escutcheon and our diplomacy are to mean anything again south of the Rio Grande Villa and his followers must be rounded up by our troops and made to pay the penalty of their hideous crimes against American citizens."[49]

In Texas, no stranger to raids, the outpouring of anger and indignation paralleled that of the rest of the country. "No self-respecting nation," wrote the *Houston Post,* "can endure forever what this nation has endured in Mexico and in our own territory at the hands of Mexican outlaws." The *San Antonio Express* called on Wilson to end the "long reign of brutality" and take Villa "dead or alive." The *Dallas Morning News* concurred: "The time has come . . . when United States troops should be sent into Mexico and kept there until they have either captured or killed Villa and dispersed his force." If Carranza objected, it stated bluntly, "his protest ought to be disregarded."[50]

In the face of this rising tide of jingoism, the Wilson administration reluctantly agreed to another Mexican excursion, although opting for a limited intervention instead of Sen. Albert B. Fall's call for an army of a half-million men to occupy Mexico. After reassuring a reticent Carranza that its only objective was to secure Villa, the White House sent a punitive expedition, under the command of Brig. Gen. John J. "Black Jack" Pershing, across the border into Mexico on March 15, less than a week after the Columbus raid.[51]

As it turned out, nothing went right for the expedition, and within months its actions brought the two countries to the brink of war. The problems began immediately, as Carranza, expecting a few American soldiers, was troubled to learn that the invasion force actually numbered over five thousand men. Pershing and his men quickly grew tired and frustrated with Villa's elusiveness and the hostile reception they received from the locals, but Carranza's worries nonetheless multiplied as their expedition increasingly took on the look of an occupying army with every mile that they penetrated deeper into Mexico and every additional soldier that they received as reinforcement. On April 13, following an encounter between a detachment of American troops and several Mexican soldiers that left several dead on both sides, Carranza finally demanded the withdrawal of the expedition, which Wilson promptly refused.[52]

By late May, things had spun completely out of control. Carranza ordered his troops to resist any further American reinforcements and to block the expedition from moving in any direction but northward. Wilson answered by sending warships to both Mexican coasts and calling practically all of the National Guard, a force of about one hundred thousand men, to protect the border. On June 21, tensions erupted in violence yet again after an American party attempted to overpower a Mexican detachment assigned to prevent their advance. Instead of giving way, as the Americans expected, the Mexican troops stood their ground. The melee, later known as "the Carrizal affair" after the town that served as the battleground, left thirteen Americans dead and another twenty-four prisoners; the Mexicans, no less ailing, reported twenty-nine casualties.[53]

Although a full-blown confrontation seemed imminent, it never came. Neither side truly wanted war. On the one hand, Carranza was well aware that because his countrymen were at each other's throats, Mexico could not effectively resist its more powerful neighbor. And

Wilson, for all his belligerence, had never wanted anything other than for the Mexican people to enjoy the blessings of democracy; he had simply been too patronizing to allow them to attain it for themselves and too quick-tempered to disregard even the slightest affront. A few days after the bloodletting at Carrizal, however, the American Union Against Militarism, a pacifist organization, convinced the president to dispatch a delegation to meet with Mexican representatives in El Paso to discuss the recent troubles. The move was a success. On June 26, the United States admitted publicly that American forces had been responsible for Carrizal. Two days later, Carranza reciprocated by releasing the American prisoners taken in the battle. More discussions ensued in the following months, and, on January 19, 1917, the White House finally decided to withdraw the failed punitive expedition. Villa would alas go unpunished for his deeds in New Mexico, but the United States would at least avoid an unnecessary and fruitless conflict.[54]

Not surprisingly, the antagonism between the two countries had impacted the Tejano community. The huge number of guardsmen stationed along the border had been particularly disconcerting for many Tejanos. Besides erecting tents and digging trenches, the troops had counted among their daily tasks the searching of Mexican homes for hidden weapons.[55] While some Tejanos welcomed the protection they offered, others decried their unprofessional behavior, which included shady business dealings and thievery.[56] Following the Columbus raid, as well as two others in the Texas towns of Boquillas and Glenn Springs shortly thereafter, racial tensions reached a fevered pitch in the Big Bend area. Many Anglo residents abandoned their homes and sought refuge in nearby settlements as rumors circulated that several of the raiders were members of the Tejano community.[57]

V

Another motive prompted the removal of Pershing's forces from Mexico. Since 1914, World War I had divided Europe into unprecedentedly large military factions, with Germany, Austria-Hungary, and the Ottoman Empire, the so-called Central Powers, on one side, and Great Britain, France, Russia, and several other countries that called themselves the Allies on the other. In an effort to cut off American supplies to Britain and break the bloody stalemate of the war, the German high command had recently decided to resume its policy of attacking all vessels—neutral or otherwise—in the vicinity of enemy ports with its deadly new weapon, the U-boat, or submarine. As Britain's chief trading partner and the harshest critic of unrestricted submarine warfare, the United States decried the move, noting Germany's recent pledge to suspend such attacks after sinking the British liner *Lusitania* and the French cross-channel ferry *Sussex* while killing or injuring over one hundred innocent American passengers in the process. With the specter of war now looming, Wilson had decided that catching and punishing Villa was no longer as important as preparing his forces for an overseas engagement.[58]

Mexico soon became entangled in the German-American estrangement. For several years, Germany had been trying to curtail American shipments to the Allies by inciting Mexican leaders against the United States and provoking a Mexican-American war, as such a conflict would likely tie the Americans down in their own hemisphere and reduce their exports of arms and other supplies. Germany's inability to do so had contributed to its resorting to submarine attacks, but the momentum had swung in German favor after the launching of the punitive expedition. Since Carranza now feared that a war with the United States was not only possible but likely, he had begun to strengthen his ties to Germany as a means of protecting his country.[59]

The result directly triggered America's entry into World War I. Cognizant that its naval policies would probably drive the United States to the Allied cause, German foreign secretary Arthur Zimmermann sent a telegram offering Mexico the lost territories of Texas, New Mexico, and Arizona if it took up arms against its neighbor to the north.[60]

Intercepted by the British in January 1917 and made public to the world a few weeks later, the Zimmermann note created a nationwide uproar. The issue of unrestricted submarine warfare, with its debates about neutral rights and freedom of the seas, was one thing; for most Americans, a great many of whom had never even set eyes on a seacoast, this was now proof positive that Germany was not only antagonistic and lawless, but also intent upon attacking them directly. If the country until then had largely been against involvement in European conflicts, the mood had changed perceptibly.[61] "The issue shifts," stated the *Omaha World Herald,* "from Germany against Great Britain to Germany against the United States."[62] For its part, the *Sacramento Bee* inveighed against Germany's "treacherous enmity" and "underhanded, nasty intriguing."[63] Even the *New Republic,* hardly the organ of firebrands and warmongers, now vilified

Germany, calling its war against the Allies "a war against the civilization of which we are a part."[64]

In Texas, editorial condemnations of German "lawlessness," "brutality," and "inhumanity" proliferated in the days following the discovery of the note. Echoing the sentiments of the *Republic,* the *Dallas Morning News* called the German government the "blight on the world's civilization" and referred to its offer to Mexico as the final "unprovoked act of aggression" against the United States.[65] But Germany was not the only target of the Texas press. Despite Carranza's assurances to the contrary and the reluctance of the White House to challenge him publicly, the *Houston Post* speculated that Mexico was most likely a willing accomplice in this high-stakes game of international intrigue. "We may find an enemy closer to us than any European power," wrote the newspaper in an editorial that surely made its readers of Mexican descent cringe with discomfort. "War upon the fields of Texas is not beyond the powers of the imagination. Home guards may be needed."[66]

The gauntlet had been tossed. Despite much deliberation, the president unsurprisingly agreed to ask Congress for a declaration of war against Germany. On April 2, 1917, a somber Wilson addressed a joint session on Capitol Hill. "The world must be made safe for democracy," he pronounced, elevating the significance of his country's quarrel with Germany. "We shall fight for the things that we have always carried nearest our hearts,—for democracy, for the right of those who submit to authority to have a voice in their own governments, for the rights and liberties of small nations, for a universal dominion of right by such a concert of free peoples as shall bring peace and safety to all nations and make the world itself at last free."[67] On April 4, the Senate approved the war resolution by the overwhelming margin of 82 to 6. Two days later, the House of Representatives responded with a vote of 373 to 50. The president signed the resolution the following day, making it official that America was now at war.[68]

In the wake of the declaration of war, the Spanish-language press joined its English-language counterpart in supporting the Allied cause, though its conformity appears to have been, at least in part, a means of deflecting the charges of disloyalty and lawlessness that editorials such as those of the *Houston Post* were sure to bring. Its about-face was dramatic. Immediately following the discovery of the Zimmermann note, the Laredo daily, *Evolución,* which was owned and edited by Nicasio Idar's son Clemente and similar to *La*

Crónica in political orientation, had derided the "vacuous" patriotism of many Americans and their often hallucinogenic Germanophobia, alleging that "the German is now the ghost writer of any calamity in America." By early April, however, the imminence of a declaration of war had the Laredo paper unquestioningly praising all things American—a stance that would prevail for the duration of the war—and calling for more amicable ties between the United States and Mexico.[69] Similarly, San Antonio's *La Prensa,* a Mexican exile daily belonging to middle-class immigrant Ignacio E. Lozano, first labeled the news stories of German-Mexican collusion in the American press as yellow journalism, but in the weeks leading up to the war adopted a pro-Allied stance and went about portraying Mexico as the innocent recipient of aggressive German overtures. With story after story detailing the extent of German deviousness and headlines like "Germany Won't Rest until It Makes Mexico Its Ally," it likely hoped to save the Mexican people of the Lone Star State from a xenophobic backlash.[70]

VI

The years leading up to America's entry into World War I were thus years of volatility for the Tejano community. With the advent of commercial farming, Tejanos again faced dispossession, political disenfranchisement, and racial violence—travails that paralleled almost identically those of their antecedents in the mid-nineteenth century. Not only that, they found themselves in a precarious position as the violent byproducts of the Mexican Revolution led to tense diplomacy and saber rattling between the United States and Mexico. Due to a recent influx of Mexican immigrants, the Tejano community was as large and diverse as ever. As the United States prepared for war in Europe, it stood to reason that this heterogeneity, as well as the events of the last few years, would affect this community's wartime actions. How exactly remained to be seen.

CHAPTER TWO

The Call to Arms

THE CALL TO ARMS THAT FOLLOWED THE DECLARATION of war against Germany elicited varied responses from the Tejano community. Like other citizens, Mexican Americans demonstrated patriotism, but also disloyalty. The Mexican nationals who lived among them were no less divided. While some joined the American colors voluntarily or at least submitted willingly to the mandates of the Selective Service Act, thousands of others—even many who qualified for draft exemptions—fled across the Rio Grande to avoid military duty.

I

The Mexican Exodus, as the Texas press called this development, commenced soon after the start of the war. By mid-April, Brownsville authorities were counting daily an average of eight to twelve wagons loaded with Mexican citizens heading south of the border. One area farmer reported losing fourteen of his Mexican laborers in one day.[1] Similar reports surfaced in Laredo, where officials identified their border town as a major exit point for Mexicans who had been working in the interior of the state and the areas between Webb and Nueces counties. By early May, U.S. immigration officers in Brownsville had reported the departure of approximately three hundred Mexican families. According to their accounts, one man even transferred his entire house—a small, two-bedroom abode—across the international bridge.[2]

Around the same time, however, many others in the Tejano community were rallying in support of the war effort. On April 9, 1917, a volunteer corps consisting of over one hundred young Mexicans and Mexican Americans in Kingsville, forty miles southwest of Corpus Christi, offered its services to the American military during a local Loyalty Day parade. In its report on the festivities, *La Prensa* noted approvingly that the youngsters "stood ready to battle for the American flag."[3] Many of their counterparts in other towns also volunteered early. In fact, two days before the Kingsville parade, a committee consisting of both Tejanos and Anglo-Americans from nearby San Benito had written President Wilson for authorization to organize a regiment from among its many Tejano volunteers. "Our Mexican-American people have smarted for several years under the suspicion as to their loyalty," read its message, alluding no doubt to the Plan of San Diego and the recent hostilities between the United States and Mexico. "We appeal to you to secure this privilege for our young men to demonstrate their loyalty to the United States Government."[4]

It is unknown whether the committee ever received an answer to its request, but a similar case in Duval County may suggest how Wilson would have replied. There, widespread volunteering among its Mexican people prompted a wealthy rancher and justice of the peace named Felipe García to borrow a page from his neighbors in San Benito. On April 30, he telegrammed General Pershing, whom the White House had recently appointed to lead the American Expeditionary Force (AEF) in the war overseas, to request permission to organize the young men into Spanish-speaking companies. In response, Pershing's office thanked García for his patriotic gesture, but informed him that the army would not be accepting volunteer units.[5]

Ethnic prejudice likely played little, if any, part in García's rejection. Indeed, the White House had only recently turned down a similar proposal from former Pres. Theodore Roosevelt. Hoping to recapture the glory days of the Spanish-American War, the leader of the legendary Rough Riders had sought to assemble and lead a division of volunteers into the battlefields of France. Political reasons had much to do with Wilson's reluctance to grant his still formidable rival such a glamorous assignment, but the recent efforts of the American military to attain the level of sophistication of European armed forces also figured into his decision. Many high-ranking officers now regarded amateur "political" generals and volunteer units as too unreliable and a hindrance to these modernization efforts.[6]

Wilson and Secretary of War Newton D. Baker remained steadfast against volunteer forces even though the military could hardly afford to turn away any willing, able-bodied men in a time of war. (At a mere two hundred thousand troops, for example, the U.S. Army paled in comparison to many of its European rivals.) Determined to fill the ranks of the army without compromising its efficiency, Wilson and Baker insisted that volunteers serve in the Regular Army, which would be enlarged by the creation of twenty divisions to accommodate the new arrivals. Integrated among the regulars, they reasoned, the recruits would profit from the leadership and training of experienced soldiers and officers. Meanwhile, a military draft—the first since the Civil War—would offset any potential shortfall of volunteers caused by the new policy.[7]

Not surprisingly, the implementation of the draft turned out to be the most difficult part of their plan. In Kansas City, police arrested two men for attempting to obtain an injunction to prevent the governor, mayor, and other public officials from enforcing the draft. A similar antidraft measure arose—and failed—in California. In Congress, the president's draft bill faced opposition from states-rights advocates, isolationists, pacifists, and a host of other dissidents. Sen. Robert M. La Follette of Wisconsin, its most vehement opponent, resented the mere presence of such legislation on the Senate floor. "Never in all my years of experience in the House and in the Senate," he remarked, "have I heard so much democracy preached and so little practiced as during the last few months."[8] To make the bill more palatable to critics like La Follette, its authors eliminated some of the most antidemocratic elements of the Civil War draft measure of 1863—iniquities such as bounties, substitutes, and purchased exemptions—and guaranteed that draftees would serve for the extent of the war. Partly as a result, the controversial measure eventually won approval in both houses. On May 19, 1917, the Selective Service Act was officially passed.[9]

Texas, along with the rest of the country, immediately felt the reverberations of the bill's passage. On May 22, authorities in Snyder arrested seven supposed members of the Farmers' and Laborers' Protective Association (FLPA) for allegedly "planning to resist conscription by force." At about the same time, an Abilene man with purported connections to the Industrial Workers of the World (IWW) fell into police custody for antidraft activities.[10] As the month neared its end, the areas along the Rio Grande made national headlines as officials in border towns like Laredo reportedly began nabbing daily between twenty and twenty-five Anglo-American draft dodgers from places as far away as Maine and New Hampshire. Most of the young detainees denied any attempts to escape conscription and instead cited pressing business concerns in the Mexican mining and oil industries as their reason for traveling out of the country.[11]

Regardless of such distractions, the government held three registrations during the course of the war. The first required all men between the ages of twenty-one and thirty-one years to report to their local draft board in June 1917. The second, a two-part event held the following June and August, enrolled those men who had turned twenty-one since the previous summer. Finally, in September of that year, the third registration extended the age limits to eighteen and forty-five years inclusive.[12]

Aliens were also required to register, but only a few were subject to the draft. During the first year of the war, the military conscripted only declarants—aliens who had already applied for American citizenship—from nonenemy countries. However, in July 1918, Congress agreed to exempt declarants from neutral countries like Mexico, as well. The decision left declarants from friendly countries as the sole group of conscriptable aliens during the last few months of the conflict.[13]

Eventually, a total of twenty-four million citizens and noncitizens registered for the draft, allowing the military to amass a wartime contingent of roughly 3.5 million men—a force consisting of about 2.8 million conscripts and over seven hundred thousand volunteers. In Texas, the rallying call found a ready audience. By the end of the war, almost one million men, including about eighty thousand Mexican citizens and thirty thousand Spanish-surnamed natives, had registered in the state. Altogether, 197,000 residents of the Lone Star State served in the military during the war. Of these, approximately five thousand possessed Spanish surnames.[14]

The recruitment effort was a rousing success for the White House. More specifically, it was a coup for the judge advocate general, Enoch Herbert Crowder, whom Wilson had appointed as provost marshal general and placed in charge of the Selective Service System soon after the passage of the draft bill. Long a student of wartime conscription, General Crowder had resolved to avoid the mistakes of the disastrous Civil War draft, whose inefficiency and corruption had set off widespread, even riotous, protests. In 1920, he could boast—albeit with a touch of overgeneralization—of having successfully transformed "conscription in America" from a "drafting of the unwilling" into a practice in which the "citizens themselves had willingly come forward and pledged their service."[15]

His overarching strategy had been simple but effective: remove conscription's image as an imposition of an autocratic military by tying the long-reviled procedure to traditional American ideals of loyalty to country and civic duty. Toward that end, his agency entrusted civilian volunteers with full responsibility for the management of draft boards. It also obtained the enthusiastic support of state and municipal organizations, local chambers of commerce, and private citizens from all walks of life. Together, they relentlessly promoted the draft as a barometer of American patriotism.[16]

Their efforts paid off. On June 5, 1917, the first registration day,

Americans all across the country celebrated as though they were observing a national holiday. Some towns hired bands to regale their registrants; others held parades. Everywhere, townsfolk cheered on their young "patriots." It was, in the words of draft expert John Chambers, "one of the first successful exercises in mass compliance through propaganda, hoopla, and peer pressure."[17]

Despite—or, perhaps more accurately, because of—these efforts at social control, Tejanos participated eagerly in both the duties and the merriment of registration day. Laredo attorney Juan V. Benavides, son of Civil War veteran Col. Santos Benavides, the highest-ranking Mexican American to serve the Confederacy, served as chairman of the Webb County Draft Board. Meanwhile, in several precincts in El Paso County, Tejanos served as chief registrants, clerks, and interpreters. Their community also contributed a Mexican American band to the El Paso registration day parade. Under the direction of Reymundo S. Gonzales, the musical group marched behind the El Paso Women's and Girls' Rifle Club and ahead of the display of the Daughters of the American Revolution. The most gripping story of the day, however, came from Brownsville. There, a patriotic oration by Brig. Gen. Charles G. Morton compelled an elderly Tejano to cross the international border into Matamoros, Mexico, to retrieve his two draft-dodging sons and have them register.[18]

The following day, *La Prensa* issued a proclamation titled "To the Line of Fire, Mexican-Texans!" Its author, former mayor Amador Sánchez of Laredo, exhorted the Tejano community to contribute men to what he called a "holy war in defense of the liberty and welfare of the entire globe." It was an impassioned message. "If the enemy is ferocious and cruel," the eloquent Sánchez argued, "it shall be a greater triumph to defeat them, for it is more of an honor to fight with lions than with lambs." A master motivator, Sánchez appealed not only to his readers' courage but also to their filial piety. Discussions about the country's manpower needs segued neatly into paeans to wives, children, and mothers with "gray, sacred manes." He concluded with a reference to history. "The future," he predicted, "will know that we fulfilled our obligation, that we sacrificed everything we could on behalf of our country and our fellow man."[19]

The war enthusiasm of Tejanos like Sánchez persisted for the duration of the conflict. In fact, many of their stories were featured in the Texas press, which likely hoped to inspire similar patriotism in other Mexican Americans. The *Corpus Christi Caller and Daily Herald,* for instance, ran an article on Francisco Hernández Jr. of San Diego, who contributed all three of his sons to the war effort. As the paper noted, the three Hernández boys were continuing a military tradition in their family begun by their grandfather, Francisco Hernández Sr., a veteran of the Civil War.[20] Likewise, Oligario Rodríguez's gusto landed him on the pages of the *Laredo Weekly Times.* After members of the draft board in his native Laredo informed him that he had been called mistakenly, Rodríguez reportedly brushed off the error and volunteered to serve. "You might as well take me now," the *Times* quoted the young Tejano as saying. "I am willing to fight for my country and am willing to put on a uniform right now. Let me take the place of someone whose mother would cry for him—I have no mother." The next day, he presented his letter of recommendation from the board to the commander at nearby Fort McIntosh and formally enlisted in the army.[21]

Another subject for these pieces was that of the privileged youngster who was willing to leave behind his comfortable surroundings to fight for his country. Perhaps the most celebrated of such cases belonged to José Antonio Navarro, who was profiled in both the *San Antonio Express* and the *Laredo Weekly Times.* A member of one of the most distinguished Mexican American families in Texas, Navarro was a graduate of the University of Texas and held the position of city auditor in San Antonio at the time of his enlistment in the 1st Texas Infantry. Both newspapers waxed poetically about the young Tejano's patriotism and compared it to that of his "illustrious" grandfather of the same name, who eight decades before had been one of only three Mexicans to sign the Texas Declaration of Independence. The younger Navarro, wrote the *Express,* was "eager to don the khaki and to fight for the State and nation for which his ancestors sacrificed, fought and suffered."[22]

In addition, newspapers were seemingly eager to highlight instances in which Mexican citizens volunteered to fight on behalf of their adopted homeland. On May 6, 1917, the *Laredo Weekly Times* recounted a dramatic encounter that had occurred the previous afternoon between a Mexican volunteer and Webb County Deputy Sheriff M. G. Benavides. "Are you registering men for the United States army service?" the young man reportedly asked. "Yes," replied Benavides. "Are you an American citizen?" "No," he responded. "I came from Mexico, but I want to join the army when the soldiers are enlisted in Laredo." After Benavides reminded him of the seriousness of such a move, he countered, "The best way for a man to gain citizenship in a country is to fight for the flag of that country. Put me down on the list and notify me when my services are wanted." In a later article on Martín Castillo, another Mexican citizen who volunteered for military duty, the *Times* declared, "These are the kind of men that the United States army wants—volunteers of that type who will make good loyal fighters and be entitled to recognition as a good American citizen [*sic*]."[23]

The patriotic fervor made an impression even on some of the youngest Tejanos. In a 1976 interview, Luis O. Varela, who was nine years old when the United States declared war on Germany, remembered proudly how his immigrant father supported the war effort and remained in the country to register for Selective Service—unlike many other Mexicans in their West Texas hometown of Clint. Almost sixty years after the end of the war, he still kept as a memento the card his father received from the board, a certificate given to all registrants to serve as proof of their compliance with the draft laws. Another young Tejano, Conrado Mendóza of El Paso, tried to register on June 5, 1917, despite being underage. Although told that the military "had little need for children," Mendóza harbored no ill feelings about his rejection, as a few months later a German submarine torpedoed a troop transport carrying many of his older and newly inducted friends, none of whom survived.[24]

Although the draft functioned smoothly for the most part, problems were not altogether uncommon. For instance, a mishap with the mail translated into jail time for Hermenegildo Domínguez, who registered for the draft in his hometown of Rockdale in Central Texas but moved soon afterward to nearby Calvin in search of employment. Because the post office delivered his draft summons to his former residence, Domínguez never knew of his conscription until authorities arrested him as a draft dodger in October 1917.[25] The aforementioned José de la Luz Saenz, who also moved shortly after registering, faced a comparable ordeal despite having provided his new address not only to the post office but also to the sheriff and county judge in his native Comal County. After waiting fruitlessly for a draft call, Saenz wrote Washington directly to offer his services, which prompted a polite but stern reply informing him that the Selective Service System had already issued him a draft summons months earlier. Only the foresight he displayed in notifying more than one office of his change of residence spared him from the legal hassles of draft delinquency.[26]

Sometimes, however, blunders carried more than legal consequences. Such was the case with Florencio Heras, a railroad worker from the small South Texas town of Alfred. Early one morning in 1917, officials apprehended Heras at his home, confusing him with a draft dodger of the same name who had recently fled the neighboring town of Benavides. Despite Heras's claims to the contrary, his captors remained convinced of his draft dodging and insisted that he register immediately. At only nineteen years of age, Heras was technically ineligible for the draft, but relented to their demands after his employer threatened to dismiss him from his job. Never able to prove his true identity, the youngster eventually found himself in the U.S. military, which sent him across the Atlantic toward the trenches of France in February 1918. Sadly, he never completed the voyage, as his troop transport fell victim to a German submarine.[27]

Maximiliano González of Martindale in western Caldwell County suffered a fate no less unjust. Seventy years of age, poor, and nearly blind, González was living with his sons Filomeno and Simón—his only caregivers—at the time of the United States' entry into the war. Not long after the conscription of Filomeno, another letter from the Selective Service System arrived at the González household, this time a draft summons for Simón. The elder González beseeched the local draft board to exempt his younger son on grounds of dependency and severe hardship, but his requests, however well founded, fell on deaf ears. Undaunted, he took his case directly to Simón's superior officers, whom he surprised one afternoon by showing up at Camp Travis in San Antonio, the last fifty cents in his pocket having gone to the young boy who served as his guide. Again rebuffed, the determined septuagenarian nonetheless persisted in his efforts for several months, but ultimately succumbed to hunger and neglect. Not long afterward, the tragedy was made twofold by Simón's death in France.[28]

While Saenz, who knew the Gonzálezes personally, attributed their troubles to ethnic prejudice, calling Martindale "one of those towns that is most unjust to our people," it is just as likely that Simón's denial of an exemption by the Caldwell County draft board stemmed from legitimate, though nonetheless unfair, grounds. This presumption is based on responses the elder González allegedly elicited from board members, who, according to Saenz, dismissed the old man by telling him that his son would be better able to provide for him with a military salary than with the meager earnings of a day laborer. As historian Jeanette Keith has pointed out, in July 1917 General Crowder attempted to lessen the number of draft deferments awarded on the basis of dependency by deeming as unqualified those draftees whose pay as servicemen would suffice to support their dependents. In so doing, the general made it all but impossible for most poor Southerners like Simón to obtain exemptions, as few earned the one dollar a day or more necessary to match the thirty dollars minimum monthly salary of a serviceman. Since most Mexicans and Mexican Americans in Texas worked in relatively unprofitable occupations like farm work and day laboring, it is thus probable that this portion of the draft laws played just as much—if not more—of a role than bigotry in scuttling many of their applications for dependency-based exemptions.[29]

Through most of the war, the presence of large numbers of nondeclarant aliens from Mexico also created problems for the residents of the state. Because the Selective Service System based quotas on total population, citizens and declarant aliens in places with many nondeclarants were forced to supply a disproportionately high quantity of draftees.[30] Some, like the editorial staff of the *Laredo Weekly Times,* vented their frustration over this injustice at the government. "The fault of the whole affair does not lie with . . . exemption board[s]," it argued, "but with the lack of the reasoning faculty on the part of some of the federal officials."[31] Others, however, misdirected their anger at Mexican nondeclarants, in some cases classifying them intentionally as Class I-A, the category most subject to the draft. One misclassified nondeclarant, a resident of Fort Bend County by the name of Angel Pérez, was assigned to the same ill-fated troop transport as Florencio Heras and, like his fellow conscript, destined to perish before even reaching France because of a German submarine (see chapter 6 for more on this episode).[32]

In any case, the Tejano community, like other ethnic groups across the country, earned praise for its contribution of manpower to the war effort. "A gratifying feature of the entire campaign for recruits is the response of the . . . young men of Texas birth and Mexican descent," editorialized the *Laredo Weekly Times,* which invoked the memory of the Civil War in its eulogy. "They have lived up to the traditions of their fathers and grandfathers who responded so gallantly . . . in the sixties, and there is no question that they will be among the men whom we shall delight to honor when the war is over." The paper also acknowledged the contributions of Mexican citizens. Many of these immigrants "offered their services," it claimed, "feeling that they owed a duty to the country where they have been living for years past, and to the liberty which is the watchword of their own country."[33]

Of course, Mexican citizens had other reasons for volunteering. As demonstrated by Deputy Sheriff Benavides's interviewee, some aliens joined the military to prove their worthiness for American citizenship.[34] In other cases, however, their motives were not unique to unnaturalized immigrants. Young men of all sorts of backgrounds—citizens and aliens, whites and nonwhites alike—entered the military out of a sincere belief in the righteousness of President Wilson's mission to spread democracy across the globe, as well as love and gratitude toward the United States—their native or adopted homeland.[35]

The war also offered an opportunity for adventure and a hero's return home. To a young Tejano like Pete Leyva, an impetuous teenager who had never wandered far beyond his native Presidio in West Texas, joining the navy seemed like the perfect way to find excitement and see other parts of the world. "I volunteered," he remembered years later. "I was just big enough and old enough to go. I went over there [to his local recruitment office] and says [*sic*], 'I want to go, and I'm going to war,' because I liked it; I wanted to go some place."[36] For his part, Frank Delagoa of San Antonio resigned from a well-paying job as a telegraph operator to help "lick the Kaiser," indicating that American propaganda likely played as much of a role as straightforward thrill seeking in his decision to enlist in the army.[37]

For other Tejanos, their second-class citizenship provided an additional set of motives, incentive that they shared with other persecuted peoples. Like the multiethnic committee from San Benito, Saenz recognized that many Americans mistrusted anyone of Mexican descent. He too regarded the war as a chance for his people to prove their loyalty to the United States and, in the process, earn their rightful place as full-fledged American citizens. Such plans resembled those of many African Americans—even the most ethnically militant like W. E. B. Du Bois—who also hoped to redeem the respect they gained from their wartime contributions into civil rights advancements after the end of the conflict. The plans also bore similarities to those of British colonial subjects. "The gateway to our freedom is situated on French soil," Mohandas K. Gandhi told his fellow Indians, urging them to support the war effort on behalf of the British. "If we could but crowd the battlefields of France with an indomitable army of Home Rulers fighting for victory for the cause of the allies, it would also be a fight for our own cause."[38] Saenz recorded comparable sentiments throughout his diary, but perhaps nowhere else more movingly than in a piece titled and addressed "To Our Government":

> Our sacrifice in battle is the ultimate act of protest against a determined group of petty citizens who have never been able to rid themselves of their racial prejudice against our people, and there are many places in Texas where such hostility is deeply marked,

> where we are denied social consideration and good schools for the education of our children.
>
> We firmly believe that the trials of war will change many previously hostile opinions, and God willing this will bring the justice and recognition that we deserve. . . .
>
> As we fall in battle, we only hope for justice. . . .[39]

Ethnic pride also fueled Saenz's desire to fight abroad. The fiercely patriotic schoolteacher believed that the Mexican people belonged to a "warrior race" and hungered to do his part to confirm this to the American public. "It will not be long," he wrote in a stirring farewell letter to his students, "before you hear of me brandishing a rifle in the trenches of France in defense of our racial pride and the honor of our flag."[40] Others felt the same way. In his rallying call in *La Prensa,* for example, Amador Sánchez warned Tejanos not to tarnish the image of revered Mexican figures such as Pres. Benito Juárez, Miguel Hidalgo, and Cuauhtémoc, the last emperor of the Aztecs. "We Tejanos should be the first in volunteering for the fight, in joining the effort, as we possess a glorious heritage that we must respect," Sánchez insisted, his contention a remarkable blend of American and Mexican nationalism. That heritage, in his opinion, forbade Mexicans from displaying "any sort of weakness or cowardice."[41]

Of course, not all motives for wanting to participate in the war effort were as seemingly noble as those of Saenz or Sánchez. On the one hand, men often chose military life for reasons as mundane as obtaining a steady wage, good food, and warm clothing. José López of El Paso, on the other hand, sought permission to join the army simply to secure his release from prison.[42]

Whatever their reasons for joining up, the first recruits began departing for basic training during the late summer and early fall of 1917. In Texas, as throughout the rest of the country, communities organized touching farewell ceremonies to send them off in proper fashion. On September 21, for example, a large gathering of friends, family, and girlfriends gave the first contingent from Maverick County a send-off fit for war heroes, cheering and applauding loudly as their "boys"—many of whom were of Mexican descent—boarded a truck destined for Camp Travis. To the delight of the crowd, the eager youngsters adorned the vehicle with a sign that read, "Eagle Pass Deer Hunters Aiming at the Kaiser."[43] Amid similar pomp and circumstance, the first contingent from Webb County also departed for Camp Travis that same week. Neither the recruits nor their well-wishers allowed the heavy rainstorms to dampen their enthusiasm.

In a procession that included public officials, troops from Fort McIntosh, and the 37th Infantry band, the men trudged through muddy streets waving goodbye to friends and onlookers before arriving at the local train station. According to the *Laredo Weekly Times,* "the Mexican American boys in the party were the happiest of the group."[44]

Similar scenes played out throughout the next several months. On February 23 of the following year, the fourth contingent from Webb County—over half of which was Spanish-surnamed—was met at the train station by scores of relatives and friends as it prepared to leave for Camp Travis. The occasion was a merry one despite the absence of a military band and the political speeches that marked the first three send-offs in the county. The Girls Honor Guard of Laredo deserved much of the credit, as its members arrived at the station to present homemade olive drab sweaters to the grateful recruits, each of whom donned the garments immediately upon receipt.[45]

II

Despite the overwhelming success of the Selective Service System, millions of potential conscripts resisted the draft. According to government officials, some men went as far as procuring jail sentences to avoid military duty. Others scrambled to find marriage partners after the government announced its intention of conscripting single men before husbands, a revelation that produced a matrimonial boom in many parts of the country. Occasionally, as with the so-called Green Corn Rebellion of eastern Oklahoma, opposition even turned violent. During this most famous of antidraft flare-ups, hundreds of poor tenant farmers and sharecroppers aligned with the Socialist Party resisted conscription through force of arms. Protesting that the conflict overseas was a "rich man's war" but a "poor man's fight," the farmers in one case ambushed a posse of law enforcement officers. Although authorities scotched their movement before it could develop fully, the rebels' plans had included destroying railroad bridges and telegraph lines to impede the work of the Selective Service System and then eventually leading a march on Washington—subsisting partially on their wagonloads of green corn, which gave the uprising its name—to force the government to end the war.[46]

In magnitude, the Green Corn Rebellion dwarfed any resistance that emanated from the Tejano community, but a two-day affair in the small town of Mikeska in Live Oak County rivaled it for sheer intensity. The troubles there began on October 5, 1917, when local sheriff Charles L. Tullis arrived at the home of Serapio Loso to apprehend two of the Mexican citizen's sons on charges of draft dodging. Tullis found the house barricaded, but eventually managed his way inside to confront the family, whereupon a gunfight ensued that left the father of the two boys dead. With the aid of the Losos' landlord, whom the sound of gunfire had drawn to the scene, the sheriff then shot and killed one of the two brothers, the other escaping.

The bloodshed resumed soon afterward. At noon the next day, five miles away from the Losos' home, Tullis and his men found the fugitive accompanied by a third brother. According to the sheriff, his attempt to arrest the draftee incited the other brother to reach for a hidden weapon, which in turn led Deputy Sheriff William James to immediately open fire on the accomplice. Mortally wounded, the brother nonetheless managed to obtain his pistol and return fire on the deputy, who also fell dead.[47] As it turned out, the killings had not only been unfortunate but also unnecessary. Both nondeclarant aliens, the boys had qualified for draft deferments and had only needed to submit the required paperwork to secure their discharge from military duty. A few months later, the surviving brother did just that and was promptly released from Camp Travis, where he had been sent after being cleared of any part in the death of Deputy James.[48]

While nowhere near as extreme, other antidraft activities involving Mexicans and Mexican Americans occurred throughout the rest of the state. In Karnes City, fifty miles southeast of San Antonio, law enforcement officers arrested a Mexican citizen named Manuel Garza for attempting to disrupt the registration of his peers, a situation that turned tragic when Garza jumped out of a squad car and sustained life-threatening injuries.[49] In the South Texas town of Aguilares, yet another incident involving the post office led to legal troubles for two Tejanos. On September 29, 1917, authorities arrested and jailed Pablo Navarro and his son Librado on two separate charges—the latter for failing to answer two draft calls summoning him to report for military duty, and the former for knowingly violating the Selective Service Act by neglecting to deliver those summons to his son. The elder Navarro had apparently refused to retrieve these notices from his mailbox during his visits to the local post office.[50]

Besides conscientious objections and the simple desire to save one's own skin—the most common reasons for draft resistance—loyalty to Mexico and a concomitant antipathy toward its longtime nemesis to the north compelled many in the Tejano community to oppose conscription. Alejandro Balderas of San Antonio, for instance, decried both the draft and his country during a meeting of Mexican and Mexican American laborers held just prior to the first registration day, claiming that he would neither register nor serve in the military despite being a native-born citizen of the United States. According to a Justice Department informant who had been observing the proceedings, Balderas added that he "preferred to be shot than to fight for the *gringos*."[51] Fellow San Antonian Francisco Gómez wanted nothing to do with the war either. Soon after its outbreak, Gómez notified his local draft board that he had become a Mexican citizen years earlier and was now only working in the city of his birth. "The Americans wanted to draft me during the war because they thought that I was an American citizen," he later told anthropologist Manuel Gamio. "But I showed them."[52]

The Green Corn Rebellion and Live Oak County episode notwithstanding, most cases of draft opposition consisted of simple evasion rather than open resistance. According to John Chambers, an estimated 2.4 to 3.6 million men avoided registering for Selective Service during the war, while 337,000 draftees—or roughly 12 percent of the nation's total—effectively dodged induction.[53]

The Mexican Exodus accounted for many of these escapees. Although reports of Mexican citizens fleeing the country to avoid the draft surfaced throughout the Southwest and even as far away as Michigan, it was Texas that witnessed the biggest waves of emigration—a distinction largely attributable to the simple fact that it held the largest Mexican population of any American state. The three registration periods triggered the most departures. On June 4, 1917, alone, approximately three thousand Mexicans reportedly abandoned the town of Mission. During the week prior to the second registration, another three thousand Mexicans were alleged to have exited the country through neighboring Laredo. Even though the exodus receded by the following September, authorities in El Paso still counted daily an average of three hundred passport applications from Mexicans wishing to cross into Ciudad Juárez in the days leading up to the third and final registration.[54] The total number of Mexicans who returned to their homeland throughout the exact period of belligerency is unknown, but we do know that 132,385 of them arrived in Mexico from the United States during all of 1917 and 1918—almost the same amount as that of the previous five years combined.[55] There is little doubt that the demographic impact of their emigration was enormous. On June 5, 1917, for example, *Evolución* reported that Brownsville and the rest of the Lower

Rio Grande Valley had been left almost entirely devoid of Mexicans, a fate which other areas of the state soon experienced.[56]

Why did so many Mexicans flee the country? The question does not call forth a clear-cut answer. Rumors alleging that all aliens—declarants or otherwise—would be subject to the draft appear to have been the most likely reason for the exodus. The origins of these reports, however, are shrouded in mystery. American officials claimed, without sufficient evidence, that German agents or sympathizers concocted the stories to frighten Mexicans, a charge that many Texans accepted at face value (see chapter 3). Since Mexican workers were vital components of the agricultural labor force in the Southwest, the line of reasoning went, their mass departure benefited Germany by diminishing America's wartime food supply.[57]

Most likely, a series of factors set off the exodus. Some Mexicans probably headed homeward because they associated conscription with political oppression. In Mexico, after all, the *leva* (draft) often involved federal troops seizing individuals right off the street, as had frequently been the case during the reign of Victoriano Huerta. "Some have expressed surprise that so many Mexicans have crossed the river through fear of the American conscription," wrote the *Laredo Weekly Times,* "[but] it is not surprising to those who know how many of them in the past have been forced into the ranks of the Mexican armies to fight the battles of those with whom they have no sympathy save that of race."[58] Moreover, the prospect of war between the United States and Mexico—a possibility some took quite seriously given Germany's recent overtures toward the Carranza administration—seems to have convinced numerous others to exit the country. On April 28, 1917, *El Demócrata Fronterizo,* a Mexican exile newspaper headquartered in Laredo, reported that many laborers were fleeing to Mexico out of fear of an anti-Mexican backlash similar to that which took place during the Plan of San Diego Rebellion.[59] Their concerns proved well founded. Accounts of Texas Rangers and other law officers rounding up Mexicans to collect the fifty-dollar-per-slacker reward offered by military authorities circulated throughout the state. On January 4, 1918, H. C. Meyer, the mayor of Rockdale, complained to Gov. William P. Hobby, who succeeded Governor Ferguson, that unwarranted arrests of Mexicans by "six-shooter deputies," as he called them, had driven so many laborers from the mining fields that the nation's supply of lignite coal was in danger.[60] Virginia Corn Yeager, who witnessed firsthand the brutal seizure of a Mexican friend by a group of Rangers near San Diego, also protested to the governor. "Any of them would go to war," she said of her Mexican neighbors, but for "the brutality of these creatures who respect no law nor individual."[61]

As fears about conscription and corrupt lawmen mounted, an atmosphere of dread permeated the Tejano community. No doubt the most unfortunate incident that stemmed from this state of alarm occurred on June 24, 1917, when Mexican citizen Tomás Ramos, angst ridden over the prospect of being torn from his wife and children to fight on behalf of a country not his own, shot and killed himself in his home near the small town of Kyle, twenty miles south of Austin.[62]

Because the government was channeling much of the state's workforce into the military, the disappearance of so many Mexicans generated widespread worries about a possible labor shortage. At the behest of owners of large commercial farms and other enterprises, General Morton issued a proclamation to Mexican citizens in Brownsville on May 5, 1917, assuring them that only declarant aliens would be liable for conscription if Congress eventually passed the draft bill. When the announcement failed to curb the tide of emigrants sufficiently, some employers turned to Austin for aid. On May 15, South Texas farm owner Lawrence Bates received an audience with Governor Ferguson to discuss the recent developments. Arguing that the exodus had virtually paralyzed the agricultural industry, Bates implored the governor to issue his own manifesto to preserve the state's dwindling supply of Mexican laborers.[63]

His request produced immediate results. Two days after the meeting, Ferguson released an official statement urging those Mexican citizens who would likely qualify for draft deferments to remain in the country. Much to his approval, the antiemigration campaign received the support of numerous English- and Spanish-language newspapers, which propagated the announcement to practically every corner of the state. It also attracted the attention of the federal government. To assist in dispelling any misconceptions about the draft, Secretary of State Robert Lansing, who had expressed concerns over the exodus's "possible effect . . . upon labor conditions in the Southern states," recruited everyone from E. Garza Pérez, the Mexican secretary of foreign relations, to John W. Shaw, the Roman Catholic bishop of San Antonio.[64] By the time of the first registration, signs in Spanish with a message from Secretary Lansing had appeared along Texas highways. "There is, without question, no intention on the part of the American government of inducting aliens into the military," read the markers, conveniently omitting any references to the draft eligibility of declarant aliens. "Mexicans and other foreigners in the United States of America . . . have no reason to be alarmed."[65]

Interestingly, the commotion over the exodus and the draft revealed conflicting notions of Mexican manhood. On the one hand, Tejanos like Saenz regarded their service as proof of their *hombría* (manliness).[66] On the other, Anglo Americans, particularly those who sought an adequate supply of cheap labor, often emasculated Mexican men and deemed them unfit for military duty. "I don't believe this class of men would be any benefit to the country if they were forced into the army," wrote J. C. B. Harkness of Frio County to J. F. Carl, secretary of the Texas State Council of Defense, "but [they] could be useful in working and gathering food stuff [*sic*]."[67] In its pitch to keep Mexican laborers in the state, the editorial staff of the *San Antonio Express* arrived at the same conclusion. As it noted, the U.S. military wanted only the "pick" of the state's half-million young men, not those who would be a "hindrance rather than a help and would only swell the pension rolls that are always more or less of a tax burden after the close of a war." Thus, it reasoned, most Mexicans were safe from the clutches of General Crowder.[68]

Many leaders of the Tejano community also took an active part in discouraging their ethnic counterparts from quitting the state. The owners of some of the largest Spanish-language newspapers were especially helpful. Besides printing notices to educate the masses about the draft, publishers such as Laredoan Clemente Idar of *Evolución* and San Antonian Francisco A. Chapa of *El Imparcial de Texas* participated in mass meetings wherein they explained the draft laws and refuted false rumors about the Selective Service System.[69] Other prominent Tejanos did likewise. In Laredo, local dignitary A. R. García joined Idar in delivering orations in Spanish regarding draft exemptions to a gathering of Mexican laborers on the eve of the third registration. A few days later, Spanish teacher J. J. Mercado, a descendant of a Civil War veteran, clarified the latest statements from General Crowder during a Mexican Independence Day celebration in Houston.[70]

In order to lure Mexicans back into the country and placate their former employers, the federal government progressively eased some of the restrictions on immigration that had taken hold since the late nineteenth century. First, on May 23, 1917, Secretary of Labor W. B. Wilson suspended the literary test, head tax, and contract labor clause for agricultural workers, effective until March 2, 1921. Then, the following year, Wilson extended the period of admission for Mexican laborers for the duration of the war and granted them permission to seek employment not only in agriculture but also in railroad work and lignite coal mining. Soon afterward, every other sort of mining and—at least in Texas and the southern parts of New Mexico, Arizona, and California—construction work made the list of government-approved occupations. Even an unofficial "Bracero Program" developed. Requiring employers to make arrangements with the government for the transportation, housing, and feeding of Mexican laborers, for whose import and export they would then assume responsibility, this scheme established the precedent for the Emergency Farm Labor Program, the official name of the Bracero Program, of World War II.[71]

Although such political initiatives never came close to satisfying the demand for Mexican workers, labor officials and the Texas press prematurely hailed the end of the crisis on more than one occasion. As early as July 1917, J. C. Jennings of the Texas Department of Labor had already proclaimed the exodus over, citing immigration reform, the draft information campaign, and the poor economic conditions in Mexico as the main reasons for its abrupt conclusion. More than a year later, in September 1918, *La Prensa* issued a similar report, only to run a front-page story shortly thereafter detailing how the third registration had provoked yet another phase of the exodus. A subsequent edition of the paper with a fresh report of its demise ultimately proved accurate, but less because of changes to immigration laws or the numerous reassurances from local, state, and federal authorities than because of the fact that the war itself appeared to be waning and many workers no longer considered the draft a threat.[72]

For Tejanos, the exodus had been a public relations nightmare. On February 15, 1918, the *San Antonio Express* ran an article that carried the headline "Temple Fails to Find Mexican Registrants." The subheadline delivered the harder jab. "Not a Man of Latin Blood Can Be Located to Fight for America," it read.[73] Some Tejanos dealt with derision personally. In his diary, Saenz recollects quarreling with a German American who needled him about the exodus. "Why didn't *you* return to Mexico," the latter reportedly asked, to which Saenz replied, "Because I don't have any business in Mexico." After specifying that he was a Mexican American, not a Mexican national, the fiery schoolteacher proceeded to upbraid his unsuspecting adversary, calling him and other enemies of the Tejano community "vile reptiles" and, perhaps even worse, "white trash."[74]

Saenz's attempt to differentiate between Mexicans and Mexican

Americans likely deterred little criticism, as it was no secret that some of the latter group also fled the country to avoid military service. As a matter of fact, a few were downright brazen about their dereliction of duty. In Ciudad Juárez, U.S. Army deserters sometimes paraded in the streets wearing their official military uniforms, while in tiny Socorro, on the American side of the border, others reportedly attended large celebrations and gatherings during temporary forays from their sanctuaries in Mexico.[75]

That said, not everyone found life as a refugee agreeable. In Mexico, many encountered bleak economic prospects and a hostile populace, with natives often making fugitives the subject of countless *burlas* (taunts).[76] Some slackers consequently reconsidered their decision to leave Texas. Hilario Ochoa of Riviera, for example, sought out the assistance of L. A. Kaufer, secretary of the Kleberg County Council of Defense, who informed state officials of the young Mexican American's willingness to join the American colors if they allowed him back into the country.[77] Similarly, Bernardo de la Garza Jr. of Laredo wound up serving in the U.S. Army after notifying his local draft board of his decision to return home.[78] A fellow Laredoan named Bernabé Vergara never made it back, however. On the morning of March 25, 1917, he drowned in the Rio Grande while trying to reach American soil.[79]

A few Tejanos expressed resentment over what they perceived as the disloyalty of some of their peers. On March 22, 1918, a group of volunteers from Brownsville issued a statement to the press after a member of the group's company deserted training camp and fled to nearby Matamoros, Mexico. "This individual has behaved like a traitor," read the pronouncement. "We are not traitors: we have pledged to support our country . . . and we will fulfill it by fighting to the end on behalf of Uncle Sam."[80] Sometimes, though, the censure carried a touch of despondency. "The sad and grave error of those who turned 'slackers,' neglecting their civic duty when the country was in danger, [cast] doubt even on the good intentions of those who willingly offered themselves for the sacrifice," lamented Saenz.[81]

Mexicans and Mexican Americans, of course, had not been the only ones who fled south of the border during the war. In fact, Mexico had been so popular as a refuge that entire colonies of draft dodgers from diverse backgrounds had eventually formed within its borders. One such settlement in Mexico City, for example, had been comprised almost entirely of socialists and upper-class liberal pacifists of Anglo-American extraction, while another near the international boundary in a remote section of Sonora had reportedly included immigrants from Italy, France, Poland, Montenegro, Serbia, Germany, Austria, and Turkey, along with many native-born Americans.[82]

Nevertheless, in Texas it was the wartime conduct of the Mexican-origin people that garnered the most criticism. Indeed, years after the end of the fighting, most discussions on their World War I legacy focused on the exodus, which remained a lightning rod for controversy. The topic even surfaced in the political arena. In his book about Mexican Americans in World War II and the Korean War, author Raúl Morín recounts how a bitter political race from the late 1920s featured one candidate releasing campaign literature that supposedly documented his opponent's view of Mexicans as "slackers." Designed to swing the Tejano vote, the flyers quoted the second candidate as arguing that Mexicans were not a "desirable type of citizens for Texas" because most of them had fled to Mexico soon after the declaration of war against Germany, returning only after the last shots were fired "to reap the harvest of this great state." Whether baseless or not, Morín recalled, the mudslinging swayed the votes of more than a few Tejanos, revealing their sensitivity regarding the issue of World War I.[83]

Such feelings were understandable. Mexican Americans in the state did indeed produce their fair share of slackers, but no evidence exists to authenticate the claim that they did so in disproportionately higher numbers than other ethnic groups. In truth, anecdotal evidence suggests that Tejanos' response to the wartime rallying cry was very much like that of other citizens. As this chapter has shown, most Mexican Americans complied dutifully with the Selective Service Act, and even many Mexican nationals, young men who in most cases were not obligated to serve militarily, volunteered to fight abroad. In the end, the Mexican Exodus, which saw thousands of Mexican citizens—along with some Mexican Americans—flee the country in fear of the draft, skewed the image of the Tejano community in the eyes of many Americans. Although its wartime contribution drew accolades from some circles, scorn for the exodus also left an imprint on the pages of history. For the Mexican people of the Lone Star State, this was one of the tragedies of World War I.

CHAPTER THREE

Surveillance

ON MARCH 3, 1917, TWO DAYS AFTER WORD OF THE ZIMmermann note's interception reached the press, the *New York Times* hailed Mexico's apparent rejection of an anti-American alliance with Germany, but warned its readers that the country and its president, Venustiano Carranza, "will still bear watching from this side of the border."[1] Attitudes of this sort, along with suspicions of Mexican intrigue, persisted throughout the war era in the United States due to reports of a considerable German presence in Mexico. As wartime fears of enemy spies and saboteurs undermining the war effort gripped the public, American intelligence not only conducted operations in Mexico but also kept close track of Mexicans and Mexican Americans domestically.[2]

The Tejano community found itself a prime target for surveillance because of its proximity to the U.S.-Mexico border and the pervasive unease with all things Mexican. In Texas, as in many other parts of the country, concerns over the possibility of German-Mexican collusion often bordered on hysteria. Throughout the war, intelligence agencies received countless tips implicating Mexican-origin individuals in nefarious activity of one form or another. To say that many of these leads—particularly those alleging the most serious crimes—were fruitless would be to make an understatement. The isolated cases of disloyalty that emanated from the barrios, though, were more than enough to validate the anxieties of the most fretful citizens and public officials. Inevitably, the unique relationship between Mexico and the United States ensured that these cases would receive extra attention from American intelligence.

I

To be sure, the Wilson administration's concern with foreign subversives was not unfounded. Germany had targeted the United States in several of its plots since the eruption of hostilities in Europe. To hinder the flow of matériel to the Allies, German agents had in July 1916 bombed the Erie Railroad docks in New Jersey, destroying thirty-four boxcars loaded with ammunition. They had also set ablaze the Kingsland munitions factory near New York Harbor several months later.

These efforts, however, were sometimes downright clumsy. In one case, a German consul carelessly misplaced a briefcase containing compromising evidence of espionage on a Third Avenue elevated train in New York City. Despite its success elsewhere, German intrigue in the United States, in the words of historians D. Clayton James and Anne Sharp Wells, was "[m]ore annoying than substantial."[3]

As the Zimmermann note fiasco made clear, it also to a large extent involved Mexico, whose president welcomed a German alliance to counter American aggression. Always looking to obstruct the shipment of American manpower and supplies to Europe, the German government coveted Mexico as a base from which to wage a campaign of espionage and sabotage against the United States. Germany also hoped to produce a second Mexican-American war by fomenting anti-Americanism among the country's various revolutionary factions and coordinating armed provocations and raids along the border. Fortunately for the Germans, the punitive expedition had made Carranza more receptive to overtures from their country, from which the so-called First Chief hoped to obtain financial and military aid in case of a war with the United States. With the Mexican president suddenly more amenable to its needs, the German secret service in 1917 moved its headquarters to Mexico and launched a series of covert activities against the United States.[4]

The American government took countermeasures against the German threat south of the border, albeit with mixed results. Under the direction of the military attaché, five different American secret services—the State Department, the army, the navy, the Department of the Treasury, and the Justice Department—conducted intelligence activities in Mexico. With the assistance of French and especially British intelligence, American officials were able to learn the identity and movements of most of the German secret service's agents, in large part due to Britain's interception of several German telegrams and the joint Allied effort at deciphering German secret codes. The Americans also attempted to dislodge German businesses from Mexico, a less productive endeavor impeded not only by the Germans' skill for camouflaging their activities but also by American business interests. As two-thirds of German business's sales in Mexico were based on U.S. goods, American businessmen pressured their government to resist interfering with the free flow of commerce and to regard their German counterparts down south as "harmless."[5]

Mexican intrigue was no less a focus for the intelligence community back home. The U.S. government's surveillance team for domestic matters included the army and navy intelligence branches and the investigative arms of the State and Post Office departments, the latter of which focused on scanning mail for disloyal and subversive content and monitoring letters, telegrams, and packages to and from Mexico and other foreign countries. Another component of this network of agencies was the Justice Department's Bureau of Investigation (later the Federal Bureau of Investigation, or FBI), which had been inspecting Mexican neutrality violations on American soil since the early days of the Mexican Revolution. After the declaration of war against Germany, the Bureau of Investigation simply added espionage and sabotage to previous concentrations such as arms smuggling, which itself took on an entirely new dimension now that the possibility existed of revolutionary factions—the usual culprits in such crimes—delivering weapons to Germans south of the border. In Texas, surveillance was aided by the state adjutant general's creation of a special investigative unit called the Loyalty Rangers. Under the direction of W. M. Hanson, a former federal marshal for the Southern District of Texas, the Loyalty Rangers worked to improve intelligence collection along the Rio Grande. Armed with the newly passed Espionage Act, which prohibited practically anything that could be defined as the aiding and abetting of America's enemies, this network of intelligence agencies paid considerable attention to the Tejano community.[6]

For many intelligence officials, the impertinent statements of some individuals substantiated fears of German-Mexican intrigue. In May 1917, in the small German settlement of Guda in northern Falls County, a reputed hotbed of anti-Americanism, authorities received two separate reports of a local Mexican's boasts that "Mexicans and Germans were going to take this country."[7] In San Antonio, meanwhile, an informant of German extraction filed a report with the Bureau of Investigation detailing his recent war-related discussion with a Mexican acquaintance, who allegedly expressed a desire "to see the germans whipp the Bigmouthed 'Gringos' and give them what the[y] had coming to them" for the last several years. "Knowing me to be of German decent," the informant wrote, "he spoke very bitter against the . . . Americans," whom the Mexican argued "would only make a laughing stock out of themselfes [*sic*], because they had not been able to get Villa."[8] Owing to the intolerant political temperament of wartime, criticism of this sort could sometimes result in legal trouble. In April 1917, for example, law enforcement officials in Mission arrested a Mexican simply for writing a letter that allegedly "abus[ed] the President and the American people in general."[9]

Obviously, in cases like these where the mail was involved the department that took the lead in surveillance was the Post Office, led by Albert S. Burleson, its autocratic postmaster general—the war era's "foremost official enemy of dissidents," according to historian David M. Kennedy. Authorized by the Espionage Act to ban from the mails any materials that violated its provisions and with the leeway to monitor the private correspondence of most "potential subversives," Burleson ruthlessly wielded his considerable powers to stifle critics of the Wilson administration, many of whom relied on the mail to circulate information.[10] The postmaster general, wrote presidential advisor Col. Edward M. House in 1918, "is in a belligerent mood against the Germans, against labor, against the pacifists, etc. He is now the most belligerent member of the cabinet."[11]

The post office worked in conjunction with other government agencies. The chief postal censor, for example, headed a national Censorship Board composed of representatives from the Navy and War departments, the War Trade Board, and the Committee on Public Information (CPI). Charged with the task of monitoring incoming and outgoing international mail not already censored by England, France, or Italy, the Censorship Board often overstepped its bounds by repeatedly reviewing domestic correspondence, which it was supposed to do only in cases of extreme necessity. Besides its work with the Censorship Board, the post office also communicated with other agencies by providing them with lists of banned publications. In turn, military intelligence, the Bureau of Investigation, and even the Loyalty Rangers also conducted investigations of suspect publications sent through postal channels.[12]

Due in large part to the efforts of the post office, freedom of the press suffered continual setbacks throughout the war. The socialist press was one of Burleson's favorite targets. Often with little provocation, Burleson banned some of the era's major radical publications from the mails, initiating the decline of the American socialist movement. The foreign-language press too fell under the heavy hand of the Wilson administration. Following the passage of the Trading-with-the-Enemy Act in October 1917, foreign-language papers were required to submit at their own considerable expense translations of any items dealing with the government, the other belligerent powers, or the conduct of the war. The post office then took on the task of combing them for subversive messages at its Translation Bureau in New York, where a staff of four hundred college professors volunteered as translators. In this environment, it is therefore unsurprising that publications of all sorts of languages and affiliations wound up toeing the administration's line for fear of losing their second-class mailing permits, a penalty Burleson meted out freely in enforcing the press censorship provision of the Espionage Act.[13]

In the case of the Mexican press, Burleson's surveillance activities were actually sensible. As part of its intense and extensive propaganda campaign in Latin America, the German Foreign Office subsidized several Mexican newspapers—including Mexico City's *El Demócrata,* the main organ of German propaganda—in exchange for favorable coverage, an expenditure American intelligence estimated at approximately $25,000 monthly. Although costly, the operation proved successful. The War Department, for example, estimated that 90 percent of the Mexican population held anti-American attitudes during the war. The reason for this level of antipathy was clear to the Wilson administration. "With the possible exception of Spain," concluded the CPI, the American government's own propaganda arm, "German propaganda has proceeded in no other country with such resolve and malicious aggressiveness, as in Mexico."[14]

The American government took several measures to counter the pro-German Mexican media. For one thing, it issued a ban on "objectionable" newspapers such as *El Demócrata, La Defensa, El Progreso, Informales Inalámbricas,* and *Redención,* a prohibition that resulted in the virtual disappearance of Mexican newspapers along some parts of the border.[15] It also imposed a paper embargo on all pro-German newspapers in Mexico, causing some to close shop either permanently or temporarily. The most successful countermeasures, however, were economic sanctions—which put an end to the *Boletín de Guerra* of Progreso, Yucatán, and turned *La Opinión* of Torreón, Coahuila, over to the Allied cause—and the hindrance of shipments of pro-German newspapers through American territory. The latter move especially affected the isolated Mexican provinces in the western part of the country, much of whose mail first passed through the United States.[16]

For the most part, nothing that drastic was needed to control the Spanish-language press north of the border. In Laredo, *Evolución* was downplaying the idealistic claims of the Allies as late as March 1917, portraying the war as a traditional European power struggle. With America's entry into the conflict, however, it devoted itself wholeheartedly to the war effort, with its publisher, Clemente Idar, even landing a job with the CPI. Most likely because it was the organ of the local Mexican exile community, cross-town rival *El Demócrata Fronterizo* was less enthusiastic about America's role in the war, although it too eventually fell into line with the mainstream. The same was true of another Mexican exile paper, *La Prensa* of San Antonio, which remained nominally neutral throughout the conflict but lent support to the American government by translating and publishing official wartime notices and lauding the exploits of Mexicans and Mexican Americans in the war effort to generate patriotism in the Tejano community (see chapter 4). Ultimately, none of the Spanish-language newspapers from Texas were ever labeled disloyal by the post office, although it is impossible to ascertain exactly whether their propriety stemmed from true patriotism—or, in the case of exile papers, gratitude toward their adopted country—or fear of retribution from Burleson and his staff.[17]

What is certain is that at least some members of the foreign-language press were keenly aware of the ever-watchful eye of the American government. In the days leading up to America's declaration of war against Germany, several pieces in *El Demócrata Fronterizo* caught the attention of intelligence officials. One informant submitted a report detailing editor and publisher Justo Cárdenas's history as a refugee from Porfirian Mexico, along with a translated excerpt from an editorial criticizing the "partisans of the war movement in the United States," including President Wilson, whom it identified as its "head."[18] Another report several days later noted how, upon instructions from Bureau of Investigation officials either to suppress the publication or seek prosecution "if practicable," the matter had been turned over to a local U.S. marshal. "As a result of the interview I am informed that Cárdenas has promised faithfully not to again publish article of like character," the report's author noted. "I am of the opinion that like article will not appear again in *El Demócrata Fronterizo*."[19]

Interestingly, members of the Spanish-language press sometimes turned on one another. In late 1917, Clemente Idar, who had been acting as an informant for the Justice Department since at least 1916,[20] wrote President Wilson's private secretary, Joseph P. Tumulty, Sen. Morris Shepard of Texas, and a local Bureau of Investigation agent to inform them of how two of *Evolución*'s competitors in San Antonio—*La Prensa* and *La Revista Mexicana*—were causing trouble for the American government by publishing "seditious propaganda" against the Carranza administration, a regime that was, as he pointed out, "officially recognized by us and entitled to all the considerations of our friendship." In his view, both papers were attempting to incite Mexicans to overthrow their current president. While perhaps tolerable during peacetime, Idar argued, such intrigue was now far too dangerous, as the country could not afford to have revolutionaries smuggle any of its precious arms and munitions south of the border. Idar was adamant in his conviction. "Disturbing the peace in Mexico, fomenting a new revolutionary movement therein and fomenting it from American territory, abusing our proverbial hospitality to refugees, means treason," he wrote.[21]

As it turned out, even the Burleson-led post office considered his fears of both papers' activities overblown. "As far as I have been able to ascertain this publication has been loyal since the war was declared," opined one postal inspector about *La Prensa.* "Insofar as the war news is concerned, [it] is strictly neutral."[22] He reached the same conclusion in his evaluation of *La Revista Mexicana.* "There is no evidence tending to show disloyalty to this government on the part of the publication in question," he wrote in a report for the chief inspector.[23]

Indeed, not long after Idar brought him to the attention of the authorities, *La Prensa*'s owner, Ignacio E. Lozano, attempted to make use of a provision in the Trading-with-the-Enemy Act that exempted demonstrably "loyal" foreign-language newspapers from translation requirements. Post office records do not indicate whether or not he, like Idar, was granted such an exemption,[24] but he did receive a strong recommendation from Postmaster George D. Armistead of San Antonio, who called *La Prensa*'s translation and publication of an entire CPI pamphlet "a splendid specimen of patriotic cooperation."[25]

Nevertheless, Idar continued monitoring his colleagues in the Spanish-language press through the duration of the war. In the fall of 1918, *El Demócrata Fronterizo*'s criticism of the "Work or Fight" laws—which required that all able-bodied men, including noncitizens, not serving in the military be employed only in what the government considered "productive work"—provoked a scathing attack from *Evolución.* In an editorial titled "What *El Demócrata Fronterizo* Is Attempting," Idar decried Justo Cárdenas for his lack of gratitude toward his adopted country, calling him a "rabid old man . . . full of passions and hatred" who deserved only "contempt" from Laredoans. His paper's "Germanophilic Labor," the subheadline read, "Is Ineffective Because *Evolución* Constantly Watches It."[26]

The post office ensnared a few U.S.-based Spanish-language newspapers even without Idar's assistance, however. In California, *El Rebelde* of Los Angeles had its second-class mailing privileges revoked for violations of the Espionage Act.[27] After publishing an anticapitalist manifesto in his *Regeneración,* a courageous act in light of the repressive wartime atmosphere, Ricardo Flores Magón was arrested on charges of, among other things, conspiracy, mailing indecent and "un-mailable" materials, and publishing false statements that undermined the American military. He was sentenced to twenty years in prison.[28] The only Tejano newspaper to be found guilty of any of Wilson's antidissent laws was El Paso's *La República,* a pro-Villa publication whose "sole purpose," as Mexican Ambassador Ygnacio Bonillas told Secretary of State Robert Lansing, was "to create alarm and strain the relations between Mexico and the United States."[29] After Lansing brought the paper to Burleson's attention, its editors, José Luis Velasco and Luis R. Alvarez, were arrested on the minor charge of failing to submit an English-language translation to the postmaster general.[30]

Burleson remained steadfast despite criticism for his disregard of Americans' civil liberties. His contention that "no newspaper which in its conscience is free from disloyal intent has anything to apprehend" from the Espionage Act's enforcement did not fly with his detractors.[31] Theodore Roosevelt accused the post office of using the new law for political purposes by "punishing papers which uphold the war but which told the truth about the administration's failure to conduct the war efficiently."[32] Both Herbert Croly, editor of the *New Republic,* and reformer Amos Pinchot complained directly to President Wilson. Likewise, in a letter to the president, Upton Sinclair wrote, "your Postmaster-General reveals himself a person of such pitiful and childish ignorance concerning modern movements that it is simply a calamity that [in] this crisis he should be the person to decide what may or may not be uttered in our radical press."[33] When Wilson confronted Burleson about such matters, the latter threatened resignation, prompting the president to backpedal. "Well, go ahead and do your duty," Wilson reportedly responded. Except for one single instance late in the war, Burleson was never reined in by his superior in the White House.[34]

II

In cases unrelated to the mail, the other agencies of the federal government's surveillance team took charge. For military intelligence, a major source of anxiety without question was the seemingly endless string of raids that had been plaguing the U.S.-Mexico border since the early days of the Mexican Revolution. By late 1917, the problem was being compounded by widespread hunger caused largely as a result of a food export embargo on Mexico, which, according to officials, the Germans were pointing to as evidence that the United

States was attempting to starve the Mexican people. As one report noted, German agents were utilizing such propaganda to stir up resentment against Americans and incite Mexicans to conduct raids across the border. Whether the tactic succeeded is unknown, but as the following chapter shows, raids into American territory continued well into the war era.[35]

Another major concern for intelligence officials was that foreign enemies were involved in a mass conspiracy to subvert African Americans, a concern that had existed since the prewar period. In Texas, which had the most investigations into these rumors, the scheme reportedly involved not only Germans, as in other states, but also its substantial Mexican population—the largest in the country. As some authorities claimed, Mexicans were helping lure blacks south of the border, where Germans were supposedly organizing militias and lying in wait until enough Americans went off to war before attacking the United States. The recruitment of African Americans was believed to serve a dual purpose: they could enlarge these units while simultaneously depleting the United States of essential laborers.[36]

There was no shortage of leads when it came to this issue. The day after America's entry into the war, authorities in North Texas were alerted to the presence of two Mexican recruiters who were telling local blacks that "white people [were] the cause of the Negroes being held down." In Mexico, the men supposedly professed, Carranza would offer them the chance to start their lives anew.[37] One citizen of the small Central Texas town of Buda reported that twenty-four local blacks were planning to depart to Mexico "to enlist,"[38] while another man in San Antonio told authorities of a recent conversation with a black lawyer named Campbell, whom he described as a "Slippery Coon" and an "adventurer" who kept company "with a bunch of Damage suit lawyers." According to the latter account, Campbell had spoken of his plans to travel south of the Rio Grande, where he claimed to fit in. "I have ready [*sic*] in the press of certain people trying to incite our Negro population," the informant wrote, "and if this be true, don't know where a better subject could be found than this man."[39] In East Texas, meanwhile, an Anglo-American woman allegedly overheard a black preacher urging his audience to support Germany and Mexico against the United States. Because "negroes were not allowed to hold offices and not allowed to vote in some of the elections," read the report, the preacher "wished Germany would wipe up the earth" with the United States and "threat [*sic*] all Americans like Americans have been treating the negroes."[40]

Of course, some leads were more reliable than others. In April

1917, authorities in Dallas received a report that a local black man by the name of Ire Cornelius had been attending meetings headed by five "well-dressed Mexicans" who were attempting to persuade blacks to immigrate to Mexico with promises of land and social equality. Little came of the matter. As investigators discovered, the original source of the tip, Cornelius's wife, had simply been spreading rumors to produce trouble for her unsuspecting husband, who had earlier threatened to leave her.[41] There were other cases of African Americans notifying authorities about Mexican subversives. In Moody, thirty miles southwest of Waco, authorities arrested a rail hand named Joel Coronado after several of his black co-workers accused him of attempting to recruit them as soldiers for his native Mexico in case it went to war with the United States. "He told me that this country belonged to Mexico," one worker was quoted as saying, "and if us Negroes would go to Mexico with him, that with the Mexicans and the Germans we could whip the United States." Not only that, he added, "after the war the Negroes would be given some land and could have all the white women they wanted." Coronado strongly denied the accusations, which were unverifiable (and perhaps the result of a preexisting enmity among the men involved).[42]

In Dallas, fears over the subversion of loyal African Americans reached their height in the spring of 1918. On May 9, Chief of Police John W. Ryan ordered all "strange" Mexicans in the city arrested on sight. "There is an organized gang of Mexican men and women now working in Texas with the intention of getting Negroes to go to Mexico," reported the *Dallas Morning News* the following day, justifying the draconian measure. "Officers have received the intimation that the Mexican propaganda is prompted by agents of the German Government."[43]

According to historian Theodore Kornweibel Jr., Anglo-Americans in Texas and elsewhere vastly exaggerated the extent of these plots. In his view, the widespread rumors of Mexican recruitment efforts likely stemmed from the fresh memories of the Plan of San Diego, as well as the belief that African Americans were naive and readily manipulated. Their supposedly childlike nature, coupled with long-standing grudges against Anglos, made them easy prey for enemy agents in the minds of many Americans. As Kornweibel notes, it should not be surprising that most reports of black subversion came from the Southern states, which had both the largest concentrations of African Americans and the worst history of racial conflict in the country. With so many of their young men off fighting, Anglo-American Southerners dreaded the possibility of Germans and Mexicans turning local blacks against them.[44] Obviously, it is very likely that some individuals did make disloyal statements, some of which might have involved threats of moving to Mexico to fight against the United States, but their very utterance does not necessarily mean that any such schemes existed beyond the realms of their imaginations. Furthermore, while it is a certainty that some Mexicans actually did attempt to draw African Americans to Mexico, it must also be noted that recruitment of this sort had been taking place since the late nineteenth century, when colonization and investment opportunities south of the border first began opening up for blacks. To automatically attach insidious motives to these activities would require ignoring altogether a unique facet of early twentieth-century Mexican and African American history.[45]

In any case, fears of African American subversion by Germans and Mexicans persisted until the war's conclusion. But they by no means disappeared automatically once the last shots were fired across the Atlantic. As Kornweibel notes, a new bogeyman in the form of Bolshevism had appeared by then, and the anxieties of wartime transferred seamlessly into those of the Red Scare era, with blacks now regarded by many as easy targets for the agents of communism.[46]

III

Yet another focus of the intelligence community was the monitoring of draft opponents. In July 1917, Bureau of Investigation agents arrested four Mexicans for propagandizing against the recruitment and enlistment of Tejanos in San Antonio. According to officials, the men had publicly condemned the use of Mexican labor for the construction of encampments for the American military, which they believed was engaging in an unjustified war. They had also helped distribute a circular titled *The Price We Pay,* a socialist publication that attributed American involvement in the war to capitalist greed and called for mass protest to repeal the draft law.[47]

Of course, the complicity of suspected draft opponents was not always easy to prove for authorities. Such was the case with Juan Ríos, who was also arrested in McAllen by Justice Department agents for distributing literature urging Mexican workers to return to their homeland. In preliminary hearings, the Mexican citizen claimed he had been recruiting laborers for employers in northern Mexico and pleaded ignorance of the draft laws, arguing that he had assumed such hiring practices were legal not only in Mexico but also in the United States. Further complicating the government's case, the

Mexican consul in Brownsville vouched for the detainee and vowed to seek his return to Mexico.[48] Similarly, one report out of San Angelo in Tom Green County had a certain Francisco Lozano scaring fellow Mexicans with stories of the American military drafting noncitizens. Upon interrogation, though, Lozano claimed only to be repeating what a German stranger had told him earlier on the road to nearby Ballinger. Unable to challenge his account, authorities were forced to drop the matter altogether, a somewhat necessary move given their fear "of the effect it would have had on Mexicans within registering age to have detained him longer at the time."[49]

Besides, these authorities likely considered Lozano's alibi plausible, as it was widely held that such rumors—and the Mexican Exodus that it produced—were the handiwork of German agents and sympathizers. "Mexicans leaving this country for fear of being drafted," read a 1918 telegram from the Southern Department to Lt. G. L. Hoff in Galveston. "Probably due to German propaganda."[50] Maj. Gen. L. R. Holbrook, commander at Fort Sam Houston in San Antonio, was less equivocal. "For several days German propagandists have been busy circulating rumors among the Mexican population about the registration," Holbrook declared in a proclamation to Mexican laborers in the United States. "These rumors are baseless, malicious, and untrue."[51]

They were also multifarious. In late 1917, panic struck Mexicans in Caldwell County after a story broke out that any adult males still in the country by the start of the new year—regardless of citizenship—would be thrown into the army.[52] Other stories in Poteet, a few miles south of San Antonio, had it that anyone who registered would be drafted, and that the military was planning to send a regiment composed entirely of blacks and Mexicans to the trenches in France.[53] But perhaps the most outlandish tale came out of Laredo. There, in the summer of 1918, a rumor was making the rounds that the American government would soon be conscripting Mexican washerwomen for service in Europe.[54]

Circulating false rumors to prompt the emigration of Mexican workers, so the prevailing belief went, was one of Germany's ways of sabotaging the American war effort. "The purpose of such propaganda is obvious," wrote James A. Harley, the adjutant general of Texas, in September 1918. "Unpicked cotton fields in Texas bear out [my] department's excuse for anxiety over the situation."[55] But it was not just the agricultural industry that suffered as the state's labor supply dwindled. "Mexicans are employed in almost all trades in this part of the country," observed the *San Antonio Express,* noting how vital they were to the railroad industry as well. "The hindrance of transportation at this time would be a great detriment to the war program, as it would be impossible to move troops."[56] As Lieutenant Hoff argued, the Mexican Exodus was "playing into Germany's hands" because Mexicans "furnish[ed] a large part of the labor . . . for the carrying on of important government work."[57]

The reasons for many Americans' belief that Mexican laborers were susceptible to German propaganda were akin to those cited in discussions of the black subversion issue. "The average Mexican," the *Austin American* stated in an editorial on the exodus, "is slow to act and think."[58] General Harley concurred. "The Mexican laboring people, or peons as they are called, are very credulous and easily deceived," he wrote. "Propagandists have found them easy prey for furthering their schemes."[59]

Some Tejanos also blamed Germans for the exodus, albeit of course without the use of disparaging, anti-Mexican stereotypes. One letter sent to President Wilson, signed "A Mexican from Glen Flora," complained about how Germans were terrorizing Mexican laborers in Wharton County.[60] The staff of *Evolución,* meanwhile, attributed the labor shortage to "German propagandists found throughout the border and their allies in the interior of the country." Now that the Wilson administration was working toward luring many refugees back from their home country, the paper asserted, the enemy was "doing everything possible to stop Mexicans from immigrating into the United States, thereby interrupting the harvest of American crops."[61]

At least initially, though, not everyone in the state was in complete unanimity about what was prompting so many Mexicans to flee across the border. "It would be a mistake to conclude that the exodus is proof of any widespread German propaganda," the *Dallas Morning News*—whose views, as evidenced by their reporting on the subversion of African Americans, would later change dramatically—argued in an editorial the day after the first registration. While acknowledging that anxiety over the draft was the most likely determinant, the paper stopped short of laying the entire blame on the Germans.[62]

Although it probably underestimated the extent of the German propaganda machine, the *News* was on firmer ground in its opinion that the exodus likely stemmed from several causes, as more than one incident made clear. For instance, in Mercedes, authorities apprehended a man by the name of Will Anderson for disseminating misinformation about the draft among the Mexican residents of nearby Donna, his hometown. Apparently, Anderson's scheme involved conducting business with the frightened Mexicans, whom he had hoped would sell their property below market value as they rushed back to Mexico.[63] The Bureau of Investigation reported something similar in San Antonio, where unscrupulous businessmen were reportedly planning to make a profit by conveying Mexicans across the border in automobiles and trains.[64] Naturally, some individuals accused Mexicans and Germans of comparable scams. One resident of Runge in Karnes County informed authorities that a certain Eliseo Muñiz, who had previously been maligning the draft, was now transporting Mexican laborers across the Rio Grande in his automobile at ten dollars a head.[65] Another report had Germans in San Marcos, thirty miles southwest of Austin, contributing to the widespread panic to purchase real estate from refugees, financial speculation that carried the frightening prospect of eventually building up the kaiser's war chest.[66] Not all such incidents involved economic motives, however. According to another intelligence report, the only discernible reasons for Lawton, Oklahoma, native James T. Chancelor's crime, which involved spreading false rumors about the draft in the barrios of Fort Worth, were alcohol and a marked antipathy toward Mexicans.[67]

IV

As we have already seen, not all investigations into Mexican criminality panned out. In one case, the Bureau of Investigation saw fit to review the activities of a mutual-aid society called La Liga Protectora Mexicana (Mexican Protective League), the reason likely being that any Mexican organization was a prime target for scrutiny. As it turned out, however, the league's founder, Manuel C. Gonzales, was a pillar of the community in San Antonio who would go on to serve admirably in the U.S. Army during the war (see chapter 7). Needless to say, the organization's file was a short one, with no indications of follow-up investigations of any sort.[68]

Some of the Bureau of Investigation's leads were patently false. In November 1917, J. C. Childres of Callahan County reported to Justice of the Peace J. H. Surles that a Mexican sheepherder named Martínez who claimed to be a former officer in the Mexican army had recently divulged a joint German-Mexican plan to invade the United States. According to Childres, whom Surles considered "perfectly reliable," Martínez was only herding sheep as a pretext and had declared that he "would be Glad to see the time this Would Take

Place [*sic*]."[69] A subsequent investigation revealed Childres to be less than trustworthy, however. In a letter to a local Bureau of Investigation agent, U.S. Commissioner W. E. Girand noted how Martínez had taken Childres's job after the latter had been terminated for "inefficiency." Concluding that the initial report was "a piece of spite work more than anything else," Girand exonerated Martínez, who had been taken to him for questioning, and released him from police custody.[70]

Reminiscent of the internal strife that afflicted other segments of the Tejano community, Mexicans themselves also sent authorities on futile searches. In El Paso, Justice Department agents and customs inspectors were alerted to a smuggling operation involving a woman named Carolina Pacos. Their informant, another Mexican female whose identity was kept secret in the official Bureau of Investigation report, told them that Pacos was in the habit of frequenting a local grocery store owned by a suspicious Turk. There, she claimed, Pacos would purchase small amounts of ammunition and smuggle them into Mexico in her undergarments. To catch the alleged smuggler in the act, the investigative team furnished customs officers with her passport photograph and waited for her next appearance at the Stanton Street Bridge.[71] After an inspection that could only have been an embarrassing experience for all parties concerned, the Bureau of Investigation was forced to concede that its examinations had "failed to substantiate that the woman was smuggling ammunition."[72]

Other episodes bordered on absurdity even without false leads. One such case took place in the spring of 1918 in Fort Worth, where authorities placed a Mexican native by the name of Valle, a resident of Bureau, Illinois, under arrest as a potential subversive. "Being a mexican [*sic*] and having with him a camera and unable to explain himself clearly," Bureau of Investigation agent F. S. Smith wrote, Valle "was considered suspicious." Such reservations diminished after officials inspected the detainee and interrogated him fully, which resulted in his release from police custody. As it turned out, Valle had simply been doing his sixteen-year-old brother, who was en route from Mexico, a favor by meeting him in Fort Worth, from where they planned to depart for Illinois. On the elder Valle's person, Smith noted, investigators had found a Liberty Loan bond.[73]

The most ludicrous of these leads involved elements of mysticism and the supernatural. In May 1917, Bureau of Investigation agents responded to rumors that Mexicans in Austin were holding meetings to plan the bombing of the state capitol building and other local structures. The main attraction at these gatherings, they were told, was a young Mexican girl with special powers of healing and clairvoyance. In actuality, their investigation turned up little more than a traveling medicine show. Sitting on a throne wearing a silk dress and a brass crown, the young soothsayer would first address the crowds about war, prophesies, and other such matters before prescribing her father's miracle salve to ailing audience members, who in gratitude would then offer whatever they could as a donation. Although the girl's father was taken into custody and charged with practicing medicine without a license, authorities were unable to find any evidence of sabotage or disloyalty. Indeed, not only were the meetings not encouraging Mexicans to return to their homeland—as some agents suspected—the little girl was actually calling on her followers to "work unceasingly in the fields and in the towns" so that "food and other supplies may be produced in abundance to help the starving people across the ocean."[74]

V

Examples like these illustrate a troubling aspect of the war's vigilance campaign: namely, that it was conducted at the expense of the civil liberties of thousands, perhaps even millions, of innocent Americans. Besides the post office's systematic attempts to compel loyalty from the press, authorities often harassed and intimidated suspects during the course of their investigations. Even when the suspicions of disloyalty proved false, other charges were sometimes substituted to punish surveillance targets, as evidenced by the seer episode. Of course, these charges were occasionally unsustainable too and some suspects walked free. Nevertheless, by then local officials had subjected them to the powers of arrest, confinement, indictment, and intimidation.[75] In the words of constitutional historian Paul L. Murphy, "the story of civil liberties during World War I is a dreary, disturbing, and in some respects, shocking chapter out of the nation's past. Americans . . . stood by on the domestic scene and saw liberty and justice prostituted in ways more extreme and extensive than any other time in American history."[76]

In the end, no Mexican or Mexican American was ever found guilty of active spying in the United States, although suspected cases of espionage did sometimes land in court. In Laredo, the arrest in late 1918 of a sixteen-year-old girl named Guadalupe Ledesma, who was charged with being a German agent, caused a considerable stir. Garnering attention as much for her beauty as for her legal quandary, the Mexican native stood accused of carrying messages for the Germans back and forth across the Rio Grande. However sensational, her trial was short-lived. In April 1919, a federal court in Laredo found Ledesma innocent of all charges.[77]

The sole enemy agent sentenced to death during World War I was a German naval lieutenant by the name of Lothar Witzke. An experienced spy despite being a mere twenty-two years old, Witzke had orders to create a major disturbance along the U.S.-Mexico border. To accomplish this task, he and two other agents had plans to travel to Arizona to induce the African American soldiers of the 9th and 10th Cavalry to mutiny, as well as to incite waves of violent strikes among the local copper miners. Unfortunately for Witzke, his companions were both double agents, one of whom was working in conjunction with American intelligence (the other agent was operating with the British). On February 1, 1918, military intelligence officials arrested Witzke in Nogales, Arizona. Several months later, a military tribunal found him guilty of espionage and sentenced him to hang, although certain legal technicalities undermining the government's case eventually led to his sentence being commuted to life imprisonment, and, in 1923, to his release to Germany.[78]

Because espionage and conspiracy were so difficult to prove in court, offenses such as smuggling resulted in more convictions. With its accessibility to anyone willing to hide a few munitions on his or her person and transport them across the border, smuggling was often carried out by destitute Mexican refugees who were willing to risk a stint in the county jail. In other cases, however, the offenders were more high-profile individuals, such as Herminio Mercado Abasta, a captain in Gen. Pablo Gonzales's revolutionary army, who was caught attempting to smuggle five thousand rounds of pistol cartridges into the northern Mexican town of Nuevo Laredo.[79]

In the years following the Allied victory in the war, Germany's influence in Mexico gradually faded. A few weeks after the armistice, the American government sent German leaders a note stating that "the German minister in Mexico is continuing to foment anti-American propaganda in that country." If the United States is "to take in good faith the German government's recent request for aid," the message continued, "it must request that the agitation in question cease and the German minister to Mexico be recalled immediately." Not surprisingly, Germany wasted little time in complying with the demand. Although the Nazis resumed German projects in Mexico during the 1930s, their success paled compared to that of the kaiser.[80]

VI

Throughout the war, disloyalty manifested itself in every part of the country. The barrios of the Lone Star State were no different. But in its surveillance of the Tejano community, American intelligence above all else acted on the widespread fears of German-Mexican collusion, fears so deep and abiding that even the shakiest of leads were pursued. For the student of history, this particular aspect of World War I merits consideration not only because of its often fascinating accounts of conspiracy and intrigue, but also because of what it says about the unfavorable views of Mexicans that existed during the period. At a time when no one could afford to be considered a potential subversive, the image of the Mexican as untrustworthy gained renewed credence. The result was that the civil liberties of many innocent individuals were sacrificed on the altar of national security.

CHAPTER FOUR

The Home Front

EVEN AS THE GOVERNMENT MONITORED MEXICANS AND Mexican Americans with a suspicious eye, contributions to the war effort poured in from the Tejano community, which still suffered occasionally from the violent spillover of the Mexican Revolution. Reflecting the divisions across the country, some Mexican Americans opposed the war, with a few even displaying outright disdain for the actions of their country. Nevertheless, shows of support for the war far outnumbered those of resistance.

I

In April 1917, soon after the United States declared war against Germany, communities throughout the country held parades in observance of Loyalty Day. In the Lone Star State, Mexicans Americans reveled alongside other Texans. On April 11, several hundred Tejanos marched together with African Americans in the Loyalty Day parade in Dallas.[1] In Corpus Christi, which held its celebration a few days earlier, thousands of men, women, and children—including many of Mexican origin—from all over Central Texas participated in the city's parade. At the head of the Mexican American procession was the Demócrata Obrera, a prominent local organization composed of about eighty Tejano businessmen.[2]

In Laredo, Mexican Americans were especially critical to the Loyalty Day festivities. Some, like G. R. Jiménez, served on the committee appointed by Mayor Robert M. McComb to plan the grand Loyalty Day parade. Jiménez and his fellow committee members eventually opted to hold the celebration on April 19 to commemorate the historic Battle of Lexington and Paul Revere's famous midnight ride.[3] At precisely 4 o'clock that afternoon, the approximately five-thousand-strong procession, which included the Mexican Banda Social and various Mexican trade unions and fraternal organizations, started traversing the designated route. With each of its participants sporting American flags, the parade navigated the town's entire downtown area and finally arrived in front of the federal building. There, thousands remained to enjoy the patriotic program put together by the Loyalty Day committee, a show that consisted mainly of recitations and patriotic addresses. Among the orators was the aforementioned Clemente Idar, publisher of *Evolución,* one of the city's most important Spanish-language dailies, who delivered his speech in Spanish. Loyalty Day, declared the *Laredo Weekly Times,* had inspired "one of the grandest and most inspiring patriotic demonstrations ever witnessed" in South Texas. "Not only were the genuine Americans wearing flags and displaying them today," it observed, "but the Mexican-Americans as well showed loyalty to their adopted country."[4]

II

Fomenting patriotism was only the first step in mobilizing the country. "It is not an army that we must shape and train for war," President Wilson declared, "it is a nation."[5] Toward this end, the White House placed federal bureaus in charge of every economic sector. Among the myriad of agencies were the Railroad Administration, the War Finance Corporation (WFC), the Food Administration, the War Trade Board, the Emergency Fleet Corporation, the Fuel Administration, and the War Industries Board (WIB).[6]

One of the most important of these agencies was the wider-ranging Council of National Defense (CND). Consisting of the secretaries of War, Navy, Agriculture, Commerce, Labor, and the Interior, and including a Woman's Committee and civilian Advisory Commission made up of leaders of industry and labor, the CND was in charge of coordinating industries and resources for the war effort. To assist them with this monumental task, council leaders requested that each state organize a state council of defense. In Texas, the State Council comprised thirty-eight members appointed by Governor Ferguson, a Texas Division of the Woman's Committee, and over 240 county councils and fifteen thousand community councils. Several Tejanos held positions on these local councils, such as in the counties of Webb, Cameron, Duval, El Paso, Willacy, and Starr, where F. O. Guerra served as chairman. Meanwhile, Adina De Zavala of San Antonio, already famous in the state for her fight to preserve the Alamo, served as state treasurer and chairwoman of parochial schools on the Woman's Committee. In late 1918, De Zavala led a statewide letter-writing campaign to promote noon prayer on behalf of American servicemen abroad.[7]

Because the outbreak of war saw many young workers leave their jobs for the armed forces and led to an overall decrease in immigration, the mobilization of American labor was an especially crucial priority for the CND. Accordingly, Wilson enlisted the backing of Samuel Gompers, president of the American Federation of Labor (AFL), whose cooperation was crucial for recruiting other trade unions for the war effort. After pledging the AFL's support for the war, Gompers received a seat on the council's Advisory Commission. Not coincidentally, most labor unions worked in concert with the government throughout most of the war.[8]

Mexicans and Mexican Americans played a key role in the war effort as laborers. Like women and blacks, they filled the jobs previously held by the Anglo-American men now in uniform. "During the First World War Mexicans performed a valuable service to the United States and her allies," historian Ricardo Romo has written. "They manned railroads, helped construct new military bases and picked cotton used in gunpowder and clothing. Mexicans who worked in mines in the Southwest also helped to provide a steady flow of copper, lead, and other minerals needed in the war effort."[9] Of course, as mentioned previously, they also formed a vital component of the agricultural labor force. One of their most significant contributions to the war effort, then, was in lending their energies to essential war production—by simply working.

Sometimes, however, Tejanos pledged their contributions to such production in roles other than laborers. On May 4, 1917, for example, two hundred Mexican American farmers in the El Paso Valley held a "war-crop meeting" in the town of San Elizario. After a series of patriotic speeches in Spanish, the group vowed to increase food production to aid the Allied cause.[10]

Volunteerism was key to mobilization. The Food Administration, for example, mostly eschewed government-mandated rationing in favor of patriotic self-sacrifice to conserve foodstuffs. Charged with the task of providing food to the troops and their allies abroad, Food Administrator Herbert Hoover appealed to the patriotism of American consumers. Taking up slogans like "Food will win the war," Americans everywhere loyally observed wheatless Mondays, meatless Tuesdays, and porkless Saturdays. Food conservation, which became known as "Hooverizing," was an unqualified success.[11] To feed themselves and save farm crops for the war effort, patriotic Americans also planted vegetable gardens, or "war gardens," in their backyards or empty lots. Tejanas took a special interest in this wartime activity. In a letter to a fellow member of the local council of defense, the chairwoman of the committee to encourage the planting of war gardens in Kleberg County identified over ninety Tejanas who had joined her effort.[12]

The Spanish-language press likewise aided the food conservation effort. Publications like *Evolución* and *El Demócrata Fronterizo* often ran notices to inform Tejanos of the Food Administration's conservation measures, in some cases translating in full the latest proclamations from government officials.[13] Announcements of stricter rationing policies—especially those pertaining to groceries, restaurants, bakeries, and hotels—usually received front-page coverage. Besides supporting the war effort, these newspapers provided a valuable service to the Spanish-speaking business community, as the penalties for violating such regulations were often prohibitive.[14]

Not all aspects of the mobilization effort fared as well, however. For one thing, the production of ships and tanks was negligible. Not only that, heavy guns were manufactured in large quantities only after the end of the war. Artillery pieces for the American Expeditionary Force (AEF) actually came from France, which, along with England, also supplied the planes for American aviators. To top it all off, the financing of the war quickly reached unheard-of levels. "The noughts attached to the many millions were so boisterous and prolific," recollected Secretary of the Treasury William Gibbs McAdoo of his efforts to calculate the cost of the war, "that, at times, they would run clear over the edge of the paper."[15]

To alleviate some of these problems (and counter criticism from Republicans), Wilson organized the War Industries Board in the spring of 1918. Under the direction of Bernard M. Baruch, the WIB, whose ostensible responsibility was to regulate war purchases, also wound up overseeing everything from price fixing to industrial growth. Like Hoover, Baruch preferred suasion to law. Occasionally, however, this took the form of threatening uncooperative individuals with public humiliation. Once, for instance, he told a recalcitrant businessman that if he ignored the WIB's requests "you will be such an object of contempt and scorn in your home town that you will not dare to show your face there. If you should, your fellow citizens would call you a slacker, the boys would hoot at you, and the draft men would likely run you out of town." However ham-fisted, such tactics more often than not succeeded and eventually set American industrial production on the right track.[16]

Also helping convince Americans to join the war effort was the Committee on Public Information (CPI), led by the zealous muckraker George Creel. The chief propaganda arm of the Wilson administration, the CPI enlisted the support of journalists, illustrators, filmmakers, and lecturers to disseminate the government line on the war, eventually distributing thousands of press releases, pamphlets, films, posters, and speeches. The agency even recruited Hollywood's elite like Charlie Chaplin, Douglas Fairbanks, and Mary Pickford to contribute to the war effort.[17]

In terms of oratory, the leading voices of the CPI were supplied by the Four Minute Men. Numbering over seventy-five thousand, the Four Minute Men were volunteer speakers whose task it was to deliver brief talks wherever ready audiences awaited—movie theaters, schools, lodges, and union halls, to name but a few such venues.[18] Several Tejanos served as Four Minute Men. In North Texas, Joe Vera was part of Fort Worth's ensemble, while Domingo Montoya performed in his native El Paso. Laredo's fourteen-man troupe—including Clemente Idar, its lone Tejano—spoke on such topics as "The European War" and "Why We Are Going to War" in Webb County theaters. Meanwhile, José Tomás (J. T.) Canales, state representative from Brownsville and civil rights advocate, was the only Spanish-surnamed individual on a council of defense list of the most popular and frequently used speakers in Cameron County.[19]

Through a series of CPI publications, the directors of the Four Minute Men advised their state chairmen on how best to train their charges. One memorandum stressed the importance of keeping to the four-minute limit, as it was believed that anything longer was bound to bore the audience, and poor speakers were considered "worse than none." Another called for the nationwide implementation of "Alien Squads" into the Four Minute Men's presentations. A successful innovation from Philadelphia, the Alien Squad presentation consisted of a short opening speech by a Four Minute Man, who would then introduce a group of eight to sixteen American servicemen of varied ethnicity. According to the communication, the servicemen's declarations of their national origins usually elicited enthusiastic responses from audiences. Above all else, though, Four Minute Men were directed to be pithy, sonorous, and direct.[20] In addition to these requirements, Mexican American Four Minute Men often needed to be bilingual. As in New Mexico, where half of the audiences facing these orators could not speak the English language, many parts of Texas contained predominately Spanish-speaking audiences. "Every speaker in these [local] theaters must necessarily speak in Spanish," noted the El Paso chairman of the Four Minute Men, "and we are dependant [*sic*] upon these few men who can speak the language fluently."[21]

One of the major projects of the Four Minute Men, and the CPI in general, was the sale of war bonds. Instead of continuing the tradition of financing wars through the sale of bonds to wealthy individuals and large businesses, Secretary McAdoo opted to tap into the passionate volunteerism of the era, designing the so-called Liberty Loans to be affordable for all but the poorest Americans. "We went direct to the people," he noted, "and that means everybody—to businessmen, workmen, farmers, bankers, millionaires, school-teachers, laborers. We capitalized the profound impulse called patriotism."[22] The strategy succeeded beyond expectations, as the four wartime loans and a fifth postwar "Victory Loan" raised over twenty-three billion dollars.[23]

In Texas, Mexican Americans staged a vigorous war bond campaign. Pvt. Manuel Vela, a volunteer in the Texas Cavalry, delivered patriotic speeches on behalf of the Liberty Loans throughout Central and South Texas. During a one-week period in the fall of 1918, Private Vela sold over fifty thousand dollars in bonds to the residents of Alice, Premont, McAllen, Harlingen, San Benito, and the surrounding areas.[24] In Laredo, Clemente Idar was an especially articulate spokesman. "If a sentimentalist were to say that he wished not to give money to send the younger generation to a foreign death, we could in all honestly remind him that every American dollar he donates signifies the shedding of one less drop of blood," he told one crowd. "These current times hold the test of loyalty for the American people."[25]

For patriotic Tejanos, the press was an essential marketing tool. Besides publishing messages from the Federal Reserve Board, Liberty Drive chairmen, and local chambers of commerce, newspapers like *La Prensa, Evolución,* and *El Demócrata Fronterizo* printed full-page advertisements, many of them sponsored by Tejano businessmen, urging their readers to purchase war bonds.[26] By and large, though, their editorial staffs delivered the pitches themselves. "We must be patriotic and generous, offering the government all of our resources so that it will quickly and assuredly lead our soldiers to triumph," advised *El Demócrata Fronterizo* during the fourth Liberty Loan. "One last effort and the victory will be ours."[27] Meanwhile, *Evolución,* its cross-town counterpart, was not above shaming its readers into spending for the war. During a particularly dry period of the first Liberty Loan, one of its headlines read "Laredo Has Not Acted Patriotically."[28]

Coercive devices of this sort were not unusual during wartime. "Every person who refuses to subscribe or who takes the attitude of let the other fellow do it, is a friend of Germany and I would like nothing better than to tell it to him to his face," McAdoo told an audience in California in the fall of 1917. "A man who can't lend his government $1.25 per week at the rate of 4% interest is not entitled to be an American citizen."[29] For its part, the Federal Reserve Board requested from each community a list of individuals whose war bond purchases were not commensurate with their financial standing, a blatant strong-arm tactic given that notice of this demand was publicized throughout the media, including the Spanish-language press.[30] Moreover, despite the emphasis on volunteerism and self-sacrifice, the federal government assigned each state a quota based on its aggregate wealth to encourage the purchase of war bonds. Because bank deposits figured into the calculation of a community's wealth, problems sometimes arose as a result of the substantial accounts some Mexican citizens held in U.S. border towns, which were nonetheless responsible for filling their overinflated quotas.[31]

While capable of eliciting selflessness and good will, the Liberty Loans also brought out the worst in some Americans. When Sen. Warren G. Harding took the Senate floor to call attention to the loan drives' devolution into the "hysterical and unseemly," his colleagues showered him with scorn and ridicule.[32] In some parts of the country, vigilantes affixed yellow cards to houses belonging to individuals who had not purchased bonds.[33]

III

The pressure to support the Liberty Loans reflected the unfortunate side effects of supernationalism. Across the country, opponents of the war—even those whose credentials as patriots were unquestionable—suffered persecution and abuse. Sen. Robert La Follette was censured by the state legislature of his native Wisconsin for his antiwar views. Meanwhile, socialist leader Eugene V. Debs's comment that his followers did not deserve to be "cannon fodder" garnered him a twenty-year prison sentence. Perhaps most appallingly, a Colorado gang assaulted a man bound to a wheelchair for daring to criticize President Wilson.[34] Fear, intolerance, and enforced conformity often surfaced in Texas, as well. In Dallas, a thirteen-year-old girl was attacked by her schoolmates—none of whom were punished—for uttering pro-German remarks. In Fort Worth, a woman filed for divorce from her German-born husband on the ground that his disloyalty to his adopted country had torn apart their marriage.[35]

Developments in Austin contributed to the hostile mood. During a special session in 1918, the state legislature banned criticism of the U.S. government, its officials, the flag, and the servicemen's uniforms. It also denied the ballot to the unnaturalized foreign-born.

A new law required that schools display an American flag on their campuses, devote at least ten minutes daily to lessons on patriotism, and, most significantly, conduct all classes—except those expressly to teach foreign languages—in English.[36] "While primarily the law was intended to prevent the teaching of German in the schools of the state," the *Laredo Weekly Times* warned its mostly Spanish-speaking readership, "it also includes any other foreign language" and its violation "carries with it a penalty for any teacher of not less than $25 nor more than $200."[37] Regardless, its effectiveness along the border remains in question, given that as late as August 1918—less than three months before the end of the war—citizens in Jim Hogg County were asking the Texas State Council of Defense for advice on what actions to take against a thriving private school run by Mexican citizens and conducted entirely in Spanish.[38]

The tensions of wartime led some to conclude that an individual's lack of English skills translated into a lack of patriotism. Even council of defense members were not immune from charges of disloyalty. In late 1917, E. L. Gammage of Rio Grande City relayed his concerns about the entirely Mexican American Starr County Council of Defense to both the Texas State Council of Defense and the Bureau of Investigation. "Not an American is on the [council]," Gammage complained, referring to ethnicity rather than citizenship, "and only two members . . . speak and write the english [*sic*] language." While conceding that the group did consist of "respectable citizens," the small-town attorney nonetheless labeled them "race haters" who discriminated against all things American. "None of them are leaders," he went on, "and none are overcharged with patriotism for Uncle Sam. They live and dream only for Mexico." Despite his best efforts, though, federal and state officials opted to leave the local council to its own devices, particularly since it appeared to be making an honest effort to fulfill all of its duties and obligations.[39]

Throughout the war, flags featured prominently in matters involving questions of patriotism. In Laredo, officials discouraged displays of the Mexican flag from the Loyalty Day festivities. "The advice not to have Mexican flags in the procession is given in a friendly way," apologized one local editorial, "and for the reason that the parade is strictly American in its nature and to show that Mexican-Americans are loyal to the country of their adoption."[40] The Mexican Independence Day of 1917 was the first in the town's history in which the Mexican tricolors were nowhere to be seen, authorities having issued an order to desist from flying flags other than those of the United States and its allies.[41] Not surprisingly, tensions over the flag issue reached a fever pitch. When a Mexican schoolgirl refused to salute the American flag in class, administrators promptly sent her home and revoked her school privileges.[42]

Perhaps as a reaction to such oppressive measures, displays of disdain toward the American war effort occasionally emanated from the Tejano community. On April 5, 1917, the *Corpus Christi Caller and Daily Herald* printed a story out of El Paso detailing how a man named Francisco Aguilar and an unidentified companion had been issued fines for trampling on an American flag. According to the account, a riot had ensued in the city's Mexican quarter as a result of their actions.[43]

The American flag played a role in similar incidents elsewhere. In Laredo, a district court sentenced Vicente San Miguel to up to five years in the state penitentiary after knifing and seriously wounding Inés Ramos and Severo Miramas in a bar fight. San Miguel had apparently attacked Ramos for wearing an American flag boutonniere and injured Miramas when the latter rushed to Ramos's aid.[44] The ominous tones of a subsequent *Laredo Weekly Times* editorial reflected the importance that some observers attached to such anti-American activities. "It is to be hoped that some of the 'bad' Mexicans here will not make it necessary for the authorities to teach them a wholesome lesson," read the piece. "Our police officers are ready at all times, and our jail stands waiting for all who violate the laws. And it might be that some of those who affect to despise the American flag might need other ministrations before the police could rescue them from an enraged populace."[45]

Tensions over the desecration of the American flag carried over into the immediate postwar period. On December 22, 1918, a ruckus erupted when a certain Félix Castillo tore down an American flag at a dance hall in the small mining town of Dolores in Webb County. Once the dust had settled, a man by the name of Pablo Morales lay dead, a murder for which Castillo was later charged by a district court in nearby Laredo.[46]

IV

If Tejanos worried that such incidents might perpetuate the image of Mexicans as inherently hostile to Americans, events along the U.S.-Mexico border likely increased these anxieties tenfold. On Christmas Day, 1917, Mexicans raided the ranch of one of Presidio County's wealthiest residents, L. C. Brite. Located just fifteen miles east of the Rio Grande, the sprawling 125,000-acre spread was an inviting target for the raiders, who looted Brite's merchandise store and terrified the local populace before crossing back into Mexico, leaving in their wake three men dead and another wounded. Two months later, raiders again struck in beleaguered Presidio County, this time attacking the more humble estate of forty-nine-year-old rancher Ed Neville. On the evening of March 25, 1918, fifty Mexicans ransacked the Neville ranch house. When U.S. troopers arrived on the scene, they found Neville's teenaged son Glen mortally wounded with gunshots to the head and knee. Their discovery inside the ravaged house was even grislier. There, sitting on the floor against a wall, was the mutilated corpse of Neville's cook, Rosa Castillo, whose breasts had been torn off and placed on either side of her body. Also in the house were Castillo's three children, all of whom had witnessed their mother's murder, one having been wounded and left for dead. While not as frequent as those of the prewar period, such attacks on American soil were no less brutal and often resulted in numerous casualties.[47]

That said, the American retaliation was generally worse. After the raid on the Neville ranch, U.S. troopers crossed the border into Mexico and located the culprits in the small village of Pilares, Chihuahua. A massive gunfight resulted in the deaths of thirty-three Mexicans. This reprisal, however, paled in comparison to what transpired after the killings at the Brite ranch. Following an engagement between the raiders and American soldiers that left ten of the Mexicans dead, Capt. J. M. Fox of Texas Rangers Company B ordered several of his men to the predominately Mexican village of Porvenir, Texas, a supposed bandit nest in the Big Bend area. With tensions still running high from the Brite affair, the Rangers summarily executed fifteen innocent Mexicans, orphaning forty-two children. Despite subsequent investigations and hearings that led to the forced resignation of Captain Fox and a complete overhaul of the Texas Rangers, no criminal charges were ever filed against anyone in Company B.[48]

The internecine conflict usually provoked panic on both sides of the border. On more than one occasion, Ygnacio Bonillas, Mexican ambassador to the United States, was forced to fire off dispatches to Secretary of State Robert Lansing expressing Pres. Venustiano Carranza's reservations about American soldiers crossing into Mexico, which the First Chief regarded as a violation of Mexican territory. In the opinion of the Mexican government, bandit raids on American soil were hardly analogous to these incursions—despite American protests to the contrary—as raiders, unlike American soldiers and Texas Rangers, were not official government troops. Nevertheless, their promises to handle the brigands themselves fell on deaf ears, as anxious American officials insisted on their right to take matters into their own hands—regardless of the illegalities involved. "I agree with you wholly as to the necessity of our having no avoidable friction with the Mexicans who live along the border," Secretary of War Newton D. Baker wrote to Secretary of State Robert Lansing in July, 1918, "but if Mexicans cross our border and commit raids, I can not agree that they should not be pursued by our patrols even if they flee across the Mexican border."[49]

Naturally, the border violence was often front-page news. Blazing headlines such as that of the August 28, 1918, issue of the *Houston Post,* which read simply "Americans and Mexicans Fight," likely did little to improve the image of Mexicans among Texans. Even the national press picked up the reports. On December 26, 1917, for example, the *New York Times* led with the story of the attack on the Brite ranch.[50]

V

On the whole, however, there was more than enough evidence of Mexican American patriotism to offset any negative media coverage, as when entire communities turned out for loan drives. On April 23, 1918, Mexicans and Mexican Americans purchased approximately seventy thousand dollars in war bonds at a rally in Brownsville.[51] In nearby Jim Wells County, officials gave much of the credit for their county's success during the fourth Liberty Loan to its residents of Mexican descent, particularly those from the small town of Premont, whose tiny community alone raised eight thousand dollars in one day.[52] No less significant, the Tejano community in Victoria County pledged over twelve thousand dollars worth of bonds during the fourth loan, with one of its rallies raising over one thousand dollars in less than ten minutes.[53]

In Laredo, B. G. Salinas offered a fifty-dollar war bond to the Boy Scout who could write the best essay on why Americans should support the Liberty Loans.[54] His fellow Laredoans at the L. Villegas Company, most of whose employees were either Mexican or Mexican American, also contributed to the war effort, resolving at a meeting during the first Liberty Loan to purchase collectively a war bond in the amount of one thousand dollars.[55] Perhaps more so than any other part of the state, Laredo, with its elite class of wealthy and propertied Tejanos claiming descent from the city's Spanish founders, saw the purchase of war bonds become a symbol of status and patriotism among Mexican Americans, several of whom spent the requisite amounts to join the $1000 Club of Laredo and the even more exclusive $5000 Club.[56]

More than a few individuals registered notable purchases. Rafael Flores, a farmer from Sejita, a hamlet in southern Duval County, made the news after walking into the Corpus Christi National Bank with a large sack of money containing proceeds from his latest cotton crop and investing the entire sum of sixteen hundred dollars in war bonds.[57] Even Mexican citizens spent considerable amounts. At a Brownsville rally during the third loan, Matamoros native José Donato bought two thousand dollars worth of bonds, one of the largest purchases of the loan drive.[58] Such purchases paled in comparison to that of Luis R. Ortíz, however. When his hometown of Laredo seemed on the verge of missing its quota for the fourth loan, Ortíz came to the rescue with an investment of thirty thousand dollars, an especially impressive sum given that at the time the annual family income after taxes was only fifteen hundred dollars.[59]

The wartime enthusiasm extended to another of McAdoo's major fundraisers, war stamps. Tejanos in the Central Texas town of Brady organized an "all-Mexican" thrift stamp society at their local Catholic church.[60] Their counterparts in San José oversubscribed their twenty-five-hundred-dollar war stamp quota by approximately one thousand dollars, in some cases pledging their hay and fruit crops in payment for the stamps.[61] The Sociedad de la Unión, one of the largest and most prestigious Mexican mutual-aid societies in San Antonio, purchased three thousand dollars worth of stamps. Its contribution, according to Francisco Chapa, publisher of *El Imparcial de Texas* and an honorary member of the organization, "showed that the Mexican citizens know what Uncle Sam is trying to do and are going to help him do it to the limit of their ability."[62] Apparently, Gov. William P. Hobby agreed, sending the group a congratulatory letter that was promptly translated, framed, and copied for the Spanish-language press.[63]

The Tejano community also contributed toward semiofficial services like Red Cross work. Tejanos organized Mexican auxiliaries to their local Red Cross chapters in both Forth Worth and San Antonio, which, along with Eagle Pass and New Braunfels, held fundraising events for the organization on Mexican Independence Day.[64] In Brownsville, several Mexican Americans served as ward chairmen in their local chapter, while in Laredo, Tejanos sometimes delivered speeches in Spanish during Red Cross rallies. In most cases, such contributions were simply part of the war effort. In Fort Worth, however, a benefit fiesta held by the town's Mexican residents in the summer of 1917 was also in recognition of the Red Cross's services in Mexico during the revolution.[65]

Some contributions were not products of organized fundraisers. A. G. Verduzco simply took up a collection from his co-workers at the Cannel Coal Company in the small Webb County towns of Dolores and Darwin and submitted the proceeds to the Laredo chapter of the Red Cross.[66] For his part, Julián Cisneros Chapa, a cotton picker from Brownsville with two sons in the army, donated a fifty-dollar war bond to his local chapter, of which he was a member and monthly contributor. Previously, he had donated over several hundred dollars raised in the cotton fields of San Marcos through appeals to his fellow Spanish-speaking laborers. "I cannot fight, for I am too old. But I can help to take care of those soldiers who are fighting for my country," the sixty-year-old Cisneros told the *Brownsville Herald*. "The American flag has protected me all my life, and I am ready to do my best to protect the flag."[67]

It was in Red Cross work that Tejanas were most active during the war. Some women, like Rachael G. Saenz of El Paso, worked as nurses with the humanitarian organization.[68] Most others, however, helped in raising funds. In Darwin, Alberta Botello de Alexander, along with several other Tejanas, organized a festival whose proceeds benefited relief efforts in France. A similar event was held in Laredo, where María C. Villarreal served as the chairwoman in charge of the bazaar. In some cases, these benefits took a rather different form. In Del Rio, on the southwestern corner of the Edwards Plateau, for example, the Ideal Dramatic Club, a theatrical troupe of young Tejanas, staged performances at various venues around town as part of its Red Cross work.[69] Perhaps as a sign of gratitude, the Red Cross also lent a helping hand to the Tejano community. In July 1918, the secretary of the San Antonio chapter of the Red Cross printed a notice in *La Prensa* to inform the wives of Mexican American servicemen that her organization would be assisting with the task of securing soldiers' pensions, with which many Tejanas had apparently been struggling.[70]

Although no less appreciated, patriotic gestures on the part of Tejanas were often more modest. In one case, Mrs. G. G. López of Brooks County donated a comforter to the soldiers at Camp Bowie in Fort Worth, most likely in response to the calls from the Texas press for warm clothing for needy doughboys. Immediately upon its receipt, Maj. J. S. Upham wrote López to thank her on behalf of his commanding general, who wished to inform her that the gift would be turned over to a deserving soldier straight away.[71] Even after the end of the war, some Tejanas continued to help out the troops. In

January 1919, for example, Tejanas from the Our Lady of Refuge Catholic Church in Eagle Pass prepared tamales for a feast held in honor of the soldiers in Camp Eagle Pass.[72] Deeds of this sort garnered the respect of the Spanish-language press. "Women will have a monument alongside that of the heroes who died for their country," *Evolución* prophesied. "They must have it."[73]

One Mexican woman received plaudits across the state for her artistic talents as well as her prowar stance. In April 1918, nineteen-year-old Concepción Macías was profiled in several newspapers for her pencil drawing titled *Belgium Waits.* A sensation in her adopted hometown of Houston, where it was put on display at the meeting hall of the Rotary Club, the piece depicted the Belgian nation as a shackled maiden overlooking a devastated countryside, stoically waiting for the Allied powers to free her homeland from German occupation. The *Houston Post* noted that Macías's work was especially impressive given her total lack of formal artistic training, surmising that her inspiration was likely drawn from her own experiences as an expatriate from Mexico, whose revolutionary travails had recently dispossessed her family of its land and wealth in its native San Luis Potosí. "She can sympathize with the poor women of Belgium," it wrote, "for she has seen and endured hardships too."[74] For its part, *La Prensa* was moved to lyrical flight: "Belgium Waits! How beautifully symbolic of the promise and the state of affairs! Yes! Belgium awaits with the highest and most noble of heroism the triumph of the cause for which it shed first blood, defying with one proud and fierce gesture the arrogance of the Teutons!"[75]

Other Tejanos likewise employed art to further the war effort. *Evolución,* for example, often ran illustrations with patriotic and anti-German themes. One cartoon simply titled *Kaiser,* by in-house artist Eduardo L. Martínez, showed Wilhelm II as a skeleton in full military regalia, no doubt attributing the mass carnage abroad to the German monarch.[76]

VI

Music was arguably the leading art form of World War I, which came to be known as a "singing war." Some wartime songs conveyed patriotic messages with a touch of humor. "K-K-K-Katy," Geoffrey O'Hara's profile of a stuttering, lovesick doughboy, and Irving Berlin's "How I Hate to Get Up in the Morning," which had servicemen threatening their buglers in unison, were popular numbers in this vein. However, the most widely known war song to come out of

America, George M. Cohan's "Over There," was pure flag-waving patriotism, its refrain of "the Yanks are coming" conveying the notion of America as world savior.[77]

The Tejano community added its own contributions to the catalog of American patriotic music. Along with lyricist J. W. Falvella, Prof. J. M. de Villar, a professional musician from Laredo, a town with a lively artistic scene, composed "The Texans Are Ready," which garnered acclaim in South Texas.[78] Several months after its release, fellow Laredoan Sgt. Joe Benavides of the 141st Infantry—then in Missouri en route to France—wrote to notify his hometown of the song's popularity among his comrades. "'The Texans Are Ready' was played here today when we reached Sedalia, Mo.," noted Benavides. "It made a great hit and was cheered and cheered."[79]

Laredo also produced Spanish-language patriotic music in the folk genre of *corridos*.[80] The anonymously written "Registro de 1918" (Registration of 1918) depicts the emotions of those young men who were about to journey to the battlefields of Europe:

> Farewell sparkling Laredo
> with your towers and bells,
> but we will never forget
> your beautiful Mexican women.
>
> Now they're taking us to fight
> to faraway places
> and they're taking us to fight
> against the German forces.
>
> Now they're taking us to fight
> in different directions
> and they're taking us to fight
> against different nations.
>
> How far is the journey
> Over the sea waves!
> great would be my joy
> if I could be victorious. . . .
>
> Farewell my beloved parents
> and the young woman I love,
> when we get to France
> we'll send you a sigh.[81]

A portion of another anonymous composition titled "Nuevo Corrido de Laredo" (New Ballad of Laredo) also dealt with World War I.

Brimming with ethnic pride, the *corrido* celebrates the town's contribution to the war effort:

It would be criminal
were anyone to say
that your sons didn't shine
in the great world war.

There are many Mexicans here
who fought in the war,
they returned decorated
for the courage they demonstrated.

Some of them were gassed,
others are missing legs,
and many other things befell them
fighting foreign causes.

Not only at the front
did they demonstrate their valor,
for that reason in Laredo, Texas,
Mexicans are appreciated.[82]

Clearly, these ballads—along with another from Texas titled "La Guerra," which declares, "We Tejanos also know how to die for a great nation"—suggest that Tejanos took immense satisfaction in the exploits of their World War I veterans, accomplishments that they no doubt hoped would improve their relations with other Texans.[83]

Meanwhile, some Laredoans recruited artists to inspire patriotism in the Tejano community. Such was the case on May 28, 1918, when the Sociedad Hijos de Juárez, a local fraternal organization, invited Mexican poet Oswaldo Sánchez to speak at one of its meetings. According to the *Laredo Weekly Times,* Sánchez riveted his audience with "one of the most ardent pro-ally speeches ever made in Laredo."[84] To those who feared the consequences of the terrible conflict overseas, Sánchez offered hope. "Civilization will not end," he declared, "because in the limpid blue of the banners which defend justice there sparkle with the tremulous splendor of lofty tragedy, the American stars, those of all the Americas of Columbus which . . . will not delay in defending themselves from the interruptions of the vandals." To the United States, he gave credit: "Latin-America, particularly our own unfortunate country, owes more to the modern civilization of the United States than to any other country of Europe, with the exception of Spain, to whom we owe our lofty doctrinarian sentiments and the incomparable language of Cervantes."[85] Sánchez's oration made such an impression on Laredoans that Clemente Idar later attempted to arrange for him a speaking tour of the Southwest through the Four Minute Men.[86]

Tejanos occasionally staged their own patriotic performances in Laredo. On October 11, 1918, *La Prensa* featured a preview of a literary and musical festival in honor of the Allies that would be held in the town's Lincoln Theater the following day. Besides original pieces from the local talent, among the acts to be performed were "Siciliana," from the opera *Cavalleria Rusticana* (1890), and an orchestral rendition of the French national anthem.[87]

VII

Throughout the course of the conflict overseas, most of the Spanish-language press maintained a steady drumbeat of patriotic messages. With obvious pride, newspapers profiled young Tejanos as they embarked for military service. In an August 11, 1917, article on the voluntary enlistment of Olegario Rodríguez and Genaro Alegría, *Evolución,* a particularly prowar daily, hailed their contribution as proof of the "elevated character" and "dignified attitude" of Mexican Americans. "We can confirm," it boasted, "that in the County of Webb, it is the Mexican Americans who have responded in the greatest numbers as volunteers."[88] The exploits of Tejano servicemen abroad also generated significant coverage in the pages of *Evolución,* with casualties often being accorded the most solemn tributes. On December 8, 1918, for example, the paper printed a notice on the death of local boy Leonardo Díaz, who had fallen in combat in early November. Díaz, its editorial staff declared, had "exalted his racial heritage."[89]

Sometimes, holidays and other significant dates provided opportunities for nationalistic discourses. In its July 4, 1918 edition, San Antonio's *El Imparcial de Texas* declared that the United States "fought not only for its own liberty, but for that of all humanity."[90] *Evolución* held similar views. "The existence of global liberty, civilization and Christianity, and all of the glorious principles associated with the freedom of man are imperiled," the newspaper editorialized on the anniversary of the declaration of war against Germany. "It is necessary that every resident of the free lands of America cooperate fully, so that the US government and its people can help bring about a happy ending to this terrible conflict."[91] With columns of this sort, the Spanish-language press did its bit to rally the Tejano community behind the Allied cause.

Not surprisingly, such contributions to the war effort garnered the attention of those outside of the Tejano community. "Americans are learning that the Mexicans are not all . . . fierce bandits," proclaimed the *Laredo Weekly Times*. "The average Mexican," it had become convinced, wanted to "help win the war for the world's freedom." The response to the fund drives for the Red Cross, Liberty Loans, and war stamps was especially gratifying to its editorial staff. "There is no race on earth that is more charitable than the Mexican," it proclaimed.[92]

Whether true or not, declarations of this sort indicate that the Tejano community's attempts to prove its loyalty convinced at least some individuals. The respect was well earned. Throughout the nineteen months of belligerency, the denizens of the Lone Star State's barrios had worked alongside other Americans on behalf of the war effort. They had rallied for the war, propagandized for the war, and spent for the war. As much as any group of Americans, therefore, the Tejano community could claim a share of the credit for mobilizing the country in its quest for victory.

1. Congressional Medal of Honor recipient David Cantú Barkley, who is believed to be the first Mexican American recipient of the Congressional Medal of Honor. *Courtesy Military Order of the Purple Heart, David Barkley Cantú Chapter #766.*

2. Statue of David Cantú Barkley in Laredo, Texas, the city of his birth. Behind it stands a black granite–faced wall bearing the names of the Hispanic Medal of Honor recipients. *Author's collection.*

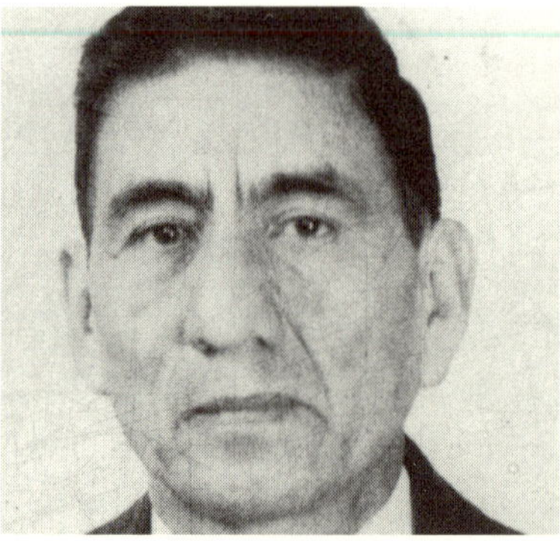

3. Schoolteacher and civil rights leader José de la Luz Saenz, whose war diary was later published (along with several additional pieces) as *Los México-Americanos en la Gran Guerra,* the only extant personal account of a Mexican American doughboy. *Courtesy Benson Latin American Collection, University of Texas at Austin.*

4. Saenz with his students in Moore.
Courtesy Benson Latin American Collection, University of Texas at Austin.

5. El Pasoan Marcos B. Armijo, winner of the Distinguished Service Cross, whose courage as he lay dying moved Maury Maverick to remark, “Nothing I’ve seen has ever impressed me as much.”
Author’s collection.

6. The Marcos B. Armijo Community Center in El Paso.
Author’s collection.

7. Octogenarian Marcelino Serna of El Paso, one of the most decorated Tejano doughboys, poses in uniform. This photograph appeared on the cover of a fiftieth anniversary program issued by El Paso's Marcos B. Armijo VFW Post No. 2753. *Courtesy Veterans of Foreign Wars, Department of Texas.*

8. Mexican American political leader José Tomás (J. T.) Canales of Brownsville, where he served as a Four Minute Man during the war. *Courtesy J. T. Canales Collection, South Texas Archives, Texas A&M University–Kingsville.*

9. Clemente Idar, Four Minute Man and owner-editor of the Laredo daily, *Evolución. UTSA Institute of Texas Culture, #084-0595, courtesy A. Ike Idar.*

10. Manuel C. Gonzales, one of the several Tejano veterans who would go on to become prominent leaders of LULAC. Gonzales served as the organization's third president during the early 1930s. *Courtesy Benson Latin American Collection, University of Texas at Austin.*

CHAPTER FIVE

Training Camp

"THE ACTIVITY IN THIS HUMAN BEEHIVE IS INDESCRIBable," marveled José de la Luz Saenz, who was eventually assigned to the Intelligence Section of the 360th Infantry, upon his arrival at Camp Travis in San Antonio. "Thousands upon thousands of men occupied with different tasks can be seen everywhere."[1] At Camp Travis and other installations, new recruits received their introduction to military life. Primarily, training camp was geared toward turning civilians into fighting men capable of defending the country against its foreign enemies. But during World War I the military also prepared for the postwar period. Servicemen were thus given instruction not only in formal drill and weapons use but also in morality, civics, and a host of other subjects. For many Tejanos, training camp served to break the shell of provincialism. By its completion, even the most naive and uneducated among them had experienced enough to realize that there was much more to life than what went on in the barrios and ranches of their home state.

I

One of the first tasks for the military was assigning new recruits to a division. Twice the size of their European counterparts, these divisions consisted of three brigades—one artillery and two infantry—and approximately a thousand officers and twenty-seven thousand men. Most draftees were assigned to the National Army divisions, numbered 76 to 92. Volunteers were usually placed in the Regular Army divisions, numbered 1 to 20, which aside from a few conscripts contained mostly Regular Army units. (Divisions numbered 26 to 42 were made up mostly of the National Guards of the several states.) Many, but not all, Tejanos served in the 90th and 36th Divisions—the Texas-Oklahoma draft and National Guard divisions, respectively.[2]

To accommodate the trainees, the military needed plenty of cantonments (temporary troop quarters). Accordingly, Secretary of War Baker organized a Cantonment Division headed by Col. Isaac W. Littel and convened the six territorial commanders of the army to select sites for these camps. The cantonments selected for the National

Army were the following: Camp Pike, Arkansas; Camp Gordon, Georgia; Camp Grant, Illinois; Camp Dodge, Iowa; Camp Funston, Kansas; Camp Taylor, Kentucky; Camp Meade, Maryland; Camp Devens, Massachusetts; Camp Custer, Michigan; Camp Dix, New Jersey; Camp Upton, New York; Camp Sherman, Ohio; Camp Jackson, South Carolina; Camp Travis, Texas; Camp Lee, Virginia; and Camp Lewis, Washington. Baker also provided the sixteen preexisting National Guard posts—three of which were located in Texas—with tents to house the National Guard divisions.[3] With the plenitude of camps in the Lone Star State, Texans had a greater chance than other soldiers to train close to home. Nevertheless, numerous Tejanos were assigned to faraway installations, such as Camp Kearny, California; Camp Cody, New Mexico; and Camp Wadsworth, South Carolina, to name but a few.[4]

Upon arriving at these cantonments, recruits often found conditions less than optimal. For one thing, many National Army camps were not even completed by the time the first recruits were delivered, the military having fallen short of its goal of completing 80 percent of construction by September 8, 1917. The preexisting cantonments were similarly raw. At Camp MacArthur, Texas, newcomers arrived to find portions of a cotton crop, while the men at Camp Wadsworth grubbed stumps to clear their company areas. Making matters worse, the army seemed at a lack for almost everything. Some men, such as those at Camp Grant, were forced to wear their civilian clothes during the first days of training. At Camp Greene, North Carolina, ten to twelve men were crowded into tents designed to accommodate only eight.[5]

Conditions were even worse for African Americans. Awaiting these recruits was segregation and mistreatment, including inferior rations and medical services. Three out of every four black soldiers were channeled into the Services of Supply (SOS), the logistics branch of the army. As the SOS supported the combat divisions by building roads, raising encampments, and digging trenches, most blacks served as manual laborers for the military. Compounding this injustice was the harshness of the prejudice they encountered. At Camp Lee, for example, an armed soldier reportedly held guard duty over a whites-only prayer meeting to ensure that no blacks were allowed entry. Camp Hill, Pennsylvania, was far worse, however. There, during the winter of 1917/18, black servicemen, some of whom had no blankets, were forced to live in tents without floors or stoves. Not only that, the army failed to provide these men with latrine facilities and changes of clothing for over four months.[6]

Tejanos—whom, as previously mentioned, the military categorized as "white"—and other minority groups were spared the indignity of segregation.[7] While a debate over the issue of creating separate American Indian units—one that dated back to 1911—did resurface soon after the declaration of war against Germany, the advocates of this form of segregation were motivated not by racism, but by well-meaning, albeit misguided, attempts to preserve the identity of a "Vanishing Race." Ultimately, of course, these efforts failed, spoiled by none other than Secretary Baker himself. The secretary of war, in the words of one leading segregationist, simply "did not believe in the segregation of troops according to race."[8] Indeed, had the pressure from influential Southern politicians and the white supremacist military establishment not been so strong, the racially progressive Baker probably would have worked harder for better treatment of African American servicemen. Instead, the so-called race question, inasmuch as it pertained to blacks, was left unsettled for the sake of political expediency.[9]

At any rate, the rough conditions of the camps—particularly the overcrowding—predisposed recruits to illness and disease. Some diseases, such as measles, mumps, diarrhea, tuberculosis, smallpox, chicken pox, meningitis, typhoid, and diphtheria, ran rampant among the recruits. The worst among these, though, was the Spanish influenza. Beginning in August 1918, the disease spread through military installations so rapidly that many Americans feared it was the handiwork of the Germans. To contain it, medical officers quarantined the camps, inspected them frequently, and ordered all windows closed. They also vaccinated unaffected soldiers and prescribed daily throat spraying and gargling. Nothing seemed to work. During one week in mid-October, four out of every thousand soldiers in the United States fell victim to the flu. Although it subsided by the end of the year, the disease by then had halted draft calls and slowed training in army cantonments considerably.[10]

Other factors hampered training. In keeping with its track record of disorganization, the military also faced a severe shortage of weapons. As a result, some men trained with dummy guns for the first few days. In the case of the 33rd Division, machine gunners spent two months in camp before firing an actual machine gun. Nature was perhaps an even larger hindrance. During the winter of 1917/18, temperatures dropped so much that the army was forced to restrict training. In the warm barracks of the Northern cantonments, recruits for the most part avoided hardship, but life in the tents of the Southern camps was altogether different. At Camp Oglethorpe, Georgia, where temperatures reached as low as four degrees below zero, trainees awoke one morning to find their clothing frozen. Their counterparts at Camp Greene hardly fared better. There, between December 10, 1917, and March 4, 1918, inclement weather allowed for only sixteen days of training.[11]

Yet to the army's credit, training still went off, however formidable the challenges. Weather permitting, recruits trained six days a week—seven hours daily from Monday through Friday with a shorter four-hour session on Saturday. The training program took sixteen weeks in total. During the first four weeks, trainees spent hours in physical drill and practicing with the bayonet. The rest of the time was devoted to recruit instruction, "school of the squad," and platoon instruction. By the second month, recruits received rifle instruction and target practice, with machine gun companies beginning sighting exercises. Training in open warfare, or "minor tactics," began in the third month, while "combined training," which consisted of maneuver, liaison, open and trench fighting, and coordination of two or more arms of service, was a staple of the fourth and final month of the program.[12]

Britain and France assisted the American military with this training regimen. To provide instruction in the new weapons and techniques of trench warfare, the two countries sent over seven hundred officers and noncommissioned officers to American cantonments. In some cases, the officers also served as guest speakers, with their lectures sometimes varying widely in subject matter. One French officer, for instance, discussed not only his experiences in the trenches but also courtship patterns in France. While some of these trainers complained of how the U.S. Army overemphasized physical conditioning, close-order drill, and rifle and bayonet practice at the expense of tactical problem solving and special-weapons use, for the most part they found morale at training camps positive.[13]

II

It was no accident that spirits were high. Although troop morale had always been a concern, the military emphasized it to an unprecedented degree during World War I, creating the army's first systematic morale program. After several counterespionage missions initially turned up reports of low morale among many soldiers, the War Department organized the Military Morale Section (MMS) under the Military Intelligence Branch of the General Staff. The MMS was charged with the task of instilling esprit de corps in the army's ranks.

Meanwhile, the Foreign-speaking Soldier Subsection (FSS) focused on raising morale among immigrants and non-English speakers. With the creation of the MMS and the FSS, writes historian Thomas M. Camfield, "maintenance of troop morale, heretofore solely the province of commanders in the field, was to become subject to centralized planning and direction."[14]

The MMS worked diligently to carry out its task. Under the direction of Brig. Gen. Edward Lyman Munson, who had previously served as director of training at the Medical Corps training camp, the MMS launched the Will to Win plan, the first part of which was designating the psychological examiners stationed at most army camps as camp morale officers. These officers were entrusted with the supervision of morale work in their respective camps and with the establishment of daily and weekly morale maintenance schedules. In accordance with the Will to Win plan, Munson also set up a liaison system with such groups as the Knights of Columbus, Jewish Welfare Board, Committee on Education and Special Training, and Bureau of Public Information. Besides conducting a nationwide advertising operation, these agencies sponsored Columbus Day lectures, films, and leisure activities designed to increase troop morale.[15]

The FSS was no less active. In pursuing its agenda, the section did everything from arranging for free legal advice for foreign-born soldiers to disseminating articles and cartoons detailing the contributions of America's many ethnic groups to the war effort. Cognizant of the importance of religion, the FSS also worked closely with ethnic religious organizations to meet the spiritual needs of its immigrant troops. Its hallmark, though, was its alliance with leaders from immigrant communities, who often made appearances in camps to bolster morale and promote loyalty through patriotic speeches. In some cases, these leaders were soldiers themselves, bilingual immigrants who distributed patriotic literature to their ethnic counterparts, explained the causes of the war to those with little knowledge of world politics, and reported to their superiors on the attitudes of the troops.[16]

Military officials understood that simple cultural sensitivity was essential to boost morale in the ranks. In October 1918, the War Department issued a general order forbidding the use of foreign-speaking soldiers as "fatigue" laborers. By then, the line of reasoning went, immigrants had done their fair share of menial work and were at risk of having their spirits broken by further fatigue duties. Another general order prohibited ethnic epithets, which officials claimed fostered discontent among foreign-speaking recruits. To the approval of immigrant soldiers, the War Department did not neglect to enforce the order, resulting in the reprimand of several guilty officers and enlisted men.[17] "This Section believes the need is urgent," noted the FSS with regard to its charges, "and that the improvement of the morale of such an important element of our cosmopolitan army will be an important factor in the final victory."[18]

One of the FSS's greatest achievements was the Camp Gordon Plan. Named after the camp wherein it reached fruition, the plan entailed organizing foreign-speaking soldiers into language-specific companies for six weeks—not to discriminate against certain ethnic groups or encourage "clannishness," the FSS was quick to point out, but as a temporary measure aimed at increasing efficiency and morale among non-English-speaking troops. To find leaders for these units, the army scoured the ranks for bilingual officers (showing preference for those who shared the same ethnic background as their prospective subordinates), and even went so far as to transfer the most qualified enlisted men to Officers' Training School when shortages arose. The opportunity to train under and alongside their ethnic peers performed wonders for the soldiers in the so-called Foreign Legion companies, which at Camp Gordon were composed of, among other groups, Italians, Russians, Greeks, Swedes, and Mexicans. According to one report, after the implementation of the plan, the percentage of foreign-speaking soldiers who expressed a willingness to fight overseas shot up to almost 100 percent—an amazing statistic given that none of these same soldiers had done so previously.[19]

Even as the war wound down, the success of the Camp Gordon Plan prompted military officials to attempt to put it into action in fifteen other cantonments. One of these was Camp Cody, where officials concentrated six hundred Mexican soldiers for training purposes and requested five Spanish-speaking officers from the FSS. Besides pledging to do its best to fulfill their demands, the subsection offered some hints about the "delicate work" of handling Mexican recruits, whom it considered "childish," "untruthful," and "super sensitive" about their "inferiority." As these men often exhibited a tendency to look out solely for themselves, it recommended assigning only "men of understanding," not the typically anti-Mexican officers from the South and Southwest, as their leaders, for otherwise "the spirit of cooperation [would] not develop" among them. Although the war's closing obviated any chance of enacting the Camp Gordon Plan to its full extent at Camp Cody, the FSS was so impressed with the results there that it notified other cantonments with sizable Mexican populations to consider following its example.[20]

III

To further boost morale, the army also instituted an education program for the troops. According to the General Staff, approximately 25 percent of draftees were illiterate, unable, it claimed, "to read the Constitution of the United States or an American newspaper, or to write a letter in English to the folks back home." As many of these men were immigrant and foreign-speaking recruits, they often could not speak or understand English either. Communication difficulties had decreased morale—not to mention efficiency—at several camps, particularly those like Camp Upton and Camp Gordon, which contained a higher average of foreign-born troops. As a way of addressing this problem, the War Department organized classes in, among other subjects, basic English reading and writing skills. It also set up library services as a supplement from which better-educated servicemen could also benefit.[21]

The program developed incrementally. At first, camp schools were headed by a single officer, who was selected by a training-camp commander. The arrival of thousands of illiterate troops and foreign-speaking recruits necessitated a change of approach. The result was that in 1918 the War Department secured the assistance of numerous community agencies, universities, bilingual soldiers, and civilian volunteers, and standardized English-language instruction in army cantonments. Thereafter, immigrant soldiers attended three hours of English classes daily for four months on average, in addition to their usual military duties. In class, the men learned the basics of the language while simultaneously receiving instruction in reveille, inspection, drilling, marching, saluting, double time, officer recognition, and other military topics.[22]

Not surprisingly, many non-English-speaking servicemen of Mexican extraction were placed in these classes. In February 1918, Camp Travis reported that roughly twelve hundred soldiers—many of them Mexican—were enrolled in its night school, which required the services of seventy-three instructors.[23] At Camp Kearny, which boasted one of the most successful programs in the country, Mexicans earned praise from supervisor Christina Krysto of the Bureau of Immigrant Education, who compared them to some of their fellow pupils. "It is customary to believe that the Mexican is indifferent to learning English and the Italians eager for the opportunity, yet some of the finest pupils in Camp Kearny are Mexican. The difference lies chiefly in the method of attack," Krysto noted. "The Mexican, quite unconsciously, plays at indifference, yet is disappointed if the lesson is not thrust upon him. The Italian reaches out for information. A Mexican, in studying a chart, will answer stolidly and reluctantly, and then, after class, will stand long and thoughtfully before it."[24]

These soldiers also had the opportunity to take classes in other subjects. For example, the army offered courses in basic French, which were designed to build a vocabulary of approximately seven hundred words. Apparently, the classes were popular, with their organizers laying claim to over two hundred thousand students in October 1918. Servicemen could also enroll in French and English history courses. Anson P. Stokes, one of the creators of the army's education program, was a key proponent of such classes, arguing that the American soldier would "be much more sympathetic with his French and English allies and prove more effective as a fighting man if he realize[d] their true character, the political and social ideas which have dominated them, and the difference between these and those of imperialistic Germany." Other available classes included Bible study, geography, algebra, stenography, and line and cartoon drawing.[25]

There were also vocational courses, many of which were taught at colleges and universities. By war's end, over ninety-five thousand men had obtained training in twenty basic trades at these institutions. More than four hundred colleges and universities also lent their efforts to the Students' Army Training Corps (SATC), a program that offered vocational courses, as well as collegiate-level classes, to postsecondary students. Participants in this program—which included several Spanish-surnamed students at the University of Texas—would be enlisted as privates in the army. As such, they were required to wear uniforms and live under strict military discipline, taking several hours' worth of military instruction daily in addition to their academic work. Although short-lived, the SATC trained thousands of automobile mechanics, carpenters, electricians, radio operators, and machinists.[26]

To help soldiers expand their literary skills, the American Library Association (ALA) furnished libraries in all the major army camps throughout the country. Open fourteen hours a day and with a full-time, live-in librarian, each of these buildings accommodated as many as two hundred patrons and between fifteen and thirty thousand volumes, with some books sometimes being housed in other locations throughout camp. In Texas, each of the four major cantonments, as well as Kelly Field, an aviation center in San Antonio, contained its own camp library. There, soldiers could enjoy from a large selection of works of fiction, history, military science, and engineering. Some collections also featured books on photography, gas warfare, and small arms, which were used in special military classes.[27] The ALA was careful not to neglect the needs of foreign-speaking soldiers, supplying some camps with books in a variety of different languages. At Camp Upton, the camp librarian noted that his holdings included "a few hundred select titles in Yiddish, Russian, Italian, Romanian, Spanish and Polish." Some of these books were "purely literary material," he noted, while the rest were educational resources on American history and government.[28]

Besides asking ethnic leaders to recommend appropriate reading matter for their immigrant soldiers, the army appealed to their communities to contribute books, magazines, and newspapers in their native language. In San Antonio, *La Prensa* relayed this message to its Tejano readers by exhorting them to mail their Spanish-language materials to nearby Camp Travis. On October 14, 1918, the paper reported that the library drive had been a "success."[29]

IV

The army incorporated a vigorous anti-venereal-disease campaign into its educational program. Besides aiming to help eliminate some of the social evils facing the country, it hoped to improve military efficiency. As the argument went, the doughboys could hardly expect to do their best on the battlefield if their bodies were suffering from the ravages of VD. Secretary Baker assigned the campaign to the Commission on Training Camp Activities (CTCA), a new agency created for the sole purpose of morally uplifting America's fighting men. The CTCA pointed to developments abroad to buttress the army's case, claiming that the Germans had lost several divisions to such diseases. For their part, it noted, the British had lost approximately seventy million "soldier-days" annually to VD.[30] According to historian Donald Smythe, "One British division reputedly lost 25 percent of its strength through such diseases. Infection required evacuating the sick to a rear hospital, where they remained almost two months, and meant a sharp decline in military effectiveness."[31] The American armed forces were determined not to allow the same thing to happen to them.

With an eagerness characteristic of most Progressive reformers,

Baker and the CTCA set about to attack the problem at its source—prostitution. The words of one contemporary expert reflected their views:

> The transmission of the disease itself is only part of the problem. From the social point of view the question is not only one of the effect of venereal disease upon the social body, serious as that is. The more far-reaching evil is the state of mind and character which lies back of it. The greatest evil to society results from the shattered ideals, lowered standards, sensualized minds, and perverted practices which are brought into home life and society by these men who represent in large measure the cream of the young manhood of the nation. To safeguard the home and society against these basic evils, we must not only abolish venereal disease, but minimize, so far as possible, prostitution itself.[32]

In accordance with Section Thirteen of the Military Draft Act, which had authorized the secretary of war "to do everything by him deemed necessary to suppress and prevent the keeping or setting up of houses of ill fame, brothels, or bawdy houses within such distance as he may deem needful of any military camp, station, [or] fort," Baker prohibited establishments of these sorts within five miles of military installations.[33] In addition, the CTCA encouraged the adoption of antivice legislation at the state and local levels. As early as October 1917, nineteen cities had closed their red-light districts, in most cases willingly. New Orleans was perhaps the most notable exception. Convinced that the shutdown of the Big Easy's infamous Storyville would only worsen health conditions by spreading vice throughout the city, Mayor Martin Behrman traveled to Washington to argue his case before President Wilson and Secretary of the Navy Josephus Daniel, only to be denied access to both men. By the war's end, the CTCA boasted a total of 110 district closures.[34]

Beyond question, the army considered the anti-VD campaign serious business. Indeed, according to James G. Harbord, General Pershing's chief of staff, "There was no subject on which more emphasis was laid, throughout the existence of the American Expeditionary Forces." One of Pershing's daily tasks was inspecting the daily venereal report. Units—especially their commanding officers—faced sanctions if their venereal rates were too high. Of course, there was also individual accountability. Aware that total abstinence from sexual activity was unlikely, military officials established stations at or near cantonments for soldiers to acquire prophylaxis. Those men who failed to obtain treatment and contracted VD risked court-martial and hard labor; those who contracted the disease, even after obtaining treatment, were shown mercy, with loss of pay during hospitalization their only penalty.[35]

Each camp participated in an indoctrination program designed to warn soldiers about the dangers of VD. Under the auspices of the CTCA, civilian physicians delivered lectures on the topic of social hygiene, providing many members of their audiences with their first exposure to sex education. Placards emphasizing the importance of self-control and responsibility surrounded recruits at every turn. One dealt with the debts a son owed to his father: "Remember—Your Father. Your Dad gave You the best there was in him. He expects you to make good. Don't splash mud on his name." A similar poster also touched on the issue of family: "Remember—Your Future Children—Give 'em a chance. Don't start 'em out with a mortgage on body or mind."[36] Other posters took a different tact, however. "How could you look the flag in the face," one asked, "if you were dirty with gonorrhea?"[37]

Particularly helpful was a pamphlet prepared by the American Social Hygiene Association titled *Keeping Fit to Fight.* Billed as a "man-to-man talk," the pamphlet spoke candidly on the subject of sex, utilizing terms like *whore* and *booze* to create a sense of intimacy with its young readers. "No matter how thirsty or hungry you were, you wouldn't eat or drink anything that you knew in advance would weaken your vitality, poison your blood, cripple your limbs, rot your flesh, blind you and destroy your brain," it reasoned. "Then why take the same chance with a prostitute?" To better educate its non-English speakers, the military had ethnic leaders translate the pamphlet into several different languages, including Spanish. Eventually, it also arranged for bilingual officers to interpret a subsequent film version of *Keeping Fit to Fight,* a necessity given that several immigrant soldiers initially misconstrued the film as pornography.[38]

The army and the CTCA also employed recreation as a weapon in their morality crusade. In a letter to Raymond Fosdick, head of the CTCA, Baker gave the Wilson administration's rationale for this tactic:

> We will accept as the fundamental concept of our work the fact which every social worker knows to be true, that young men spontaneously prefer to be decent, and that opportunities for wholesome recreation are the best possible cure for irregularities in conduct which arise from idleness and the baser temptations.

Specifically, the two institutions focused on athletics and music. According to a congressional report on camp activities, by the spring of 1918 the CTCA was retaining the services of thirty-one athletic coaches, twenty-seven song coaches, and fifteen theater managers.[39]

CTCA staff members worked diligently on their music programs, staging concerts for soldiers at army cantonments throughout the country. Sometimes, the entertainment was provided by professional singers, such as Margaret Wilson, the president's daughter, a capable soprano who performed for Allied troops both domestically and abroad. In other cases, the soldiers themselves produced shows, some of which were of excellent quality. *You Know Me, Al,* a musical comedy produced at Camp Wadsworth, actually played for ten days in New York. Another musical, *Yip, Yip, Yaphank!* was a hit both with the troops and with critics like Alexander Woollcott of the *New Yorker,* who called one of its songs "the best and truest thing that America contributed to the songbook of the war." Produced at Camp Upton, the musical boasted as its composer and lyricist none other than a young Irving Berlin, a private with the 20th Infantry.[40]

To encourage group singing, the CTCA organized quartets, glee clubs, and choruses, as well as competitions between regiments and companies. In their view, singing was not simply a form of entertainment. "Let us not cease to drive home to the men in our camps that we are not teaching them songs just for the fun of it or to pass the time away," wrote one advocate of the CTCA, "but because singing helps to win the war."[41] Singing, it was argued, helped morale and discipline by enabling soldiers to forget, if only for a short while, the drudgery of military life. It also fostered patriotism, which the soldiers would need in spades once the time came to confront the country's adversaries. Through the singing of such patriotic melodies as "America, the Beautiful," "Battle Hymn of the Republic," and "The Star-Spangled Banner," the CTCA expected to homogenize a diverse military, with its thousands of immigrant servicemen, and provide it with a common American identity.[42]

Because they both enhanced conditioning and served as a distraction from unsavory activities, athletics were another key aspect of the CTCA's recreation program. Many recruits were initially unfamiliar with the concept of organized play, probably due to the fact that so many of them derived from immigrant and lower-income backgrounds. Consequently, coaches often used children's games like foot races and tug-of-war as a prelude to more complicated sports. With the introduction out of the way, servicemen were then free to partake of the myriad of diversions the military had set up for them. These included boxing, football, rugby, basketball, volleyball, tennis, golf, wrestling, and swimming. Even sports as exotic as jujitsu had their fanatics in some camps. Baseball, another favorite, was believed to provide practice for grenade-throwing. Tag was said to develop physical alertness.[43]

Boxing was by far the most popular sport in army cantonments. Like baseball and tag, boxing reputedly held benefits for those servicemen destined for the battlefields of France. Specifically, the CTCA likened boxing to bayonet fighting. As Edward F. Allen, who authored a book about the CTCA during the war, wrote, "Both [activities] require agility of body, quickness of eye, good balance, and control in giving a punch or thrust, and an aggressive fighting spirit that breaks down or weakens defense, and makes openings for an effective 'finish.'" All sports, but especially boxing, supposedly promoted military efficiency by developing self-control, agility, mental alertness, and initiative. They also carried the added benefit of offsetting what many contemporary observers saw as the "feminization" of the modern-day male, who, in an urban and industrial age, no longer possessed the autonomy and independence of the pioneers and farmers of yore.[44]

Occasionally, military installations staged intercamp competitions and other sorts of exhibitions featuring the "science of boxing." In Texas, Cpl. Mercy G. Móntez of the 304th Mechanical Repair Shops, Fort Sam Houston, became a prominent figure in such matches, with previews and reports of his fights appearing regularly in the press, in some cases accompanied by pictures of him in fighting stance. In 1918, "Kid" Móntez, as he was better known in boxing circles, started out slowly, dropping a decision to Carl Fleming of Kelly Field in March, but the Tejano fared considerably better in subsequent engagements. In August, he defeated the heavier C. A. Conrad of the 144th Cavalry by decision, and several months later knocked out a fighter nicknamed Young Bradley, a former member of the 86th Infantry, in the second round.[45]

The Tejano community participated in the anti-VD campaign through more than just CTCA-sponsored athletic contests. Dr. Frank Gonzales of Dallas, for example, was one of the physicians selected by the army as a guest lecturer. "Be a man," he told an audience of four hundred soldiers at Camp Travis. "Be proud of your citizenship, and use it in a way that will make the folks at home proud of you. Go back home and marry the girl back home. Be home-makers and home-keepers." His take on the importance of religion reflected the military's emphasis on inclusivity. "Whether you be Jew, Catholic or Protestant," he declared, "when you get back home, go back to the old church and take a part in it. You need it and it needs you, and you'll be better off for it."[46] As with the library drives, the Spanish-language press lent its support. "Nothing could give us more satisfaction than a campaign of public morality in every sense of the term," proclaimed *Evolución.* "It is our belief that it will benefit the community and society in general. We are not of the opinion that brothels, gambling houses, and saloons are good for business, for, in truth, what they truly yield is simply more crime."[47]

Tejano soldiers also benefited from the services of the Young Men's Christian Association (YMCA), which was recruited by the CTCA to assist with the task of morally uplifting servicemen. The YMCA sponsored concerts, lectures, and amateur theaters, and built recreational and social facilities in all the major army cantonments, including auditoriums that seated approximately three thousand spectators. At Camp Travis, where Mexicans and Mexican Americans abounded, it even set up a department solely for the use of Spanish-speaking soldiers and their guests. In charge of the department was D. Macum, who reached out to the Tejano community by having *La Prensa* publicize the opening of the new facility. As part of this goodwill effort, Macum also welcomed local musicians and Mexican organizations to participate in the upcoming fiestas planned for the recruits.[48]

For the most part, the CTCA's efforts met with success. To be sure, some soldiers continued engaging in illicit sex. "Wine, women, and song" and similar answers were not uncommon to postwar questionnaires asking veterans about their former off-duty pastimes. Nevertheless, the indoctrination program appears to have made a profound impression on other soldiers. Besides one study's findings that 96 percent of the recruits with VD at American cantonments had contracted the disease prior to commencing their military service, military officials proudly noted that infection rates among troops dropped by an astounding 300 percent during the war.[49]

V

On the whole, military life was an intense experience for all soldiers, not just Tejanos. Some sensitive souls were genuinely disturbed by the nonchalant attitude they were supposed to take in ending another human being's life. Others simply felt disoriented by all the amazing things they had never before encountered.[50] Saenz, for example, was impressed with all the sights and sounds of an army cantonment. "It fascinated us to witness so many rifles firing and to hear the call of so many bugles," he wrote in a letter to his wife shortly after arriving at Camp Travis, "to say nothing of the many balloons and airplanes that hover over our heads like vultures."[51] If the urbane Saenz, who by his mere literacy distinguished himself from many of his colleagues in terms of sophistication, was dazed by his new surroundings, then it stands to reason that less-educated recruits must have experienced greater awe.

According to historians D. Clayton James and Anne Sharp Wells, "The Army and assisting civilian agencies imposed middle-class standards of living on draftees in the training camps." Not only was this evident in their lessons on sexual morality and civic duty, but also in their emphasis on things as mundane as personal hygiene. Sixty percent of recruits had never even experienced indoor plumbing prior to their arrival in camp. Now the military expected them to bathe at least thrice weekly, change their underwear every other day, and put on a new pair of socks daily. It also expected them to keep clean shaven with the use of a handy new tool called the safety razor, whose promotion during the war would revolutionize the shaving technique of an entire generation. The army taught soldiers that these practices—and American institutions in general—were superior to all others.[52]

What was more, military service allowed Mexican-origin recruits from varied backgrounds to interact, further broadening their horizons. Some of these men were more assimilated to American culture. Jesse Pérez, for example, possessed impeccable English-language skills and a decidedly "white" bearing from having grown up around Anglo-Americans in his native South Texas. The son of "Big" Jesse Pérez, a former Hidalgo County deputy sheriff and Texas Ranger, the younger Pérez himself had served in a Texas Ranger company prior to entering the military, a rare experience in that era for anyone of Mexican heritage.[53] In contrast, other Mexican and Mexican American servicemen spoke little or no English and in some cases had no idea why America had gone to war. In his autobiography, Maury Maverick, a member of one of the Lone Star State's best-known families who would go on to become a congressman and mayor of San Antonio, describes how, as a young lieutenant in the army, he once asked one of his men, a soldier by the name of Pedro Salazar, why the recruit was fighting for his country. "I don't know, Lieutenant, why I are in de war," Maverick quoted Salazar as responding. "But de draft board, he send me here." Later, Maverick was almost court-martialed for his vigorous defense of two Mexican-origin deserters, a defense in which he alleged that, given the two soldiers' complete lack of knowledge of either American customs or the English language, the American government should not have drafted them in the first place.[54]

However bewildering initially, military life eventually settled into a routine for recruits. The mornings were the busiest time of the day. Fifteen minutes after reveille, which took place at 5:45 A.M., the men began their setting-up exercises. Then, from 6:30 to 7:00, they retired to the mess hall for breakfast. (With an average intake of 4,761 calories, the men enjoyed much heartier meals than their counterparts in other armies.) The half hour after breakfast was allotted to the policing of quarters, which included making beds, folding blankets, and polishing shoes. Afterward came two drills, "school of the soldier" and "school of the squad." Rounding out the morning was inspection of quarters and a half-hour's worth of drills and lectures. What the recruits did in the afternoon depended on the stage of their training, but activities generally consisted of hikes, rifle practice, and tactical maneuvers.[55]

Also helping to acclimate the recruits to their new environment was basic camaraderie, in some cases between Anglos and Mexicans. In his memoir about the war, Texan Chris Emmett recounts how a camp mate named Bill Goodson befriended a Mexican corporal, the "happy possessor of a pass which permitted him to come and go from the camp at will." Not long after the two men began hitting it off, Emmett notes, Goodson could be seen on the city streets "answering to the name of 'Sanchez' and . . . exhibiting this 'homre's' [*sic*] pass as the evidence of his right."[56] As in other wars, the collective experience of military service created powerful bonds among some men, who became "war buddies." As Joe Garza of Corpus Christi later recalled, "I shared a tent with three Anglos and they treated me just like everyone else. Growing up the way I did, I can't describe what this meant to me."[57] The title of an article in a camp yearbook aptly describes this phenomenon: "Many Soldiers, Many Types: War Made Strange Bunkies, But The Army Made Them All Americans."[58]

That is not to say that the military was free of discord. As noted previously, even staff members of the FSS sometimes harbored prejudices. Not only that, serious interracial troubles involving recruits did arise occasionally. In October 1917, for example, two soldiers from Camp Bowie, Melvin Foreman of McKinney and R. P. Parish of Plano, were arrested in Fort Worth on charges of murdering Elicio G. Ornelas, a nineteen-year-old service car driver from San Antonio. Apparently, the soldiers had hired Ornelas to drive them to Kelly Field. During the trip, the pair struck the young driver with a heavy rock, robbed him, and then left him for dead. A few months later, Camp Bowie again made the news after two of its Mexican-origin soldiers attacked another civilian, in this case a man named S. S. Allen, who alleged that the two knifed him after he resisted their efforts to take away his whiskey. In neither crime, however, was race identified as the primary motive.[59]

How much did prejudice and discrimination affect the daily lives of Tejano soldiers? The evidence suggests that their general experiences were akin to those of other "white" ethnic troops—positive and worthwhile in the main, but by no means devoid of the occasional derogatory name-calling (*wop, dago,* and *bohunk,* e.g.) and other forms of hostility from intolerant peers. Saenz, whom one officer once called a *greaser* in a face-to-face encounter, put the matter into perspective when describing the army leadership. "We have officers very worthy of our respect," he wrote, "but we also have others who only merit our contempt." Quite apparently, the military possessed a wide assortment of individuals, including its share of bigots, but the presence of these unpleasant sorts does not seem to have ruined training camp for Mexican-origin soldiers.[60]

Indeed, for many of these men, it was as pleasant as anyone could have hoped for. In Saenz's case, military life, though arduous, still allowed sufficient time for the cultivation of friendships. Saenz and several of his fellow Tejanos made a daily routine of eating lunch together. Ever the teacher, he often lectured his friends on Mexican history, exhorting them to fight in Europe with the intention of bringing further honor to their people. Of course, not all of their interactions were as solemn. On some occasions, for instance, Saenz helped a less eloquent companion compose love letters to his sweetheart, whom the latter intended to marry immediately upon his discharge from the army.[61]

Predictably, several Tejanos reported enjoying their time in the military. Laredoan Higinio Valdez Jr. of the 14th Cavalry had nothing but good things to say about training camp to his hometown papers. "[Valdez] has told the press that he has found military life extremely agreeable," wrote *Evolución.* According to the young cavalryman, all of the local boys, many of whom were Tejanos, had been "very well treated" by the army. Sgt. Joe Benavides of the 141st Infantry, Camp Travis, a fellow Laredoan, gave a similar account to the *Laredo Weekly Times.* Benavides, the paper noted, "says he enjoys army life" and that "all the Laredo boys at Camp Travis are well trained and eager for the time when they are ordered to prepare for the voyage that will take them to France."[62]

VI

As training camp wrapped up, such a voyage drew nearer for many Tejanos. Most were now well versed in the ways of the military; they knew how to operate their weapons, they could follow orders, and they had the physical conditioning to carry them out. The army had also provided them with an education on several nonmilitary subjects, such as civics and morality, in the hope of producing more balanced individuals. But as it happened training camp had gone a long way toward accomplishing this end simply by exposing them to people from all walks of life and to things they had never seen before as civilians. They were no longer raw recruits; they were full-fledged American soldiers. Halfway around the world, the country's allies awaited their arrival.

CHAPTER SIX

Over There

THE LIVES OF TEJANO SERVICEMEN FOLLOWING TRAINING camp were like those of most other men in the armed forces. Not everyone saw combat, but for those who did travel overseas to fight the experience was both eye opening and life changing. From the ship ride across the Atlantic to the last days in Europe as an occupation force, World War I for American troops was equal parts tragedy and adventure.

I

The trip to France brought the doughboys one step closer to the conflict abroad. After taking passenger coaches or sleeping cars from their training camps to the designated embarkation camps on the East Coast, they underwent inspections, indoctrination, and instructions on shipboard behavior. They also received new issues of clothing and equipment. The actual boarding came a few days later. Following their departure from port, the men endured days of crowded living and strict discipline. Loneliness and homesickness were prevalent, but the military at least made an attempt to lessen the misery of sea travel by staging daily boxing and wrestling matches and frequent band concerts. Other diversions included animal fights, such as one between a bulldog and a badger, and more serious activities like religious services, which the soldiers attended in droves.[1]

Of course, the war made this oversea voyage perilous. The first and gravest disaster involving the ferrying of American soldiers to Europe occurred on February 5, 1918, when a German submarine torpedoed and sank the *Tuscania* off the coast of Ireland. At more than 550 feet and 14,348 gross tons, the Cunard-owned troop transport carried about four hundred crew members and two thousand doughboys. Among the servicemen aboard were members of the 20th Engineers and the 32nd Division, as well as three air squadrons and several medical units. The ship finally sank below the waters near the Rathlin Island lighthouse five hours after being struck. British destroyers combed the area in the aftermath of the attack, rescuing thousands, but not all lived to exact revenge on their German assailants. The final tally of *Tuscania* dead was 166 servicemen and 144 crew members.[2]

For weeks after the attack, the Texas press kept its readers abreast of the latest developments in the story, as many Texans were aboard the ill-fated ship. Among these were several Tejanos. Most, like Marcos Armijo of El Paso, who saved a nurse from drowning after falling overboard, survived the disaster. But some were not so fortunate. Nine Tejanos—Sixto Flores and José Ybarra of Laredo, Rosendo Díaz of Alice, Florencio Heras of Alfred, Angel Pérez of Rosenberg, Guadalupe Garza of Benavides, Lucio Ramos of San Antonio, Cirilo Rodríguez of Bergsmill, and Juan Pérez of Buerne—perished in the frigid waters off the Irish coast. In Alice, the Tejano community held a ceremony to honor the victims of the attack.[3]

Once in Europe, the previously narrow horizons of many servicemen expanded, as they had during training camp. Mostly provincial and naive, the troops were awed by the castles and landscapes of the Old World. Even for the more cosmopolitan among them the sights and sounds of Europe were a treat, allowing them to witness firsthand many of the settings for the works of masters like Shakespeare and Voltaire. For some Tejanos, the experience of being begged for handouts by ethnically white British and French peasants was also striking. "I thought that our humble Mexican laborers were the most backward people in the world," Saenz wrote in a letter to his children. "After all, other people portray us that way so often that we ourselves have come to believe it. As you can see, this journey has served us [Tejanos] well, if for no other reason than to see and compare with our own eyes."[4] Even for the meekest of Tejanos, a sense of empowerment was the likely result of such experiences, perhaps awakening some to the possibility that a person of Mexican origin could be of equal or even higher station than an Anglo-American back home.

Overall, the doughboys' reactions to France were mixed. For the most part, the troops got along well with French villagers, whom they often found amusing. "The people here are the smallest people I have ever seen anywhere," wrote Pablo Gonzales, a wagoner with the 111th Ammunition Train. Gonzales attributed their small stature to smoking. "The people are sure wild about American tobacco. The first thing the kids learn to say is, 'give me a cigarette.' They begin to smoke when they are about seven years old and they don't seem to grow very much after that age."[5] The young men also enjoyed the company of the attractive French peasant girls, as attested to by the popularity of the drinking song "Mademoiselle from Armentiéres."

Later, one veteran recalled that most Americans would claim to hail from Mississippi just to hear the girls pronounce it "Meeseeseepee." Still, for many, France eventually came to be associated with army life, which was enough to rob the country of its quaintness and charm for the most homesick soldiers.[6]

Interestingly, though not surprisingly given the legacy of colonialism and racism Mexican Americans inherited from their ancestral homeland,[7] what some Tejanos seemed to like least about France was their hosts' civility toward blacks, even when the respect extended to their own compatriots. "About the only thing I can hold against the French people is they think too much of the Negroes, call them black Americans and some of the French think they are American Indians," complained Gonzales. "Some of the French girls are married to negro soldiers. I guess tho [*sic*] it is only the lower classes that pull stunts like that."[8] Curiously enough, Gonzales, likely one of the many Tejanos who by virtue of their Spanish lineage considered themselves "white" (see chapter 1), was himself married to an Anglo-American. Saenz was also baffled by the prevalent race mixing, surmising that the contribution of African colonials to the French war effort was perhaps a reason for the willingness of some of the local women to fraternize with black men. In any case, he wrote in describing the first time he and a companion encountered interracial couples, "We did not like it."[9]

Besides sightseeing and interacting with the locals, doughboys also trained in France. American officials disagreed with their British and French counterparts about how best to proceed in this regard. On the one hand, three long years of stalemate on the western front had convinced the Allies that the AEF needed instruction in trench warfare and gas drills. On the other hand, the American high command believed that trench warfare had stolen the offensive mentality of the war's belligerents, preferring instead to practice for a war of movement. Weaponry was another point of contention. To the chagrin of the French, Americans to some extent eschewed bombs and automatic weapons in favor of the rifles and bayonets so predominant in previous conflicts, demonstrating their insufficient appreciation for the effect of recent technology on war. Despite admonitions to the contrary, Americans stuck to their choice of arms.[10]

II

By the early part of 1917, World War I was very much a war of attrition. Following a brutal offensive in the early days of the fighting that took the Germans as far as the Marne River, only a few miles east of Paris, the French and the British had managed to halt their advance and drive them back to the Aisne. Thereafter, the conflict settled into a two-front war characterized—especially on the western front—by trench warfare and bloody stalemate. Although the Germans attained more significant results on the eastern front, the last two and a half years by and large had seen only costly assaults that garnered little in the way of territorial advancement in any direction.

By April of 1917, however, matters had begun to change. As Adm. Sir John Jellicoe, Britain's First Sea Lord, confessed to American naval officials, not only was Germany now winning, but the rate of shipping losses to German submarines would also soon make it "impossible for [the British] to go on with the war."[11] In February of that year, Kaiser Wilhelm—at the behest of Field Marshal Paul von Hindenburg and his chief of staff Erich Ludendorff, Germany's chief strategist during the war—had ordered the resumption of unrestricted submarine warfare to cut off the Allies' access to American food and supplies. The risk of drawing the United States into the war was offset by their conviction that an isolated Britain would fall to its knees within a few months, which, in the opinion of the German high command, was not nearly enough time for the Americans to mobilize their forces for war. Besides, Adm. Eduard von Capelle, German secretary of state for the navy, told the German parliament, "America from a military point of view means nothing, and again nothing and for a third time nothing."[12]

To some extent, Capelle was correct in his assessment of the Americans as potential adversaries. In early 1917, the U.S. Army counted a mere two hundred thousand troops in its ranks, a miniscule amount compared to the armies of the major European belligerents. But German officials miscalculated the amount of time it would take for the Americans to mobilize. By the end of the war, the United States had trained and equipped four million soldiers. Moreover, many of these—namely those men of the 1st, 2nd, 26th, and 42nd divisions—had arrived in Europe within a few months of America's entry into the war. In good part due to this impressive mobilization effort, Ludendorff's "end-the-war" offensives, which were designed to gain victory on the western front before American troops could be delivered in significant numbers to reinforce the Allies, were doomed to failure.[13]

The first engagements of the war involving sizable American forces occurred at the battles of Belleau Wood and Château-Thierry.

At Belleau Wood, the Americans halted a German advance in June 1918 with a ferocious counterattack that left them with almost ten thousand casualties, two thousand of which were fatal. The following month, during the battle of Château-Thierry, French and American forces combined to rescue Paris from Ludendorff's fifth and final "end-the-war" offensive, earning the 38th Infantry the nickname of the "Rock of the Marne." Among the Tejanos at Belleau Wood was El Pasoan Juan Salorio, a volunteer serving with the 2nd Division. Another Tejano, Refugio Serna of San Antonio, was wounded in his left foot at Château-Thierry. During his time on the front lines, Serna helped save several of his comrades by providing them with armed cover as they escaped enemy troops.[14]

In mid-July, Allied supreme commander Ferdinand Foch of France ordered a counterattack in the Marne salient, where German forces now found themselves overextended. Known as the Aisne-Marne offensive, the move caught the Germans off guard and forced them to retreat. American forces ably assisted the French in virtually eliminating the German salient within a few weeks. The 32nd Division, for instance, captured the town of Fismes in early August after a forward push of almost twelve miles in seven days. During the advance, Marcos Armijo of the 125th Infantry, who had previously proven his mettle by saving a nurse from drowning after the sinking of the *Tuscania,* lost both his legs to an artillery shell. Shortly after being struck, Armijo amazed his companions by lifting himself upon his elbows and rolling cigarettes. Incredibly, he survived for another three days, joking and attempting to keep morale high in his unit the whole time. "My friends, how I lament not being able to keep fighting alongside you," Lt. Maury Maverick remembered the young private saying, "but you who can still fight should not let the Kaiser escape." Maverick later told the press, "Nothing I've seen has ever impressed me as much." Reportedly, General Pershing himself recommended Armijo for the Distinguished Service Cross, which was awarded posthumously in October 1918.[15] "By [his] display of nerve," Armijo's citation reads, "he conveyed to his comrades an unconquerable spirit of fearlessness, pluck, and will power."[16]

The success of the Aisne-Marne offensive turned the tide of the war. Since the Allied victories at the battles of Belleau Wood and Château-Thierry, the German high command had been plagued by internal strife, with Ludendorff's decision-making a specific target of criticism from the General Staff. Although the domineering Ludendorff treated his detractors with contempt, even he had grown pessimistic, describing August 8, when a British and French tank armada overwhelmed the front at Amiens, as the "black day of the German army."[17]

By September, the First United States Army, whose assemblage in late July had been made possible by the arrival in Europe of sufficient American troops, was ready for its first mission. Together with a detachment of several French divisions, the Americans were to reduce the St. Mihiel salient. A successful assault on the area, Foch had concluded, would release the Paris-Avricourt railroad in the region of Commercy. On September 12, the Americans launched a full-scale attack. After four days of continuous rain, ground conditions were appalling, but the doughboys managed to seal off the salient by early the next day, well ahead of schedule. The offensive was over within a few days, resulting in yet another German defeat and, in Pershing's view, doing "more than any other operation of the war to encourage the tired allies."[18]

The St. Mihiel offensive was the first taste of action for some doughboys, many of whom distinguished themselves in the battle. On the second day of fighting, Moisés Carrejo, a Taft native with the 360th Infantry, assisted one of his sergeants in attacking an enemy pillbox. Located atop a hill, the emplacement had provided a safe position for a German machine gunner to mow down several of the duo's comrades. Although climbing the mound proved too difficult for his companion, Carrejo mustered the energy to reach its summit and overtake the enemy soldier. Worthy of note, he accomplished this task while armed only with a pistol.[19]

Marcelino Serna, a Mexican immigrant from El Paso, was also in the thick of the fighting. During an exchange of fire with a German soldier, Serna, a scout with the 355th Infantry, received a slight bullet wound to the head. With his dazed but still fully conscious adversary in full pursuit, the German sought refuge in a nearby trench, which Serna bombarded with two hand grenades. To the doughboy's surprise, twenty-four Germans, including two officers, emerged from the smoke-filled trench, sixteen others having been killed in the explosion. Serna took the Germans prisoners and protected them from another American soldier intent on gunning down the entire group, reminding his over-excited partner that it was against the laws of war to kill prisoners. As a result of these exploits, Serna was awarded the Distinguished Service Cross in April 1919. For subsequent actions, which included killing and capturing several more enemy soldiers and destroying two German machine-gun emplacements that had pinned down his company, he received the French Croix de Guerre and the Victory Medal with three bars.

By the end of the war, the Mexican citizen had been decorated personally by generals Foch and Pershing and had also acquired the French Medaille de Militaire, the Italian Croce al Merito di Guerra, and several other medals.[20]

For some Tejanos, St. Mihiel was also their last taste of action. During the battle, Luis Rodríguez's comrades found him dead in a German trench. Apparently, the Losoya native had been on a reconnaissance mission when he encountered the fortification, which had been abandoned save for one lone soldier. Both men received mortal bayonet wounds in the ensuing struggle. The image of the two corpses, resting against each other as if locked in eternal combat, made a deep impact on those who arrived at the scene later.[21]

During the course of the fighting, the horrors of war became increasingly apparent to American troops. In his diary, Saenz described how everyone at the front had lice—including the rats. He recalled the haunting moans of the wounded and dying in Red Cross hospitals, adding that on some battlefields you could almost hear the dead cry in agony. Especially appalling to him were the corpses that lay everywhere. The remains of one German soldier he came across, he noted, consisted only of a head with its heart and lungs still attached. In another combat zone, he stumbled upon a pile of dead soldiers and their horses, their rotting flesh amalgamated almost beyond recognition by artillery shells. These scenes, no matter how grisly, eventually became so commonplace that soldiers learned to shrug them off. As Saenz pointed out, sentimentalizing simply made it too difficult to cope—particularly since some of their responsibilities included dog-tagging and burying their dead comrades.[22]

Saenz also described the drooling, purplish corpses of soldiers who had fallen victim to another of the war's terrible innovations—poison gas. First used in large scale by the Germans against Russian troops on the eastern front in 1915, gas warfare was later adopted by the Allies, who had initially denounced it as a violation of the laws of war. If inhaled in sufficient quantities, poison gas—the three most common forms of which were chlorine, phosgene, and the blister-inducing "mustard"—would lead to death by asphyxiation. According to Saenz, its ubiquity at the very least made everyone at the front miserable, producing headaches, diarrhea, and a nausea so intolerable that even the hungriest of soldiers found it difficult to touch their food.[23]

Several Tejanos who were gassed survived the ordeal. One of them was Laredoan Ignacio Rodríguez of the 143rd Infantry, who in a letter to his mother in September 1918 noted that he was recovering in a French hospital from injuries stemming from a gas attack, as well as bayonet wounds to his right arm and side.[24] In another case, Pablo Pérez, gassed at St. Mihiel, was thought dead by his comrades in the 360th Infantry. Although he was happily reunited with them after several weeks of infirmity, Pérez continued suffering from breathing irregularities and dysphonia and had to be readmitted to the hospital for treatment in December 1918.[25]

Eduardo Barrera, one of Pérez's closest friends in the 360th Infantry, also experienced gas warfare firsthand. A rancher from the small town of San Diego whose equestrian skills landed him a position as horse orderly, Barrera had been ordered by one of his commanding officers to guide him on horseback to the front. As the officer conducted business in the trenches, Barrera waited for him in a small wooded area nearby, where he was spotted by enemy troops. Despite being attacked with poison gas, which necessitated that he place gas masks not only on himself but on his horses, he maintained his post the entire night awaiting his companion, who as it turned out was hardly as conscientious. Shortly after the attack, the officer had fled back to the rear on motorcycle without bothering to check on Barrera. Indeed, the Tejano only discovered the following day what had transpired, when hunger finally forced him to return to his station.[26]

Navigating through the combat zones—which were riddled with corpses, land mines, and barbed wire—was often a nightmarish experience in its own right. Once, during night patrol in No Man's Land, Francisco Hernández encountered several German troops conducting their own patrol. In the resulting skirmish, Hernández killed three of the men with his bayonet. Meanwhile, in his role as messenger, Eulogio Gómez of the 360th Infantry, a native of Brackettville in Kinney County, repeatedly braved the battlefields alone, establishing himself as one of his unit's most successful runners despite a complete lack of formal schooling and an ignorance of most geographical concepts. To avoid losing his bearings during an assignment, Gómez eschewed tools like compasses and simply drove small stakes along his route to help him find his way back, making sure to retrieve each one on his return so as to avoid confusing himself on a later mission. Unlike many of his better-educated colleagues, Gómez never once got lost.[27]

Interestingly, some Tejanos thought little of wandering off into dangerous territory. Such was the case with Moisés Carrejo, who, along with four other Tejanos, routinely ignored the military's prohibition against eating the few crops still remaining on the battlefields—a disobedience borne less of hunger and more of a desire to prove one's courage by venturing beyond the friendly trenches. Their recklessness eventually brought about disaster, however. Spotted by the enemy after collecting grapes on one of its forbidden excursions, the group was bombed in the trenches as it enjoyed its harvest. Three of the men, including Carrejo, perished in the incident.[28]

Lulls in action and breaks in troop movements usually allowed time for other activities. During one such let-up, several Mexican American soldiers in the 90th Division paid their final respects to a fallen comrade, José "Pepe" González of Brooks County. Although they arrived too late for the funeral, the doughboys offered prayers for his soul at his French gravesite. Sometimes the activities were not as solemn. Several days earlier, some of these same soldiers had been ordered to report for delousing, a humiliating but necessary ordeal that required everyone to shave and undress entirely. Francisco de Hoyos, however, persuaded his superiors to allow him to keep his prodigious mustache, in which he took obvious pride.[29] Meanwhile, Pablo Gonzales celebrated a birthday during a respite in the latter stages of the war. According to one of his letters, he received a pair of gloves and another present from one of his sergeants. He also enjoyed beefsteak and hotcakes as his early day meals, so much so in fact that he "didn't care for much else" by suppertime. "In all I think I spent a good birthday," Gonzales wrote his wife, "even though I am in the battle zone."[30]

Such breaks, however, were in short supply following the St. Mihiel offensive, as even before its conclusion Pershing had begun ordering some units to the Verdun sector sixty miles to the northwest. It was there that the Meuse-Argonne offensive, destined to be the last major campaign of World War I, took place. On September 26, American troops, along with the French Fourth Army to its left, launched an assault northward against heavily fortified German forces in the Argonne forest. At the same time, British, French, and Belgian armies attacked the enemy lines from the west and northwest. Progress for everyone was steady for the most part, but the Americans encountered dense woods and rough, hilly terrain, encumbering their advance. The Second United States Army's successful drive against German observation and artillery positions east of the Meuse River, eliminating a trouble spot on the Americans' right flank, helped matters considerably. By early November, American forces were within reach of the city of Sedan, and German forces were in complete disarray.

Right up until its culmination, the Meuse-Argonne offensive

produced some of the most intense fighting of the war. Símon González of the 360th Infantry, whose conscription left his blind father helpless and alone across the Atlantic (see chapter 2), transferred his hatred for the predominately German American draft board in his hometown of Martindale unto the enemy troops. "I am here because of the Germans in Martindale!" González would reportedly exclaim. Never kneeling to recharge his rifle, he would stalk his foes in the customary hunting style of the Texas prairie, often laughing at the sight of their death or retreat. Nothing would infuriate the former day laborer more than losing a comrade-in-arms. On such occasions—the only times anyone ever heard him swear—all his anti-German venom invariably spewed forth. Ultimately, though, González too fell in battle. First struck by a mortar shell, which practically tore him in half, his body was then riddled with machine-gun fire.[31]

Hipólito Jasso, his cohort in the 360th Infantry, also fell victim to a mortar shell during the Meuse-Argonne offensive. His thorax ripped wide open by the blast, Jasso inspired his colleagues with his stoicism. Not only did he endure his pain without complaint, he actually made light of his heinous injuries, arguing that they were "nothing" even as his heart and lungs threatened to spill out of his chest with every word he spoke. In what most likely seemed like a miracle to most observers, Jasso lived to tell the tale. Indeed, soon after undergoing surgery, he escaped from the hospital and returned to his company. What was more, he managed to convince the commanding officer, who eventually realized the futility of arguing with his subordinate, to allow him to remain on the condition that he continue to receive treatment for his wounds.[32]

Several Tejanos received decorations for bravery during this last stage of the war. One of them, Laredoan Francisco García of the 141st Infantry, fell near the village of St. Étienne. He was awarded the French Croix de Guerre posthumously.[33] Two others soldiers, Graviel García of the Central Texas town of Somerville and Concepción Ortíz of Eagle Pass, earned the Distinguished Service Cross of the United States. A private with the 325th Infantry, García was recognized for his rescue of a wounded comrade in No Man's Land, during which he himself was severely injured. Meanwhile, Ortíz, Company I, 125th Infantry, died near Romagne while delivering messages "of great importance" across a valley wracked by machine-gun fire.[34]

David Cantú Barkley of the 356th Infantry received the highest honors of any Mexican American serviceman during World War I. On November 9, 1918, the young San Antonio resident of mixed

Anglo-American and Mexican descent and another soldier volunteered to swim across the icy Meuse River to determine the strength and location of German formations on the opposite bank. Barkley succumbed to cramps and drowned as he returned from his reconnaissance mission, but his partner arrived safely with the information they had gathered together. Their report contributed to the success of one of the last Allied assaults against German forces during the Meuse-Argonne offensive. For his bravery, Barkley received posthumously the French Croix de Guerre, the Italian Croce al Merito di Guerra, and the Congressional Medal of Honor, the highest award for valor of the United States Armed Forces.[35]

Two days after Barkley's death, the belligerent powers signed an armistice at Compiègne, marking the end of the four-year-long conflict. For the war-torn European nations, the cease-fire was a welcome relief. Being latecomers to the war, however, Americans were not quite unanimous in their reactions to these developments. Some, like Col. George S. Patton, recovering from a leg wound in a French hospital and still itching for another chance at the enemy, actually lamented the war's closing. Still, news of the armistice elicited joy among most of the participants, along with a dose of sadness for those comrades who had been lost forever. Upon its official announcement, Pershing paid tribute to these fallen warriors and thanked his men for their role in the Allied victory.[36]

The United States lost relatively few men during World War I because of its late entry. Approximately 114,000 American servicemen died in the conflict. Although by no means paltry, this sum is dwarfed by those of the other major powers, most of whose fatalities ran either close to or above the million mark. Britain, for example, lost one million men, while France lost 1,700,000. On the other side of the conflict, Austria-Hungary lost 1,500,000 men. The highest death rate, however, belonged to Germany, which lost an incredible two million men.[37] About one hundred Spanish-surnamed servicemen from Texas perished during the war, a figure that represents about 2 percent of their entire contingency. As the total death rates for Texas and the country at large are roughly 2 percent also, it appears that Tejanos did not die in either disproportionately high or low numbers.[38]

Even as the fighting raged in Europe, many Tejano servicemen had taken the time to write home. Some, like Eulogio Gómez, were illiterate in both English and Spanish and relied on their more educated companions to help them compose simple letters to their loved ones.[39] Others, like Laredoans José Villarreal and Adán

Abrego, produced memorable documents. Villarreal enlivened his correspondence with insightful descriptions of France and its local customs, while Abrego expressed pride in his Mexican heritage. Describing his combat experiences with a fellow Tejano during Mexican Independence Day, Abrego wrote, "Durán and I celebrated the fifteenth and sixteenth of September fighting like our ancestors did in 1810." Those "glorious dates" meant a great deal to them, he added, because back then "our beloved Mexico was working toward liberating itself from slavery, a feat it eventually accomplished with bloody sacrifice."[40]

Equally eloquent was Polidoro Sosa of San Antonio, who expounded on the life-changing experiences of military life. "The travelers of yore would say that an expedition was good and enjoyable, and I thought it couldn't be so," Sosa wrote his mother, "but now that I myself am on the 'road' I say the same, and I add that what makes a man a man is the world, for in it one sees things that, while inexplicable, shape his character." His closing carried an element of fatalism. "I trust you will be content to hear me say such things, and, while I am not happy to be so far away from you, I am not sad to find myself on the path that God destined for me."[41]

Another prolific letter writer, Pablo Gonzales, filled his correspondence with reassuring reports to comfort his family, whom he knew fretted about his safety and welfare. Although conceding in his letters to his wife that he was "a little lonesome" and "longing for the day when peace will be declared and I can be home again," he begged her not to worry about him. "Dear, have patience for I think the worst is about over and it won't be long until we are returning." Likewise, his father received glowing descriptions of his experiences in the trenches. "I guess the people . . . think we suffer all the hardships in the world here, but Papa we don't, and don't you let them kid you into believing that [we] do," he wrote. "Our eats are the best that can be had under the conditions and they keep feeding us until we cannot hold any more." He added confidently, "It's a settled fact that the American soldier isn't going to starve." Gonzales also made sure to acknowledge the folks back home for doing their bit for the war. "I am very glad you purchased the Liberty Bonds and if you could have done more I am sure you would have done so," he told his wife. "Anyway, the money you invested in the bonds you are sure of."[42]

In other cases, though, letters from the front lines revealed not so much intellectual and emotional depth, but instead the naïveté and exuberance more common to young men. "Just as delighted to be here as I can be. My health is fine, and all I'm thinking about is just how to help get the Kaiser," Peter T. Garza, a cotton sampler from San Antonio, wrote from France in May 1918. "Instead of sampling cotton—as I used to in San Antonio—I'm getting ready to sample the Huns, and impatient to get a whack at them."[43] Juan Benitos of Corpus Christi, meanwhile, sprinkled his letters with a touch of humor, such as using "fat as a hog" to describe his friend and fellow doughboy Eugene Martínez. "We hope to end this war by Christmas if we can get a good chance at the Germans," the spirited Benitos told his mother after seeing his first action at the front. "I am having a good time."[44]

Letters from soldiers also assured families and friends of their well-being. In one case, Louis Gonzales of the 102nd Infantry was mistakenly listed as killed and then later as missing in action. Wounded and unable to write home, Gonzales took several months before contacting his worried mother, with whom he was reunited in May 1919.[45] Similarly, San Antonian Marcos Peña had initially been registered as killed in the *Tuscania* disaster. To the relief of his parents, a letter from Peña soon disproved these reports. Amazingly, however, Peña was erroneously listed as dead again in the summer of 1918. Once more, it was a letter from Peña, who was recovering from wounds in a French hospital at the time of its writing, that restored hope to his grieving parents, although their son's tendency to downplay his injuries kept them skeptical about his true condition for several weeks. Once it was firmly established that he was alive and well, the family sent his letters to the Department of War to confirm its error. Even after the emotional turmoil they underwent, Peña's parents maintained a positive outlook. Whatever the circumstances, his mother told the press in September 1918, "he is alive and that is enough for us."[46]

Such remarkable stories lent faith to other families whose sons had fallen in combat abroad. To cite one example, the mother of the articulate Polidoro Sosa pointed to Peña's case in particular as her reason for believing that her son might still be alive. "She talks profusely," *La Prensa* noted in its November 1918 profile of María Sosa, whose other son Miguel was also in the military, "sometimes with a profound sadness but on other occasions almost joyfully, dominated by a great confidence that her son hasn't died." Despite having already received his official death notice from Secretary of War Baker, the widowed matriarch of the Sosa family clung to the hope that Polidoro was lost somewhere in Europe, or perhaps a prisoner of the Germans. Also keeping her hopeful was the fact that so far no newspaper had published his name along with the other war dead. Besides, she told *La Prensa,* her son had written her every month up to and including September of the current year, so October's letter was not yet due. If it did not arrive on time, then perhaps she would finally resign herself.[47] In the end, she never did receive another letter. As his death notice specified, Polidoro had truly fallen at the battle of St. Mihiel on September 13. The official cause was listed as death by wounds.[48]

III

Racial and ethnic stereotypes appear to have influenced military life for Tejanos and other minority soldiers. For American Indians, the widespread belief in their "instinctive" warrior nature brought prestige and respect, but also some of the most perilous duties as scouts, messengers, and snipers. Conversely, many Anglo Americans considered blacks docile, submissive, and lacking in self-control, undesirable qualities for soldiers that buttressed the military's segregation policy and the usual relegation of African Americans to labor units.[49] Stereotypes of Mexicans as fighters were more complex. Since the previous century, many Anglos had regarded Mexicans as vicious and cruel, but inherently cowardly.[50] Such ideas persisted well into World War I. Indeed, seventeen years after the war's conclusion, renowned historian Walter Prescott Webb was still analyzing Mexicans in similar terms. Their "cruelty may be a heritage from the Spanish of the Inquisition," he wrote in his landmark study of the Texas Rangers, although he also made sure to take into account Mexico's Aztec heritage. For the most part, Webb was unimpressed with the martial abilities of the Mexican, arguing that, while "skillful and devastating with the knife," as "a warrior he was, on the whole, inferior to the Comanche and wholly unequal to the [Anglo] Texan."[51] Not everyone held Mexicans in such low esteem, however. In an article published in August 1918, the *Houston Daily Post* noted that the capacity of the Mexican soldier to function on meager rations and inadequate provisions had been the marvel of the American military since the days of the U.S.-Mexican War. Despite such hardships, it noted, "the Mexican common soldier can and does fight bravely after the Mexican fashion and is obedient to his superior officers even to the point of charging a machine gun single handed."[52] These mixed assessments may have played a role in keeping Mexicans from being segregated, as well as saving them from some of the most dangerous assignments of the war.

Preconceptions aside, World War I servicemen of Mexican heritage received their fair share of tributes for their courage on the battlefield. A few years after the war, Col. Louis Mervin Maus of the U.S. Army noted how Mexican-origin soldiers had "given excellent displays of their valor in the trenches and in the line of fire," adding that "many of them can be found [buried] today among the honorable heroes in the fields of Flanders and France."[53] Maury Maverick was even more generous in his comments. "I must say," he remarked shortly after his arrival from France, "that I never saw a braver group of people than those Mexicans."[54]

As mentioned earlier, numerous servicemen of Hispanic descent were recognized officially for their heroism in battle. The U.S. government alone wound up awarding thirteen Spanish-surnamed servicemen, five of whom were Texas residents, medals for valorous service during World War I. (Except for David Cantú Barkley, who won the Congressional Medal of Honor, all of these servicemen received the Distinguished Service Cross.) In addition, some of these awardees, as well as other Hispanic servicemen, also received decorations from France, England, and other Allied countries.[55]

A few Tejanos served as officers during the war. Three, including one Mexican-born soldier, were from El Paso. Another, James L. Garza of San Antonio, served as a second lieutenant in the 24th Infantry. Capt. Augustine De Zavala of the 143rd Infantry, meanwhile, was a Spanish-American War veteran and the grandson of Lorenzo de Zavala, a Texas patriot of the revolutionary era.[56]

Tejanos also served as noncombatants, in some cases garnering acclaim for their work. Some were assigned to roles as cooks, teamsters, and even musicians. Others were placed in labor units. According to *La Prensa,* the 25th Construction Company of the Air Service, which was composed mainly of Tejanos, received high praise from Secretary of War Baker for their service in Pennsylvania.[57]

The Tejano community was also represented in the navy. Pete Leyva of El Paso served aboard a destroyer during the war. Lively and athletic, the young West Texan mingled with superior officers and professional baseball players during the frequent ball games staged by his fellow sailors. He also received the opportunity of seeing President Wilson in person during a European trip after the war. Despite losing a portion of one finger during an engagement at sea, Leyva remembered his three years in the navy fondly. "I loved it," he told an interviewer in 1976. "If I had a chance, I'd go [back] now."[58]

Less idyllic was the naval tenure of Leopoldo García. Enlisting in Galveston several years prior to America's entry into the war, García was a coxswain aboard the USS *Cyclops* during the early part of 1918. After helping fuel British ships in the South Atlantic, the *Cyclops* departed toward Maryland from Brazil on February 20. Several days later, it made an unscheduled stop in Barbados, where it took on additional supplies. After its departure, however, the ship vanished without a trace. Often attributed to the Bermuda Triangle, the loss of the *Cyclops* and its over three hundred crew and passengers has become part of seafaring lore.[59]

Following the end of the war, thousands of doughboys remained in Europe for several months to occupy Germany. This force, which Pershing organized as the Third United States Army, consisted of six divisions—four Regular and two National Guard—and was led by Maj. Gen. Joseph Dickman.[60] Those Tejanos who stayed behind seemed to have made the best of their somewhat unenviable situation. In March 1919, one group staged a fiesta in the German village of Zeltingen to commemorate the birthday of former Pres. Benito Juárez of Mexico, indicating, as the civil rights advocacy of many Tejano veterans would later demonstrate, that patriotism toward and a willingness to fight on behalf of the United States did not necessarily entail an abandonment of ethnic identity.[61] Others partook of activities, such as athletics, designed to keep morale up in the military. Mexican-descent soldiers were spectators as well as participants at several such sporting events, boasting contestants in both the one-mile run and the one-hundred-yard dash in one competition organized by the 90th Division.[62]

The military also provided soldiers in the occupation force with instruction on everything from basic literacy skills to college-level courses on a variety of subjects. Saenz, who himself took up studies in geometry, geography, and German while awaiting his return to the states, was selected to teach a night class of his choosing as part of this program. To better serve the Tejano community, the former schoolteacher opted to make it a beginner's English course for his Spanish-speaking comrades.[63]

During the postwar period, Tejanos continued to be exposed to people from different walks of life. Juan Salorio later recalled one friendship that resulted from an awkward incident in France:

> I went to a café in Paris where all the English speaking soldiers came together, the Australians, the Americans, the Canadians, the English, etc., for the owners of the café were Americans. Once when we were speaking of all the nations the old barmaid

> began to say that in Mexico there wasn't anything but Indians and that they didn't even know the Spaniards there. I told her that I was an "American-Mexican" and that my country was Mexico, which was on the border of the United States, and that Spanish was spoken there and that I could prove it. I told them to call a Spaniard who had never been in Latin America and they would see how we could talk. About this time a Spaniard who was a street cleaner passed by and they called him in and we began to talk first in French and then in Spanish. I told him that I was Mexican but he told me that I was wearing an American uniform. I then told him that I was an American citizen because I had been born in the United States but that all of us recognized Spain as our mother country and that there were more than a hundred million inhabitants in Latin America who spoke Spanish. He then invited me to take a drink but I wouldn't let him pay for it. I saw that he was very poor and I paid. He invited me to eat on Sunday at this house and he prepared a delicious Spanish meal and took me to the Spanish club and presented me to many pretty Spanish girls.[64]

The last days in Europe were bittersweet. As they prepared to depart for America, some Tejanos exchanged gifts and mementos with their friends and comrades-in-arms, most of whom they would likely never see again. Then, with final goodbyes out of the way, it was at last time for the trip back home. For those men belonging to the occupation force in Germany, the first steps involved a long march and then a train ride to France. From there, the doughboys embarked on one of the many troop transports waiting to take them stateside, a process that often took until the wee hours of the morning to complete. Once everyone boarded, the trip across the Atlantic commenced. In some ways, it resembled the voyage of a few months back. Quarters were cramped, seasickness was prevalent, and the hours seemed like days. To pass the time, some Tejanos enjoyed concerts by the army and navy bands or partook of the many games of chance—including the Spanish card game Malilla—that broke out among their companions. Yet, now there was elation to go along with the anticipation everyone felt. There was also the satisfaction that comes with doing a job well. "Perhaps this strong demonstration of our loyalty and manhood," wrote Saenz as his ship made its way to Boston in June 1919, "has highlighted how we [individuals of Mexican descent] fulfill our obligations as faithful citizens."[65]

IV

For those Tejanos who survived military service during World War I, life would never be the same. Their journey had taken them far from home. They had endured the rigors of military life, learned new skills, and, in more than a few cases, participated in some of the heaviest fighting of the war. For most, wartime service had offered a unique opportunity to experience more than ever possible in the safe confines of the barrios. That a broadening of outlook and perspective characterized the postwar lives of many of these servicemen should therefore not be surprising. How exactly this transformation would affect the Tejano community as a whole is a subject for the next chapter.

CHAPTER SEVEN

Aftermath

VETERANS OF WORLD WAR I RETURNED HOME CONQUERING heroes. Throughout the country, cities and towns staged homecomings and victory parades in tribute to their troops' sacrifices overseas. Main Streets everywhere teemed with confetti and ticker tape. But disillusionment, not just glory and euphoria, awaited servicemen in the postwar era. For those of Mexican descent, the end of military duty also meant readjusting to the harsh realities of life in early twentieth-century America. In Texas, where accolades and celebrations juxtaposed alongside prejudice and discrimination, discontented veterans spearheaded the civil rights movement in the Tejano community. As it turned out, the vigor with which they combated bigotry and intolerance altered the course of Mexican American history.

I

On the morning of September 10, 1919, General Pershing performed his last duty as commander of the American Expeditionary Force (AEF). At 10 o'clock sharp, "Black Jack" spurred his mount and slowly rode it down the streets of New York City, where huge crowds had gathered to officially welcome the American troops home. In addition to standard-bearers and staff, Pershing led a symbolic unit composed of the 1st Division, U.S. Army, and a provisional regiment containing soldiers from other combat divisions. Beginning on 110th Street, he continued until reaching Washington Square, where he dismounted and took a car to the Waldorf. There, as the victory parade—the largest of the post–World War I era—gradually came to a conclusion, he reviewed his beloved doughboys for another hour.[1]

Celebrations both spontaneous and planned had been taking place throughout the country for months, with some commencing immediately upon the troops' arrival. Such was the case in Boston on June 7, when the 360th Infantry landed aboard the USS *Mongolia.* As the soldiers waited for the ship to maneuver into its berth, a local welcome committee approached the vessel in small boats and showered the joyful passengers with candy, chocolates, and cigarettes.

The revelry intensified when the guests of honor began to disembark. As the *San Antonio Light* noted,

> [t]he shower of sweetmeats . . . was renewed from the dock. Bushels of kisses—candy ones—were thrown at them [the soldiers]. A flight of a thousand toy balloons of various bright colors was released by women of the Red Cross, bands played, flags waved and the soldiers aboard the vessel cheered in mighty chorus and showered the throng below them with German coins and tokens.[2]

Not surprisingly, the reception did not go unappreciated by the men in uniform. "We will never forget the beautiful spectacle that Boston—cradle of liberty of the United States of America—presented to us," José de la Luz Saenz wrote in his diary. "Today, tears of joy flowed in much the same way that tears of rage would have flowed had an invading despot set up his army tents on the very soil upon which our loved ones now await our return."[3]

Shortly after arriving at port, servicemen were transferred to neighboring installations for processing. After a thorough delousing, the men often had little else to do but wait for their next orders, free time that some—like Saenz—occupied by enjoying the local sights. Once processing wrapped up, their units were transported to nearby railroad depots, where they subsequently boarded trains that carried them to their local demobilization centers.[4]

Back home in Texas, no doubt unbeknownst to most of the men of the 36th and 90th divisions, the press was closely following their every move. The *Corpus Christi Caller* was typical in its vigilance. From late April, when Pershing notified the 90th Division that it would be leaving Europe in a matter of weeks, until late June, when the vast majority of Texas servicemen were finally reunited with their families, the *Caller* released a steady stream of articles detailing the movements of those units composed primarily of Texans, especially those from its hometown. On June 9, in an article titled "Men of the 90th Division Again Touch Home Soil," it hailed the return of the Texas-Oklahoma draft division. "There are one hundred or more Nueces county lads in the division," it wrote, "and their arrival home is naturally awaited with the keenest anticipation."[5]

Still, the paper called for a greater show of gratitude toward the troops. "Unheralded and unsung our Corpus Christi boys who have been fighting our battles against the despicable Hun are returning home," it hyperbolized, condemning the "spirit of indifference" of some members of its local community. "We are doing nothing, publicly, to show these splendid young men that we appreciate the sacrifices that they made. . . . [N]ow that these boys are returning it is a patriotic duty that we owe to them to see to it that we publicly manifest our appreciation of their splendid services."[6]

Nearby in Laredo, in an editorial titled "The Boys Are Coming Home: How About a Reception?" the *Laredo Weekly Times* echoed these sentiments. "Quite a number of the young men who went from here to the army of Uncle Sam to do his fighting for him, and many reaching the bloody battlefields have been returning home in 'broken lots' for several months past," it lamented, "and yet no big reception, no homecoming oration has been tendered them in Laredo like in other places over the country, perhaps for the reason that they didn't return in crowds." With the arrival of the 141st Infantry—in which Laredoans, including many of Mexican extraction, were strongly represented—the city had no more excuses to continue its negligence, the newspaper argued.[7]

In actuality, the press need not have worried. In North Texas—which was due to receive thousands of returning troops, particularly those of the 36th Division, at Camp Bowie for demobilization—plans for a huge reception got underway as the arrival date neared. Seemingly everyone wanted a part in the festivities. One planning conference, for example, included representatives of the Rotary Club, the American Legion, the Kiwanis Club, the War Camp Community Service, the Salesmanship Club, the Church Women's Federation, the Ad Men's Club, and several other organizations.[8] In San Antonio, where the return of troops from the 90th Division at Camp Travis was eagerly anticipated, the local Chamber of Commerce took control of the preparations for the troops' welcome. "It is hoped that the reception will be highly animated," noted *El Imparcial de Texas*, "so as to befit the sacrifices in Europe by the youngsters who form this heroic division."[9]

Without question, the celebrations surpassed everyone's expectations. When the first units of the 36th arrived at Camp Bowie in mid-June, the entire Dallas–Fort Worth area was ready to offer its favorite division a hearty welcome. On June 14, approximately two thousand soldiers of the 111th Engineers, 131st Machine Gun Battalion, 111th Ammunition Train, and 144th Infantry were treated to a gigantic picnic at Fair Park in Dallas. Following a parade from Union Station to City Hall, the troops boarded streetcars for the ride to Fair Park, where a vast array of homemade dishes prepared by the women of Dallas awaited them in Machinery Hall. "If I could tell you how sincerely glad we are to welcome you back it would not be necessary to bring you to this hall and spread this feast for you," Mayor Frank W. Wozencraft told the guests. "My gratitude is so supreme that I am going to spend my life seeing that the men who wore the khaki get their just dues," added Rev. John G. Slayter, the speaker of the day. "A country that bestows honors and emoluments upon its heroes deserves to live." As the men enjoyed their copious fare, a band regaled them from the speaker's platform, at one point inciting them to stand at attention with a spirited rendition of the French national anthem.[10]

Among the men of the 90th Division, Saenz's 360th Infantry—composed entirely of Texans and affectionately known as "Texas's own"—received by far the grandest reception. Early in the afternoon on June 17, a crowd of several thousand gathered at the Southern Pacific station in San Antonio to greet the troops. The arrival of the first train set off factory whistles and church bells throughout the city, signaling to its residents that the time had finally come to commence the celebration. The roar of the waiting throng—in large part parents, wives, and children of the soldiers—and the playing of the municipal band added to the din. As the men detrained, Mayor Sam C. Bell, who had proclaimed a city holiday, extended a personal welcome to the unit's commanding officers.

When everyone had arrived, the men kicked off the scheduled parade. Buoyed by the music of their regimental band, they walked to their first stop at Alamo and Commerce streets. There, they got into parade formation. Onlookers lined the circuitous parade route, which took the troops from Alamo Plaza to Houston and St. Mary's streets, and then through a Roman-style Victory Arch near the grandstand on the plaza. Sporting bronze tans and full fighting equipment, the young heroes provoked deafening ovations from the crowd, with some young women even showering them with daisies, roses, carnations, and other varieties of flowers.[11]

As several Civil War veterans looked on, state and local officials took turns singing the regiment's praises. "You have written one of the prize pages in American history," declared Judge S. J. Brooks. "You men have proved that this generation is worthy of the men who consecrated this place [the Alamo] in 1836." Harry Hertsberg, the local state senator, likewise invoked the Texas Revolution. "You have come back to us and we welcome you in the shadow of that historic building over there where war spilled the lifeblood of Texas nearly 100 years ago," he told them. "It must be to you a great satisfaction to realize that if those heroes were here today they would be proud of you even as we are."[12]

Later that night, at the Travis Hostess House, the new arrivals resumed the merrymaking. As with the 36th Division in Dallas a few days earlier, a banquet had been prepared for the war-weary troops, in this case an assortment of chicken, tamales, ham, bacon, scrambled eggs, rolls, and coffee, in addition to a dessert of cantaloupe, ice cream, and cake. Those men not completely satiated on those treats later took a swim at the Travis Club or spent the remainder of the evening dancing at the nearby Community House.[13]

In addition to Dallas and San Antonio, other towns held receptions for their returning servicemen. In Alice, forty miles west of Corpus Christi, local officials organized a mammoth two-day celebration for the combined purposes of welcoming the troops home and generating support for a proposed bond issue to boost highway construction in Jim Wells County. Beginning on the evening of June 13, more than one thousand revelers, among them one hundred newly arrived veterans, attended a grand ball that lasted until 2 o'clock the following morning. Besides a resumption of the ball, which commenced shortly before noon and ran on until the evening hours, the next day's activities included a goat-roping contest, a friendly baseball game between Alice and Kingsville, and speeches by local dignitaries in support of the highway bond issue. Perhaps fittingly, however, the main event of the jamboree was an air show staged by two fliers from Kelly Field in San Antonio, who dazzled the crowd with a series of daredevil maneuvers. According to one observer, the display by the two pilots amounted to nothing less than "ethereal gymnastics."[14]

Some Texans planned their official welcomes for Independence Day. Jim Hogg County, for example, arranged an old-fashioned Fourth of July barbecue in Hebbronville for all its returning veterans. Besides community leaders like Robert Lee Bobbitt, several doughboys were slated to speak about their experiences "over there." For its part, Laredo organized a smoker for the holiday, although it eventually postponed the event to accommodate several late-arriving servicemen. Sponsored by the Laredo Volunteer Fire Department, an organization that contributed fifty of its own members to the American colors during the war, the gathering promised plenty to eat and drink and was open to every Laredoan who had donned the American uniform. That said, "an especial invitation [was] extended to those loyal Mexican-American boys who served their country or their adopted country so well during the war," noted the *Laredo Weekly Times*.[15]

Similarly, the Tejano community in Corpus Christi planned a

barbecue in honor of its sons in the 36th and 90th divisions. Part homecoming and part memorial, the reception would include entertainment, but also a solemn high mass for Fernándo Gonzales, who died in Europe and was buried in a French cemetery. According to the committee in charge of the event, its community also intended to invite "American" soldiers.[16]

Private receptions likewise abounded. In April 1919, the friends and relatives of Leopoldo R. Vásquez held a get-together for the young veteran in his hometown of Asherton in central Dimmit County. Vásquez, who had risen to the rank of sergeant during his wartime service, had only recently obtained his discharge from the military. A few weeks later, on June 25, the loved ones of José Gómez threw a similar reception in San Marcos. There, a sumptuous feast and a piñata for the children in attendance were the highlights of the afternoon.[17] Meanwhile, on the day after his arrival in San Antonio with the 360th Infantry, Saenz attended a dance in honor of another Tejano who, like him, had just returned from Europe. The tributes apparently extended not only to the guest of honor but also to every veteran present, for Saenz was moved to remark on how the manifestation of support from his "people" had delighted the well-traveled guests, those who, in his words, had defended the Tejano community's "name and racial pride."[18]

Seemingly wherever they turned, the newly arrived servicemen were met with warm salutations. On June 19, the *Corpus Christi Caller* ran two full pages of advertisements from local businesses that wished to pay tribute to their local heroes. "All the world is proud of you and honors you for the service you have rendered to your flag, your country and humanity," declared the First State Bank of Corpus Christi. "Come and let's shake hands." The Reed Automobile Company ran a similar ad. "We rejoice in your safe return to Corpus Christi and extend our profound gratitude for the everlasting service you have rendered our Union and the world," it read. Some messages were less tactful, however. "We are happy to have you back again," pronounced M. Lichtenstein and Sons, a local garment store. "Of course you are ready to get back into civies [civilian attire] again, and . . . you will want clothes in tune with the spirit of the times . . . clothes to meet your new ideas and your new body developed in the camps. We have the clothes you are looking for."[19]

Other newspapers provided their own tributes. Some, like *Evolución,* made it a point to inform the community whenever a Laredoan arrived from the European battlefields. Its notices often contained glowing accolades, as when Leopoldo Gallardo and several other veterans pulled into town on June 23. Their victory, it proclaimed, "filled the American army with glory."[20] Three days later, an editorial titled "The Texans In The Global Conflict" appeared in *El Imparcial de Texas*. "The Lone Star State distinguished itself above many of its counterparts in the American Union," the article stated. At St. Mihiel, "the Texan soldiers who formed the 36th and 90th Divisions fought with a valor bordering on recklessness, and it was those divisions that managed to defeat the German troops head to head."[21]

The servicemen's businesslike discharge from the armed forces offered them a break from the hoopla of the homecoming parades and celebrations. After turning in their gear, the men received their release papers, a bond for sixty dollars, a pair of shoes, a coat, a uniform, and a passport that covered transportation costs for their rides home. With demobilization over, the new veterans were finally set to begin their lives anew.[22]

More than a few of them found civilian life agreeable, particularly when their military service earned them special privileges. "When we [veterans] got back, we got preference in all the jobs," recalled navy man Pete Leyva. In El Paso, where he settled after returning from his tour of duty, Leyva received work as a truck driver with the city waterworks, courtesy of a mayor who made it a point to take care of fellow veterans. Later, when Leyva left his job with the city, his status as a veteran of World War I again netted him gainful employment, this time as a sheriff deputy.[23] Marcelino Serna, El Paso's most decorated doughboy, also benefited from the city's generosity toward veterans. Like Leyva, Serna received a job with the city waterworks—and his U.S. citizenship—soon after arriving from Europe. In subsequent years, visiting military dignitaries paid homage to the dignified World War I hero.[24]

For other veterans, honors and accolades arrived posthumously. On February 17, 1919, Maj. Gen. DeRosey C. Cabell, commander of the Southern Department, presented the Congressional Medal of Honor to David Cantú Barkley's mother in a ceremony held at the Gunter Hotel in San Antonio. A few days later, the *San Antonio Express* ran a short piece on the event along with photographs of Barkley and his mother, who would later become active in leading fund drives during World War II. Wearing her son's medal and official military hat, which she covered with a traditional Mexican mourning veil, the former Antonia Cantú cut an impressive figure—solemn yet proud. Her son was only the second person whose remains lay in state at the Alamo, the first being the widely respected Gen. Frederick Funston. In 1921, Public School No. 32 in San Antonio was renamed

David Barkley Elementary School, and, twenty years later, the army opened Camp Barkeley (the misspelling was due to a clerical error in Barkley's military records) eleven miles southwest of Abilene in Taylor County.[25]

Distinguished Service Cross recipient Marcos B. Armijo also earned his share of posthumous tributes. On November 17, 1932, veterans in his native El Paso organized the Marcos B. Armijo VFW Post No. 2753. The post served as a gathering place for the town's many veterans, where old doughboys like Marcelino Serna and Modesto A. Gómez, one of the few Tejano noncommissioned officers, were looked upon with awe by other members. The post was also the font of numerous community-building efforts. Among its pet projects were the establishment in 1935 of an ROTC unit in El Paso's Bowie High School—a program once neglected by administrators because of the school's predominately Mexican national student body—and the creation of the Marcos B. Armijo Park in the town's south side two years later. Largely as a result of the efforts of the Armijo post, the Marcos B. Armijo Park would later become a multi-million-dollar complex with, among other things, a community center, library, and indoor pool.[26]

II

For many Tejano veterans, the immediate postwar era was likely a time of peace and contentment. By the 1920s, with the assassinations of Venustiano Carranza and Emiliano Zapata, the famous revolutionary general from Morelos, as well as Pancho Villa's acceptance of a peace offering from the federal government, the Mexican Revolution had begun to wane. Although violence occasionally erupted—as with the brutal and unwarranted murder of the retired Villa in 1923—the new decade witnessed a gradual stabilization of war-torn Mexico and, concomitantly, the areas along the Rio Grande.[27] These developments, along with the end of the "war to end all wars" across the Atlantic, no doubt led some Tejanos to conclude that a new era of peace was finally at hand, that perhaps they had indeed helped "make the world safe for democracy."

Yet some veterans struggled to readjust to American society. The story of Salvador Peña offers a telling, albeit extreme, example. After returning from France, Peña reenlisted in the 12th Cavalry Regiment, only to desert to Mexico a short while later after a comrade's death while patrolling the Rio Grande forced him to reevaluate his career choice. He lived in Mexico for several years under a different identity and even tried his hand at bootlegging, but was eventually caught and forced to serve a one-year sentence in a Brownsville jail. In the end, his standing as a World War I veteran earned him special permission from Pres. Harry S. Truman—a former doughboy himself—to stay in the United States, where he spent the rest of his life uneventfully as a truck driver in Laredo and a contented retiree in San Juan.[28]

For others, large-scale troubles complicated their transition into civilian life. To begin with, the dreaded Spanish influenza—an epidemic that infected a fifth of the world's population and killed more soldiers worldwide than the Great War itself—carried over from 1918 and into the first several months of the postwar era. "So many people died daily that you couldn't dig enough graves," remembered El Pasoan Severiano Torres Ortíz years later. "You'd fill one up, and someone else would be digging another." Such developments made it difficult for many veterans to settle into their new lives comfortably, particularly since, as Torres recalled, so many of them were already "sick from the gas bombs dropped there [in France]."[29]

III

In the years following the war, an increasingly negative mood gripped American society. Some veterans felt abandoned by their country, which they considered ungrateful and insensitive to their problems, such as unemployment and emotional and physical scars. Their compatriots, meanwhile, had grown tired of war, self-sacrifice, and foreign commitments. In short, they had had enough of President Wilson and his idealism. On March 19, 1920, the Senate rejected the Versailles Treaty, the peace treaty that officially ended the war, because many of its members disapproved of a provision calling for the creation of a League of Nations—an organization intended to arbitrate international disputes and thereby preclude future wars. The league, argued its most vehement opponents, would undermine American sovereignty to international authority. In the presidential election of 1920, Republican Warren G. Harding won via landslide by advocating an end to Wilsonian Progressivism and a "return to normalcy."[30]

The postwar era also witnessed the emergence of the Lost Generation, a circle of writers whose works were marked by a profound sense of disillusionment with American society, in large part due to the war. Among these authors were Ernest Hemingway, F. Scott Fitzgerald, John Dos Passos, Sherwood Anderson, Hart Crane, Sylvia Beach, Ezra Pound, and Gertrude Stein, who gave the group its name. Some, like Hemingway in *A Farewell to Arms* (1929) and Dos Passos in *1919* (1932), tackled war-related themes directly. No one, however, was more scathing in criticizing the motives for the war and the treatment of the returning veterans than Pound. In "These Fought in Any Case" (1920), the poet argued that American doughboys had

> walked eye-deep in hell
> believing in old men's lies, then unbelieving
> came home, home to a lie, home to deceits, home to old lies
> and new infamy;
> usury age-old and age-thick
> and liars in public places.[31]

The bitterness was even greater for minority groups. Native American veterans returned to reservations still plagued with high unemployment, illiteracy, and governmental neglect, leading some to alcoholism and drug use.[32] African Americans were no better off, as poverty and Jim Crow awaited most black servicemen back home. "After the fighting, and my return to this country . . . it made me wonder why can't all men be treated equally," recalled one. "What did we fight for? Democracy. Are we living it?"[33]

Mexican Americans encountered similar conditions upon their return. For one thing, many of them found few opportunities to escape poverty—a persistent problem in the barrios of the Southwest—because well-paying jobs were often denied to anyone of Mexican descent. The result was that most Mexicans and Mexican Americans were trapped in low-level employment such as farm work, which in some parts of the Lower Rio Grande Valley often paid as little as sixty cents for a ten-hour work day.[34]

Racial prejudice and segregation complicated matters further. Veteran Manuel C. Gonzales, founder of the Sociedad de la Unión, later recalled that during the immediate postwar era, "as you travelled from Laredo to San Antonio by car or train, the roads were dotted on public restaurants with signs that read: No Mexicans Allowed." According to Gonzales, whenever Tejanos asked for service at any such establishment, waitresses would invariably answer: "I am not allowed to serve Mexicans."[35] In many parts of the state, public schools were also segregated. According to Houstonian Alfred J. Hernández, who would later become a prominent jurist in his hometown, segregated "Mexican schools" were usually "little shack[s] between the black and white schools," separate but by no means equal.

"They were worse than the black school," he opined. "And the black schools were supposed to be bad." Other legal rights suffered in this environment. Tejanos, for example, were not allowed to serve on juries, meaning that persons of Mexican descent could never truly be tried by a jury of their peers. Meanwhile, in some parts of the state, Tejanos were turned away at the polls either by force or through such devices as "white primaries," which barred all but "white" citizens from participating in political primaries—often the only elections that actually mattered in a one-party state like Democratic Texas.[36] Perhaps most alarming, anti-Mexican violence remained rampant. Between 1921 and 1930, at least ten Mexicans fell victim to lynch mobs in the United States. According to historians William D. Carrigan and Clive Webb, between the years 1848 and 1930—which saw 597 reported cases of Mexican lynchings—the chances of a person of Mexican descent being lynched were comparable to, if not higher than, those of an African American in the South.[37]

For veterans, the bigotry and neglect sometimes hit too close to home. "There were a number of men who had served in the war. Then when they came home, they found that they were not served drinks [at some fountains], and were told that 'no Mexicans were allowed,'" one Tejano recalled.[38] According to Saenz, "After demobilization from service in World War I it took only three days after we had received our Honorable Discharge to throw us out from restaurants and deny us service as human beings."[39] The prevailing hypocrisy of the postwar era was not lost on veteran Manuel C. Gonzales. "In time of war we were recognized as 'Americans' and many of our comrades laid their lives upon the alter [*sic*] of sacrifice for our country," Gonzales later wrote. "In time of peace are the good people of our country to receive us as 'Americans,' or are we to step back into the role of 'an alien' until another war is had?"[40] In the South Texas town of Falfurrias, the exclusion of Mexicans from an American Legion Fourth of July dance sent one decorated veteran into a fury. The Tejano reportedly tore off the decoration from his lapel and, as he trampled it underfoot, was heard to exclaim, "If shedding my blood for you [Anglo-]Americans does not mean any more than this, I do not want to ever wear your colors, from now on I am ashamed of having served in your army."[41]

Yet another troubling incident occurred when Saenz and *mutualista* (mutual-aid society) leader Luis Rodríguez organized a movement to erect a monument in tribute to the Mexican Americans who fell in World War I. After first receiving positive feedback from San Antonio Mayor C. M. Chambers, who in 1924 promised to raise such a memorial in the main plaza facing the courthouse, Tejano veterans were later disappointed when the mayor reneged on his vow.[42] Undaunted, Saenz carried on the campaign through the rest of the decade. As late as 1929, fellow veterans like Alonso S. Perales were still pledging their support to the cause. Their fallen comrades had demonstrated that "the descendants of Hidalgo and Cuauhtémoc" were "conscientious citizens who know how to fulfill their obligations" and thus "worthy of all the rights and privileges of citizenship," Perales wrote in *La Prensa.* "It is only natural that we honor the memory of these heroes of our noble race."[43] In the end, though, the effort went for naught, embittering Saenz. "In France, there are so many monuments dedicated to its war heroes that the country has actually placed a limit on the type and amount of shrines that people can erect," he noted.[44] That Mexican Americans were not seen as worthy of a single such tribute, in his view, was downright insulting. Still intent on commemorating the Tejano war dead, Saenz published his diary—along with several additional pieces—as *Los México-Americanos en la Gran Guerra: Y Su Contingente en Pro de la Democracia, la Humanidad, y la Justicia* in 1933.

Injustices of this sort spurred many former doughboys into action. No longer willing to put up with second-class citizenship, Tejano veterans—like their African American counterparts—dedicated themselves to the struggle for equality and civil rights.[45] Eventually, their hard work would result in the creation of the League of United Latin American Citizens (LULAC), one of the oldest and most influential Hispanic civil rights groups in history.

It was perhaps inevitable that Tejano veterans took on this new role as civil rights leaders. Most veterans—regardless of their ethnicity—gained self-confidence and a broader worldview from their overseas experience. They had fought a mostly offensive war, and, at Pershing's insistence, had done so successfully as a distinctive American force. These details, coupled with the culmination of the war a mere few months after the first significant infusion of American troops, made it easier for them to take the lion's share of the credit for restoring peace to the world.[46]

Moreover, wartime service altered how minority soldiers saw themselves and their place in society. According to Philip Frazier, a Native American who served in the 355th Infantry, "the war game has shown us how to make a stand for truth in the face of death. The American Indian has proven himself a worthy American citizen . . . thus, with a broader mind and a larger heart, we are coming home."[47] In an anonymous letter to *The Crusader,* a leading black newspaper, an African American veteran conveyed his newfound self-assurance. "I am ready for any call, to the limit or beyond," he proclaimed. "I fought in the world war for 'democracy' and I am willing to do anything . . . for the liberation of my people."[48] Judge Goodwin, a fellow African American veteran, asserted his status as a full-fledged American. "I feel that I was faithful to my duty and was ready to give all for Democracy. As a Negro I feel that at least I might have full citizenship rights."[49] For many, the war had awakened a virulent political consciousness and led them to a common conclusion: wartime sacrifices had earned their people the rights and privileges of American citizenship, interests for which, if necessary, veterans were now ready to lead the fight.

Even before his return to the United States, Saenz was expressing similar visions of a politicized cohort of Tejano veterans leading the struggle for Mexican American civil rights. "It is my hope," he wrote prophetically, "that my racial counterparts who have taken part in this campaign form a nucleus of men who will labor together to lift the name of our community."[50]

His wish was fulfilled not too long after the armistice. In 1921, several Tejanos—among them veterans like John C. Solis, Pablo Cruz, and Leo Longoria—founded the Order of the Sons of America (OSA) to advance the cause of equal rights for Mexican Americans. According to Manuel C. Gonzales, veterans were the driving force behind the creation of the OSA. They had fought for democracy abroad and now wanted it for themselves.[51] A similar fraternal organization, the Sons of Texas, was formed the following year. Among its leadership was veteran Alonso S. Perales. In 1927, Gonzales branched off from the OSA to found the Order of the Knights of America (OKA), and a few months afterward Saenz and other civic-minded Tejanos formed yet another group, the League of Latin American Citizens. The Sons of Texas and the OKA were based solely in San Antonio, but the OSA eventually included councils in Somerset, Pearsall, Corpus Christi, as well as the Alamo city. Meanwhile, the League of Latin American Citizens had councils in Harlingen, Brownsville, Laredo, Peñitas, La Grulla, McAllen, and Gulf.[52]

Each of these organizations emphasized the rights and duties of American citizenship, reflecting the fervent Americanism of many of its veterans. The OSA, the Sons of Texas, and the League of Latin American Citizens, for example, restricted membership to U.S. citizens.[53] The Sons of Texas pledged to further "the intellectual, economic, and social betterment of American citizens of Mexican descent." Similarly, the OSA's constitution stated that the organization's central goal was promoting the "intellectual and social progress of the Spanish-speaking people in the United States" by influencing "all fields of social, economic, and political action in order to realize the greatest enjoyment possible of all the rights and privileges and prerogatives extended by the American Constitution."[54] Every OSA meeting ended with a prayer authored by George Washington.[55]

On more than one occasion, the new civic groups rushed to the defense of their needy brethren. In 1923, the OSA took up the case of Juan Morales and Victor Fuentes, who stood accused of killing an Anglo-American man in Corpus Christi. Convinced of their innocence, members held public meetings to inform the public about the issue and subsequently defrayed the pair's legal expenses. Two years later, a similar case ended in victory for the organization, which after three years of campaigning finally convinced Gov. Miriam "Ma" Ferguson to issue a pardon to Sabás Castillo, another unjustly accused Tejano. For their part, the Sons of Texas were especially active in discrimination cases. In 1924, they issued a formal complaint to P. F. Stewart, Bexar County superintendent of schools, regarding his district's policy of segregating schoolchildren of Mexican descent, particularly in the small towns on the outskirts of San Antonio. That same year, they pressed charges against a restaurateur in nearby Devine who discriminated against a fellow Son, World War I veteran Julián Suárez. Unfortunately for the group, neither case proved successful.[56]

However well intentioned, the Sons of Texas and its kindred groups simply lacked the political clout to exert much influence in local and state affairs. Cognizant of this fact, several leading Tejanos called for a general conference to unite the various organizations. On February 17, 1929, delegates from across the state met in Corpus Christi. Veterans figured prominently in the convention, with Gonzales serving as secretary and joining Saenz and Perales to speak on behalf of unification. "I have become convinced," pronounced Saenz, "of the necessity that exists of forming one single union of all those elements which like us fulfill all their duties toward this country, and who on the other hand are not recognized in their rights as citizens" despite having "taken up arms in its defense." Perales concurred. "Never as now will we have a better opportunity of uniting ourselves . . . to claim our rights and our prerogatives as citizens of this country." Those rights and prerogatives, he reminded his audience, "will be the only things that we will bequeath to our children."[57] After several spirited orations, the assembly voted in favor of a merger.[58]

Veterans also played other roles in the process of unification.

Gonzales and Saenz served on the executive committee chosen to administer the union until a constitutional convention could be held several weeks later. Perales and another fellow doughboy, Fortino Treviño, were among those entrusted with the task of choosing a name for the new organization. Perales proposed Latin American Citizens League, but eventually the committee opted for League of United Latin American Citizens, the key word *united* a reference to its coalitionist origins. With that, LULAC was officially born.[59]

Like those of its predecessors, LULAC's constitution expresses ethnic pride and devotion but with a decidedly Americanist bent. "We solemnly declare for now and for ever to maintain a respectful and sincere veneration for our racial origin," wrote the document's architects in Article 2. "And we pride ourselves in it." Still, the founders laid a greater emphasis on the rights and obligations of American citizenship, a requirement for membership in the organization. They vowed to "use all the legal means" necessary to combat discrimination, but also aimed on proving themselves worthy of equal rights. Foremost among their goals was becoming "better, more pure and perfect type of true and loyal citizens of the United States of America."[60] They would accomplish this by, among other things, promoting English (the official language of the group) and instilling into their children's hearts and minds American customs and values. As proof of their patriotism, members chose "America, the Beautiful" as the group's official hymn and the Stars and Stripes as the official flag, in addition to implementing George Washington's prayer from the ritual of the OSA.[61]

The organization grew rapidly. In fact, by the time its first Supreme Council met on June 23, 1929, eighteen new councils had surfaced throughout the state. Most of these chapters, such as those of Floresville, Laredo, Crystal City, Uvalde, Del Rio, and Eagle Pass, were located in either South or Central Texas—areas with substantial Tejano populations. But others, like that of Sugar Land in Fort Bend County, were outside of traditional Mexican strongholds. Within the next several years, LULAC also expanded to California and New Mexico, the latter of which would produce the organization's first non-Tejano president, Filemón T. Martínez, in 1939. Its last forays were into the Midwest and the East. During the 1950s and 1960s, the first councils were opened in Illinois, Indiana, Wisconsin, and Minnesota. The 1970s, meanwhile, saw the organization reach out to Puerto Ricans and Cubans by opening councils in Florida and New York. By this time, it had become the largest Hispanic civil rights group in the United States.[62]

Several World War I veterans from Texas went on to become prominent LULAC leaders. Alonso S. Perales served as the first vice president (1929–30) and then the second president (1930–31). Manuel C. Gonzales, who acted as the organization's legal counsel and executive secretary under several administrations, was elected the third president (1931–32). Modesto A. Gómez served as organizer general during the administration of *nuevomexicano* Filemón T. Martínez (1938–39), another World War I veteran. He became the fifteenth president (1943–44) a few years later. His successor, William Flores, a native of Socorro, had served in the army from 1917 to 1919. One of the most dynamic leaders in El Paso, where he served as secretary, director, president, and district governor, he was elected the sixteenth president (1944–45) and remained active with the organization for the next several decades.[63]

In the years following its establishment, LULAC compiled a list of accomplishments that attest to the profound influence its founders had on American society. In the area of education, LULAC helped establish the School Improvement League in 1934, and, in the 1950s, the Little School of the 400, which later served as the model for Head Start. It was also involved in the creation of SER–Jobs for Progress, the largest employment agency for Hispanics in the United States, and the Mexican American Legal Defense and Educational Fund, which would later become the leading representative of Mexican Americans in civil-rights lawsuits. LULAC members also furthered the careers of several notable Tejanos, such as Reynaldo Garza, who became the first Mexican American U.S. federal district judge in Texas; Raymond Telles, whom Pres. John F. Kennedy appointed the U.S. ambassador to Costa Rica in 1961; and Henry B. González, who in 1956 became the first Mexican American ever elected to the Texas Senate. With the backing of LULAC, González would make history again four years later by becoming the first Tejano to ever win election to Congress.[64]

LULAC's greatest triumphs, though, were in the legal arena. In 1954, its attorneys took the case of *Hernández v. State of Texas* all the way to the Supreme Court, which eventually ruled against the exclusion of Mexican Americans from Texas juries. In addition, LULAC members were instrumental in *Del Rio ISD v. Salvatierra* (1930) and *Delgado v. Bastrop ISD* (1948), the cases that ended the segregation of Mexican American schoolchildren in Texas public schools.[65]

The organization was also active during the Great Depression, when poverty, local anti-Mexican drives, and a statewide Immigration Service deportation campaign produced a mass departure of

Mexicans and—more alarming still—Mexican Americans from the state. Once prized as a source of cheap labor, persons of Mexican origin were now considered competition in the meager job market. Not surprisingly, state politicians rushed to the defense of "native" Texans. Rep. Martin Dies, for one, argued that of the state's two million Mexicans at least half were illegal and thus merited deportation. Rep. John C. Box, for his part, cosponsored a bill calling for stricter enforcement of the nation's immigration laws, his target being Mexican citizens. Within LULAC, it fell to Alonso S. Perales and J. T. Canales to stave off these attacks against the Tejano community. Before a congressional committee on immigration in 1930, Canales argued against immigration quotas on the grounds that such measures hurt agricultural interests in the state, while Perales protested Box's attempt to portray Mexicans as an inferior race. Due in part to their efforts, the Box bill failed to become law.[66]

IV

Some two decades after the signing of the armistice at Compiègne, memories of the deportation drives, together with those of World War I surveillance activities, apparently intermingled in the reactions of many Mexican Americans to the bombing of Pearl Harbor. According to author Raúl Morín, the news out of Hawaii led one Mexican American youth from Los Angeles to joke about the implications of another global conflagration on his community: "*Ya estuvo* (This is it). . . . Now we can look for the authorities to round up all the Mexicans and deport them to Mexico—bad security risks."[67]

Despite his cynicism, the *angeleño,* like Morín, a native of the town of Lockhart in Central Texas, wound up serving during World War II. Morin's explanation of his generation's impetus for contributing to the war effort echoed those of many World War I veterans years earlier:

> We felt that this was an opportunity to show the rest of the nation that we *too* were also ready . . . to fight for our nation. It did not matter whether we were looked upon as Mexicans . . . the war soon made us all *genuine* Americans, eligible and available immediately . . . to defend our country, the United States of America.[68]

The aftereffects of this new conflict on the Tejano community also paralleled those of World War I. Serving with honor, Mexican American G.I.s failed to produce a single deserter, traitor, or mutineer and held the distinction of receiving more decorations for bravery and Medals of Honor, in proportion to their population, than any other ethnic group in World War II.[69] Despite this, Tejanos returned to find their home state as prejudiced against Mexicans as ever. The incident that best encapsulated the anti-Mexican bigotry of the post–World War II era involved the refusal of a segregated funeral home in the South Texas town of Three Rivers to bury the remains of a Tejano veteran by the name of Félix Longoria. In response to the snub, a newly minted civil rights organization called the American G.I. Forum, under the direction of World War II veteran and LULAC member Dr. Hector P. García, staged a protest that garnered national attention, eventually leading to Longoria's burial in Arlington National Cemetery in 1949 at the behest of Sen. Lyndon B. Johnson. "The Félix Longoria affair" catalyzed the growth of the forum, which, along with LULAC, would lead the fight for Mexican American civil rights in the coming decades.[70]

Interestingly, at least one Tejano veteran of World War I also wound up serving during World War II. In 1942, forty-three-year-old Manuel M. Téllez of Laredo managed to talk his way into reenlisting in the military, which hesitantly assigned him to a motor transportation company at Kelly Field in San Antonio. The former doughboy, whose grandfather had served during the Civil War, had initially been turned away and told, "You old people go home and work around the house."[71]

As the years passed, World War I veterans lived out their lives in many different ways. Most, like the war hero Marcelino Serna and even the troubled Salvador Peña, eventually settled into a normal home life and retired comfortably, if not wealthily. Others broke the norm, however. Always unconventional, Saenz continued his fight for Mexican American civil rights well into his later years through his work with LULAC and his writings in both Spanish- and English-language publications. He also wrote two manuscripts—one a memoir about his childhood and the other an unusual discourse dealing primarily with visions of the afterlife he received during a coma induced by heart failure in 1940. He retired after World War II, a war to which his family contributed three servicemen and a cadet nurse, and later joined his son at what is now Sul Ross State University to complete his bachelor of arts degree. In 1947, in recognition of his lifelong devotion to the field of education and the Tejano community, admirers in his native Alice named an elementary school after him. He died soon after in 1953.[72]

For Tejano veterans, the post–World War I era brought both joy and struggle. Welcomed grandiosely, servicemen reveled in their hero status, with some even receiving preferential treatment in the postwar job market. Nevertheless, poverty and discrimination continued to plague the Tejano community. A disenchantment with the inequities of postwar America, coupled with a newfound confidence and heightened sense of citizenship, drove many veterans into the sphere of social activism. Among the founders and leading forces behind such civic organizations as the Order of the Sons of America, the Sons of Texas, the Order of the Knights of America, and the League of Latin American Citizens, veterans also played a central role in consolidating them into—and later directing—the League of United Latin American Citizens, which would go on to make monumental strides in the area of Mexican American civil rights. In so doing, they forever transformed the social and political landscape of the United States.

Conclusion

HELD ON SEPTEMBER 16, 1989, THE CEREMONY HONORING David Cantú Barkley as one of the country's Hispanic Medal of Honor recipients was the result of pure chance. One day, after reading a piece in the *San Antonio Express-News* about a local Korean War hero, Rubén Hernández, Barkley's grandnephew, contacted the story's author, Jim Kenney, a member of the Congressional Medal of Honor Historical Society. At first concerned only with whether the society was interested in some of his family's World War I mementos, Hernández eventually revealed Barkley's heritage to a fascinated Kenney. "And then [Kenney] just came over one afternoon," Hernández later recalled. "All of a sudden, we were going to put on this ceremony . . . and things just started rolling from there."[1]

It would not be the last tribute Barkley, the Mexican American, would receive. He was, for example, one of the four Hispanic servicemen profiled in Enrique Castillo's *Veteranos: A Legacy of Valor,* a 2001 historical play that combined drama, music, dance, and actual Department of Defense footage. Additionally, in May 2003, the Laredo city council approved a design for a monument in honor of Hispanic Medal of Honor winners, the centerpiece of which would be a tribute to Barkley, the city's most decorated war hero. Erected shortly thereafter, the memorial featured a bronze statue of the fallen doughboy set before a black granite–faced wall bearing the names of all the Hispanic awardees. Laredo would pay him homage twice more: on October 1, 2004, when a local group of Purple Heart recipients officially established the Military Order of the Purple Heart David Barkley Cantú Chapter No. 766, as well as on November 8, 2006, when, in an event presided over by state and local officials, the Laredo Community College campus chapel was renamed the Pvt. David B. Barkley Cantú Veterans Memorial Chapel. (In both these cases, Barkley's full name was arranged according to the traditional practice in Hispanic countries of placing the father's surname first.)[2]

I

During World War I, thousands of Tejanos answered the call to arms and served their country with honor, with many, like Barkley, sacrificing their lives on behalf of the Allied cause in war-torn Europe. But the large and heterogeneous Tejano community responded to the war in uneven fashion. Some Tejanos withheld their support entirely or contributed to the war effort only out of fear of reprisal. Most tellingly, many of them—even some American citizens—fled the country after the start of the war to avoid the draft. As it happened, Tejanos received similarly inconsistent treatment from the American government. Throughout the war, the intelligence community worked tirelessly to identify potential Mexican and Mexican American subversives. The government's surveillance team remained ever alert for any signs of sabotage or espionage from the Tejano community to benefit the German war effort—this even as another facet of the government, the military, displayed a cultural sensitivity in dealing with the special needs of Tejanos and other ethnic servicemen that resembled the approach of Jane Addams and other settlement-house reformers. It had been a brief, but memorable episode.

But would it prove significant in the long run? As this study has suggested, the answer is an unqualified yes. What is more, it is important for many of the reasons that Chicano scholars have deemed World War II a defining moment in Mexican American history.[3] Maggie Rivas-Rodríguez, for example, has asserted that the first serious participation by Mexican Americans in mainstream society occurred during World War II. By working side by side with Anglos, she contends, these Mexican Americans "discovered, if there was any doubt, that white Americans were, after all, human, no worse and no better." Insights of this sort, coupled with the more forceful sense of citizenship characteristic of many returning World War II veterans, "imbued the ongoing Mexican American civil rights movement with new leadership and a new attitude of entitlement—Mexican American men had, in large numbers, served their country as Americans; now it was time to reap the benefits of full citizenship rights."[4] Yet, as we have seen, this phenomenon was hardly unique to World War II. Over two decades before, the Mexican people of Texas had contributed much of their time, energy, and resources to the World War I effort not only on the battlefield but also on the home front. Tejano doughboys had undergone a life-changing transformation during the war by training and later fighting alongside counterparts of all ethnic, economic, and educational backgrounds. Returning to the Lone Star State as men of the world, war-hardened individuals less inclined to accept second-class citizenship after putting their lives at risk for their country, they proved instrumental in the founding of several civic groups and eventually helped combine them to form LULAC, the largest and oldest-surviving Hispanic civil rights organization in the country.

To be sure, Chicano historians have been right in stressing the impact of World War II. After all, its convulsions, along with those of the Great Depression, did help produce a dramatic resurgence in the area of Mexican American civil rights, one led in large part by an increasing number of Mexican Americans who identified more with the United States than with Mexico—the so-called Mexican-American Generation.[5] More recently, however, Benjamin Heber Johnson has reminded us that this was nothing new, arguing convincingly that the brutal backlash against the Plan of San Diego Rebellion of 1915 had likewise "Americanized" many Tejanos and driven them toward civil rights work. According to Johnson, these Tejanos had eventually recognized the futility of armed resistance against racial discrimination and instead opted to seek protection under the U.S. Constitution by claiming their full rights as American citizens.[6] With regard to civil rights, this examination of World War I confirms that the second decade of the twentieth century was indeed a turning point, a watershed experience during which the seeds of later advances, including many of the post–World War II period, were sown. Despite its scholarly neglect, the first global conflagration undoubtedly merits acknowledgment as a significant catalyst for positive change in Mexican American history.

II

Since the guns fell silent over the western and eastern fronts, servicemen of Mexican heritage have compiled a distinguished record in the American military. Up to 750,000 ethnic Mexicans served during World War II, accumulating twelve Medals of Honor. One decorated Mexican American, Guy Gabaldón of Los Angeles, was credited with securing about one thousand enemy soldiers and civilians, a record for any military conflict in history. Later, Mexican-descent soldiers, having earned six Medals of Honor during the Korean War, added another ten such awards during the war in Vietnam. Perhaps the most well-known of these Vietnam veterans, Roy P. Benavídez, has had everything from a navy ship to a G.I. Joe action figure dedicated to him.[7]

Also since then, Hispanics have surpassed African Americans as the nation's largest minority group, and with this population growth has come a greater representation in the armed forces. According to the Department of Defense, nearly 9 percent of the enlisted men and women in the army, navy, air force, and marines in the year 2000 were Hispanic, most of them Mexican in origin. In 2003, military officials estimated that approximately 55,400 Mexicans and Mexican Americans were serving on active duty.[8] That year, with the start of the Second Gulf War, an unease reminiscent of that of an earlier time gripped the Tejano community. Some relatives of the Mexican American soldiers stationed at Fort Bliss, Texas, the country's largest military base, expressed dissatisfaction as their loved ones prepared to depart to the Middle East. "It's his job," said the mother-in-law of one soldier. "But I don't like what he is going to do. I don't like this war." Her major complaint concerned what she perceived to be a lack of justification for the war, but she acknowledged that, in the case of other soldiers of Mexican descent, loyalty to their ancestral homeland, with its longstanding tensions with its powerful northern neighbor, could also complicate matters. "The Mexicans in the U.S. Army are trapped between two walls," she observed. "They have Mexican heritage on one hand and duty to the United States on the other. It's a very hard place to be." Yet, despite what could only have been trying times at home, her son-in-law was seemingly secure with his place in the army. "I'm an American and I'm proud to be a soldier," he remarked prior to shipping out to Iraq. Another Fort Bliss Mexican American who would be joining him on the trip concurred. "My family in Mexico says 'What are you doing?' But I'm here now and I'm an American."[9]

III

For historian Emilio Zamora, it was almost as if fate had intervened that day back in the late 1970s. Then an instructor and director of the Ethnic Studies Center at Texas A&I University in Kingsville (now Texas A&M University–Kingsville), he had just concluded a lecture wherein he had mentioned what little he (or most anyone else) knew about José de la Luz Saenz. It was then that he was approached by a young female student. "I want to thank you for recognizing my grandfather," said the student, whose last name was Saenz. During the ensuing conversation, she mentioned her ancestor's participation in World War I and, particularly noteworthy for a historian, that he had documented his experiences in a war diary. "Would you like to see it?" Zamora remembers her asking. As with Barkley's story, family history and a bit of serendipity had come into play.[10]

In subsequent years, Zamora came in touch with several other of Saenz's descendants, many of whom, including his son Enrique, he interviewed formally. He was also made privy to their collection of the former doughboy's photographs, writings, and other historical material, which, at Zamora's recommendation, they ultimately donated to the Mexican American Library Program, a unit of the Nettie Lee Benson Latin American Collection at the University of Texas at Austin. Eventually, Zamora published the first scholarship focused exclusively on Saenz. In an article titled "Fighting on Two Fronts: José de la Luz Saenz and the Language of the Mexican-American Civil Rights Movement," he put forth that his subject, although "one of the least-known figures in Mexican American history," was among its most significant civil rights advocates of the first half of the twentieth century—a "brilliant strategist." After decades of relative obscurity, Saenz, like his fellow Tejano with the posthumous Medal of Honor, had been rediscovered.[11]

Notes

Introduction

1. José de la Luz Saenz, *Los México-Americanos en la Gran Guerra: Y Su Contingente en Pro de la Democracia, la Humanidad, y la Justicia* (San Antonio: Artes Gráficas, 1933), 13–18, 112, quote on 112, original letter composed on August 18, 1918, translation mine; Emilio Zamora, "Fighting on Two Fronts: José de la Luz Saenz and the Language of the Mexican-American Civil Rights Movement," in *Recovering the U.S. Hispanic Literary Heritage,* vol. 4, ed. José F. Aranda Jr. and Silvio Torres-Saillant (Houston: Arte Público, 2002), 214–19.
2. Craig Phelon, "The Hero Who Hid His Heritage," *San Antonio Express-News Sunday Magazine,* May 21, 1989, 6–7, 14–19, quote on 14; Michele A. Heller, "On the Front Lines," *Hispanic,* August 1993, 36; "Texan Who Concealed His Origin Is 38th Hispanic Medal of Honor Recipient," *Vista,* January 4, 1992, 25.
3. The only published works that focus exclusively on the participation of Mexican Americans in the war effort are Carole E. Christian, "Joining the American Mainstream: Texas's Mexican Americans during World War I," *Southwestern Historical Quarterly* 92 (April 1989): 559–95 and Phillip Gonzales and Ann Massman, "Loyalty Questioned: Nuevomexicanos in the Great War," *Pacific Historical Review* 75 (November 2006): 629–66. For a good overview of the historiography of the American World War I experience, see Dennis Showalter, "The United States in the Great War: A Historiography," *OAH Magazine of History,* October 2002, 5–13. Among the works on women in World War I are Lettie Gavin, *American Women in World War I: They Also Served* (Niwot: University of Colorado Press, 1997); Maurine Weiner Greenwald, *Women, War, and Work: The Impact of World War I on Women Workers in the United States* (Westport, Conn.: Greenwood Press, 1980); Barbara Jean Steinson, *American Women's Activities in World War I* (New York: Garland, 1982); and Susan Zeiger, *In Uncle Sam's Service: Women Workers with the American Expeditionary Force, 1917–1919* (Ithaca, N.Y.: Cornell University Press, 1999). For a first-rate study of American Indians in the war, see Thomas A. Britten, *American Indians in World War I: At War and at Home* (Albuquerque: University of New Mexico Press, 1997). Although books about the World War I experiences of African Americans appeared shortly after the conclusion of the hostilities in Europe, the most recent studies are far superior to their predecessors. See, for example, Arthur E. Barbeau and Florette Henri, *The Unknown Soldiers: African-American Troops in World War I* (New York: Da Capo Press, 1996); Mark Ellis, *Race, War, and Surveillance: African Americans and the United States Government during World War I* (Bloomington: Indiana University Press, 2001); and Theodore Kornweibel Jr., *"Investigate Everything": Federal Efforts to Compel Black Loyalty during World War I* (Bloomington: Indiana University Press, 2002).
4. The only book-length military histories specifically on Mexican Americans are Jerry D. Thompson, *Vaqueros in Blue and Gray: Mexican Texans in the Civil War* (Austin: Presidial Press, 1976; reprint, Austin: State House Press, 2000); idem, *Mexican Texans in the Union Army* (El Paso: Texas Western Press, 1986); and Raul Morin, *Among the Valiant: Mexican*

Americans in WWII and Korea (Los Angeles: Borden, 1963). Maggie Rivas-Rodríguez, ed., *Mexican Americans and World War II* (Austin: University of Texas Press, 2005), meanwhile, is a collection of essays on Mexican Americans in World War II. In addition, there are a few works based on the war remembrances of Mexican American Vietnam veterans, such as: Roy P. Benavídez and John R. Craig, *Medal of Honor: One Man's Journey from Poverty and Prejudice* (Washington, D.C.: Potomac Books, 2005); Everett Alvarez Jr., and Anthony S. Pitch, *Chained Eagle: The Heroic Story of the First American Shot Down over North Vietnam* (Washington, D.C.: Potomac Books, 2005); Charley Trujillo, *Chicanos in Viet Nam* (San Jose, Calif.: Chusma House Publications, 1990); and Lea Ybarra, *Vietnam Veteranos: Chicanos Recall the War,* foreword by Edward James Olmos (Austin: University of Texas Press, 2004). Pete Billac, *The Last Medal of Honor* (New York: Swan, 1990), also tells the story of Benavídez's heroism in Vietnam.

5. Although an excellent study overall, Christian, "Joining the American Mainstream," offers no information of this sort, with Gonzales and Massman, "Loyalty Questioned," providing only the number of *nuevomexicano* casualties.

6. For more on the evolution of military history, see Allan R. Millett, "American Military History: Over the Top," in *The State of American History,* ed. Herbert J. Bass (Chicago: Quadrangle Press, 1970), 157–82; idem, "The Study of American Military History in the United States," *Military Affairs* 41 (April 1977): 58–61; Richard R. Kohn, "The Social History of the American Soldier: A Review and Prospectus for Research," *American Historical Review* 86 (June 1981): 533–67; Peter Karsten, "The 'New' American Military History: A Map of the Territory Explored and Unexplored," *American Quarterly* 36 (1984): 389–418; Edward M. Coffman, "The New American Military History," *Military Affairs* 48 (January 1984): 1–5; idem, "The Course of Military History in the United States since World War II," *Journal of Military History* 61 (October 1997): 761–75; Peter Paret, "The New Military History," *Parameters: The Journal of the Army War College* 21 (Autumn 1991): 10–8; Paul Kennedy, "The Rise and Fall of Military History," *MHQ: The Quarterly Journal of Military History* 3 (Winter 1991): 9–12; and Sandra L. Myers, "Frontier Historians, Women, and the 'New' Military History," *Military History of the Southwest* 19 (Spring 1989): 27–37.

7. For examples of new military histories of World War I, see Niall Ferguson, *The Pity of War: Explaining World War I* (New York: Basic Books, 1999); Nancy Gentile Ford, *Americans All! Foreign-Born Soldiers in World War I* (College Station: Texas A&M University Press, 2001); James H. Hallas, ed., *Doughboy War: The American Expeditionary Force in World War I* (Boulder, Colo.: Lynne Rienner, 2000); Gary Mead, *The Doughboys: America and the First World War* (New York: Overlook, 2000); and Mark Meigs, *Optimism at Armageddon: Voices of American Participants in the First World War* (London: Macmillan, 1997).

8. Ferguson, *Pity,* 295.

9. John Keegan, *The First World War* (New York: Vintage, 1998), 8–9.

10. Coahuila native José Canal also published a diary, titling it *Hazañas de Un Mexicano en Las Trincheras de Francia.* However, no copy of this 1919 work has yet been found. For more on this, as well as a positive assessment of the accuracy and validity of the Saenz diary as a historical document, see Zamora, "Fighting on Two Fronts," 231–32 n. 4, 233 n. 9.

11. Phelon, "The Hero," 6–7, 14–19; Heller, "On the Front Lines," 36. Prior to World War I, four servicemen of Hispanic ancestry had earned the Congressional Medal of Honor. Since then, Barkley and over thirty other Hispanics, mostly Mexican Americans, have received the award. See Virgil Fernández, *Hispanic Military Heroes* (Austin: VFG, 2006), chap. 3.

12. Traditionally, historical studies on World War I David M. Kennedy, *Over Here: The First World War and American Society* (New York: Oxford University Press, 1980) and Barbeau and Henri, *Unknown Soldiers,* for example—have portrayed racial and ethnic minorities as victims of an intolerant and xenophobic society with inflamed wartime passions. This book adheres to the more recent trend away from victimization history and toward more nuanced interpretations that emphasize how these groups responded actively to the internal and external pressures of the period in shaping their own futures. For other studies in this mold, see Ford, *Americans All;* Britten, *American Indians in World War I;* and Robert Zecker, "The Activities of Czech and Slovak Immigrants during World War I," *Ethnic Forum* 15 (Spring–Fall 1995): 35–54.

Another current historiographical trend is worthy of note. Whereas earlier works—particularly those, like Mario T. García, *Desert Immigrants: The Mexicans of El Paso, 1880–1920* (New Haven, Conn.: Yale University Press, 1981) and Richard A. García, *Rise of the Mexican American Middle Class: San Antonio, 1929–1941* (College Station: Texas A&M University Press, 1991), that employed the "generational model"—have depicted the World War I–era Tejano community as essentially Mexican in orientation, this study abandons notions of "collective identities" and instead highlights the complexities, ambiguities, and contradictions of the Chicano experience. For a look at how the field of Chicano history has moved beyond victimization history and the homogenization of culture and identity, see Alex M. Saragoza, "Recent Chicano Historiography: An Interpretive Essay," *Aztlán* 19 (Spring 1988): 1–77; and David G. Gutiérrez, "Significant to Whom? Mexican Americans and the History of the American West," *Western Historical Quarterly* 24 (November 1993): 519–39.

Chapter 1

1. For a balanced and scholarly biography of the Mexican leader, see Paul Garner, *Porfirio Díaz* (Harlow, England: Longman, 2001).
2. Gilbert G. González and Raul A. Fernández, *A Century of Chicano History: Empire, Nations, and Migration* (New York and London: Routledge, 2003), especially chaps. 2 and 5; Lawrence A. Cardoso, *Mexican Emigration to the United States, 1897–1931* (Tucson: University of Arizona Press, 1980), 1, 5–7, 18, 22, 28–30.
3. For an excellent English-language account of the revolution, see Alan Knight, *The Mexican Revolution,* 2 vols. (Cambridge: Cambridge University Press, 1986). Meanwhile, for the effects of the revolution on the U.S.-Mexico border, see Charles H. Harris III and Louis R. Sadler, *The Border and the Revolution: Clandestine Activities of the Mexican Revolution, 1910–1920* (Silver City, N.Mex.: High-Lonesome Books, 1988); Glenn Justice, *Revolution on the Rio Grande: Mexican Raids and Army Pursuits, 1916–1919* (El Paso: Texas Western Press, 1992); Linda B. Hall and Don M. Coerver, *Revolution on the Border: The United States and Mexico, 1910–1920* (Albuquerque: University of New Mexico Press, 1988); and Don M. Coerver and Linda B. Hall, *Texas and the Mexican Revolution: A Study in State and National Border Policy, 1910–1920* (San Antonio: Trinity University Press, 1984).
4. Ricardo Romo, "The Urbanization of Southwestern Chicanos in the Early Twentieth Century," in *New Directions in Chicano Scholarship,* ed. Ricardo Romo and Raymond A. Paredes (La Jolla, Calif.: University of California at San Diego, 1978), 194.
5. Arthur F. Corwin, ed., *Immigrants—and Immigrants: Perspectives on Mexican Labor Migration to the United States* (Westport, Conn.: Greenwood Press, 1978), 110, 116; González and Fernández, *A Century of Chicano*

History, chap. 2; Emily Skop, Brian Gratton, and Myron P. Guttman, "*La Frontera* and Beyond: Geography and Demography in Mexican American History," *Professional Geographer* 58 (February 2006): 90.

6. Benjamin Heber Johnson, *Revolution in Texas: How a Forgotten Rebellion and Its Bloody Suppression Turned Mexicans into Americans* (New Haven, Conn.: Yale University Press, 2003), 59–62; García, *Desert Immigrants,* 202–3, 225, 227. For more on the Spanish-language press in the early twentieth century, see Nicolás Kanellos, "A Socio-Historic Study of Hispanic Newspapers in the United States," in *Recovering the Hispanic Literary Heritage,* ed. Ramón Gutiérrez and Genaro Padilla (Houston: Arte Público, 1993), 110–17; Richard Griswold del Castillo, "The Mexican Revolution in the Spanish-Language Press in the Borderlands," *Journalism History* 4 (Summer 1977): 42–47; and Juan Gonzales, "Forgotten Pages: Spanish-Language Newspapers in the Southwest," *Journalism History* 4 (Summer 1977): 50–51.

7. U.S. Department of State, *Papers Relating to the Foreign Relations of the United States, 1916* (Washington, D.C.: GPO, 1925), 477.

8. Charles H. Harris III and Louis R. Sadler, "The 1911 Reyes Conspiracy: The Texas Side," *Southwestern Historical Quarterly* 82 (April 1980): 328.

9. Patrick L. Cox, "'An Enemy Closer to Us Than Any European Power': The Impact of Mexico on Texan Public Opinion before World War I," *Southwestern Historical Quarterly* 105 (July 2001): 59–61; Charles H. Harris III and Louis R. Sadler, *The Texas Rangers and the Mexican Revolution: The Bloodiest Decade, 1910–1920* (Albuquerque: University of New Mexico Press, 2004), 165–70.

10. Texas Congress, House, *Journal of the House of Representatives of the First Called Session of the Thirty-Fourth Legislature: Convened April 29, 1915 and Adjourned May 28, 1915* (Austin: Von Boeckmann-Jones, 1915), 380.

11. Hall and Coerver, *Revolution on the Border,* 17–21.

12. Justice, *Revolution on the Rio Grande,* 6; Harris and Saddler, *The Border and the Revolution,* 61–62.

13. National Association for the Protection of American Rights in Mexico, "Map Shows 551 American Lives Sacrificed to Mexican Lawlessness," map with accompanying report, December 1919, Albert Sidney Burleson Papers, Center for American History, University of Texas at Austin.

14. Cox, "An Enemy Closer to Us," 61.

15. State, *Foreign Relations,* 476–77.

16. For more on the U.S. occupation of Veracruz, see Robert E. Quirk, *An Affair of Honor: Woodrow Wilson and the Occupation of Vera Cruz* (New York: McGraw-Hill, 1964).

17. Robert A. Calvert, Arnoldo De León, and Gregg Cantrell, *The History of Texas* 4th ed. (Wheeling, Ill.: Harlan Davidson, 2007), 204–8.

18. David Montejano, *Anglos and Mexicans in the Making of Texas, 1836–1986* (Austin: University of Texas Press, 1987), 92–99; Jerry D. Thompson, *Warm Weather and Bad Whiskey: The 1886 Laredo Election Riot* (El Paso: Texas Western Press, 1991), 45–48.

19. Calvert, De León, and Cantrell, *The History of Texas,* 176, 209, 218, 250–52; Johnson, *Revolution in Texas,* 27–31; Montejano, *Anglos and Mexicans,* 103–10.

20. *La Crónica* (Laredo, Tex.), April 9, 1910, quoted in Johnson, *Revolution in Texas,* 31.

21. From the *Houston Chronicle,* quoted in Cox, "An Enemy Closer to Us," 66.

22. O. Douglas Weeks, "The Texas-Mexican and the Politics of South Texas," *American Political Science Review* 24 (August 1930): 616, 619.

23. William Leonard, "Where Both Bullets and Ballots Are Dangerous," *Survey* 28 October 1916, 86–87.
24. Calvert, De León, and Cantrell, *The History of Texas,* 266; Montejano, *Anglos and Mexicans,* 143.
25. Montejano, *Anglos and Mexicans,* 114–16, quote on 115.
26. Johnson, *Revolution in Texas,* 31–34.
27. Ibid., 34–35.
28. Harris and Sadler, *The Texas Rangers and the Mexican Revolution,* 210–12. For the full text of the Plan de San Diego, see U.S. Congress, Senate, Committee on Foreign Relations, *Investigation of Mexican Affairs,* vol. 2, 66th Cong., 2nd sess. Sen. Doc. 285 (Washington, D.C.: GPO, 1920), 1205–7.
29. James A. Sandos, *Rebellion in the Borderlands: Anarchism and the Plan de San Diego, 1904–1923* (Norman: University of Oklahoma Press, 1992), 81–82. Translations of "¡Ya Basta!" were printed in newspapers across the Lower Rio Grande Valley. See, for example, *Brownsville Herald,* August 28, 1915.
30. Montejano, *Anglos and Mexicans,* 117–25; John R. Chávez, *The Lost Land: The Chicano Image of the Southwest* (Albuquerque: University of New Mexico Press, 1984), 80.
31. Cox, "An Enemy Closer to Us," 63.
32. James E. Ferguson to Woodrow Wilson, July 7, 1915, r 335, series 4, case #2446, Woodrow Wilson Papers, Library of Congress, Washington, D.C.
33. Testimony of Capt. Everette Anglin, in U.S. Congress, *Investigation of Mexican Affairs,* 1: 1307; Sandos, *Rebellion in the Borderlands,* 109.
34. Johnson, *Revolution in Texas,* 85–87.
35. *San Antonio Express,* August 12, 1915.
36. "Necktie Party," *Lyford Courant,* August 6, 1915, quoted in Johnson, *Revolution in Texas,* 86–87.
37. *San Antonio Express,* September 11, 1915.
38. Johnson, *Revolution in Texas,* 108–20; Charles H. Harris and Louis R. Sadler, "The Plan of San Diego and the Mexican-United States Crisis of 1916: A Reexamination," *Hispanic American Historical Review* 58 (August 1978): 390–92.
39. "Los Sediciosos," in *Major Problems in Mexican American History,* ed. Zaragosa Vargas, Major Problems in American History (Boston and New York: Houghton Mifflin, 1999), 214–15.
40. *Brownsville Herald,* September 8 and 17, 1915.
41. *San Antonio Express,* September 11, 1915.
42. Inspector in Charge, Brownsville, to Supervising Inspector, Immigration Services, El Paso, September 14, 1915, File #53108/71-N, RG 85, Records of the Immigration and Naturalization Service (INS), National Archives and Records Administration, quoted in Sandos, *Rebellion in the Borderlands,* 110.
43. Sandos, *Rebellion in the Borderlands,* 110.
44. Arthur S. Link, *Woodrow Wilson and the Progressive Era, 1910–1917* (New York: Harper and Row, 1954), 109–35; Johnson, *Revolution in Texas,* 106–7, 134.
45. James A. Sandos, "Pancho Villa and American Security: Woodrow Wilson's Mexican Diplomacy Reconsidered," *Journal of Latin American Studies* 13 (November 1981): 300.
46. James A. Sandos, "German Involvement in Northern Mexico, 1915–1916: A New Look at the Columbus Raid," *Hispanic American Historical Review*

50 (February 1970): 76–81; Friedrich Katz, "Pancho Villa and the Attack on Columbus, New Mexico," *American Historical Review* 83 (February 1978): 101.

47. Chávez, *Lost Land,* 81.

48. *New York Times,* March 11, 1916.

49. Quoted in ibid., March 10, 1916.

50. *Houston Post,* March 11, 1916; *San Antonio Express,* March 11, 1916; *Dallas Morning News,* March 11, 1916.

51. Michael C. Meyer and William L. Sherman, *The Course of Mexican History,* 5th ed. (New York: Oxford University Press, 1995), 540–41; Link, *Woodrow Wilson,* 137.

52. Link, *Woodrow Wilson,* 137–38.

53. Ibid., 138–41.

54. Ibid., 142–44.

55. Elmer Ray Milner, "An Agonizing Evolution: A History of the Texas National Guard, 1900–1945" (Ph.D. diss., North Texas State University, 1979), 52.

56. James Alexander Garza, "On the Edge of a Storm: Laredo and the Mexican Revolution, 1910–1917" (master's thesis, Texas A&M International University, 1996), 86.

57. Justice, *Revolution on the Rio Grande,* 11.

58. D. Clayton James and Anne Sharp Wells, *America and the Great War, 1914–1920* (Wheeling, Ill.: Harlan Davidson, 1998), 1–20.

59. Friedrich Katz, *The Secret War in Mexico: Europe, the United States, and the Mexican Revolution* (Chicago: University of Chicago Press, 1981), 328–29, 341.

60. Ibid., 350.

61. Barbara W. Tuchman, *The Zimmermann Telegram,* Trade ed. (New York: Ballantine Books, 1985), 184–87.

62. From the *Omaha World Herald,* quoted in Tuchman, *The Zimmermann Telegram,* 184.

63. From *Sacramento Bee,* quoted in Tuchman, *The Zimmermann Telegram,* 186.

64. "In Defense of the Atlantic World," *New Republic,* February 17, 1917, 59–61, quoted in Thomas J. Knock, *To End All Wars: Woodrow Wilson and the Quest for a New World Order* (Princeton, N.J.: Princeton University Press, 1992), 117.

65. From the *Dallas Morning News,* quoted in Cox, "An Enemy Closer to Us," 77–79.

66. From the *Houston Post,* quoted in Cox, "An Enemy Closer to Us," 79.

67. Quoted in Knock, *To End All Wars,* 121–22.

68. James and Wells, *America and the Great War,* 26–27; Link, *Woodrow Wilson,* 282.

69. *Evolución* (Laredo, Tex.), March 3 and 13, 1917, translation mine. My assessment of the paper's wartime tone comes from having read each of its issues from April 1917 to November 1918, in addition to several previous and subsequent issues.

70. *La Prensa* (San Antonio, Tex.), February 9, 1917 and March 18, 1917, translation mine. For more on the founding of this paper, see Onofre di Stefano, "'Venimos a Luchar': A Brief History of *La Prensa*'s Founding," *Aztlán* 16 (Spring–Fall 1985): 95–118.

Chapter 2

1. *Corpus Christi Caller and Daily Herald,* April 11, 1917.
2. *San Antonio Express,* May 5 and 10, 1917.
3. *La Prensa* (San Antonio, Tex.), April 10, 1917, translation mine.
4. Quoted in *San Antonio Express,* April 8, 1917.
5. *Evolución* (Laredo, Tex.), May 11, 1917. Both the telegram and the reply from General Pershing's office are quoted fully in Saenz, *Los México-Americanos,* 14.
6. John Whiteclay Chambers II, *To Raise an Army: The Draft Comes to Modern America* (New York: Free Press, 1987), 136–41; Mead, *Doughboys,* 69.
7. John S. D. Eisenhower and Joanne T. Eisenhower, *Yanks: The Epic Story of the American Army in World War I* (New York: Free Press, 2001), 23–24.
8. H. C. Peterson and Gilbert C. Fite, *Opponents of War, 1917–1918* (Seattle: University of Washington Press, 1957), 21–24, quote on 22.
9. James and Wells, *America and the Great War,* 32–33.
10. Peterson and Fite, *Opponents,* 23–24, quote on 24.
11. *New York Times,* May 31, 1917; *Corpus Christi Caller and Daily Herald,* May 31, 1917.
12. Mead, *Doughboys,* 70–71.
13. Ford, *Americans All,* 52–57.
14. Ibid., 51. The nationwide figures can be found here, while the totals for Texas—excluding the specific numbers for the Mexican citizens and Spanish-surnamed natives—are in Rupert N. Richardson, Adrian Anderson, and Ernest Wallace, *Texas: The Lone Star State,* 7th ed. (Upper Saddle River, N.J.: Prentice Hall, 1997), 336.

    As the introduction points out, Mexican Americans, whom the government lumped with other "whites," receive no specific attention statistically in World War I military records. The exact number of servicemen, volunteers, draftees, and registrants of Mexican descent is therefore unknown. In this study, the totals for the Tejano community are approximations, with the respective figures for registrants and servicemen coming from samples of the nearly one million registration records for Texas in RG 163, Records Relating to Registrants, Records of the Selective Service System (World War I), National Archives and Records Administration, in the case of the former, and the war service card records housed at the Texas Military Forces Museum in Austin, Texas, in the case of the latter. (Unfortunately, the information on the war service records does not include citizenship status.)

    As it pertains to this study on the Tejano community, the shortcomings of these samples are noteworthy. To begin with, even the most expert sampling provides only approximations. The samples utilized in this study, moreover, were of archival collections almost a century old, and some of the war service card records have, for one reason or another, been lost over time. While the collection at the Texas Military Forces Museum is nearly complete and has likely yielded a reasonably accurate estimate, the limitations of the sources must be taken into account. Finally, not all Spanish-surnamed individuals in the state were of Mexican descent—though an overwhelming majority were—and, as the example of David Cantú Barkley shows, some Tejanos possessed non-Spanish surnames because of their mixed ancestry. For more on the Hispanic population in early twentieth-century Texas, see Brian Gratton and Myron P. Gutmann, "Hispanics in the United States, 1850–1990: Estimates of Population Size and National Origin," *Historical Methods* 33 (Spring 2000): 137–53. For information on intermarriages involving

Mexicans, see Ana Cristina Downing de De Juana, "Intermarriage in Hidalgo County, 1860 to 1900" (master's thesis, University of Texas-Pan American, 1998); Johnson, *Revolution in Texas,* 13; and Thompson, *Warm Weather and Bad Whiskey,* passim.

15. Enoch Crowder, *The Spirit of Selective Service* (New York: Century, 1920), 125, quoted in Kennedy, *Over Here,* 152.

16. James and Wells, *America and the Great War,* 32–33.

17. Eisenhower and Eisenhower, *Yanks,* 25; Chambers, *To Raise an Army,* 180–84.

18. *Laredo Weekly Times,* September 16, 1917; Mary Elizabeth Bush, "El Paso County, Texas, in the First World War" (master's thesis, University of Texas at Austin, 1950), 19–27; *Houston Post,* June 6, 1917.

19. *La Prensa,* June 6, 1917, translation mine.

20. *Corpus Christi Caller and Daily Herald,* September 22, 1917.

21. *Laredo Weekly Times,* August 12, 1917.

22. *San Antonio Express,* August 17, 1918; *Laredo Weekly Times,* September 1, 1918.

23. *Laredo Weekly Times,* May 6, 1917 and September 29, 1918

24. Interview with Luis O. Varela by Daniel Varela, November 18, 1976, Interview No. 274, Institute of Oral History, University of Texas at El Paso [hereafter referred to as IOH-UTEP]; interview with Conrado Mendoza by Mike Acosta, December 4, 1976, Interview No. 252, IOH-UTEP, translation mine.

25. *La Prensa,* October 22, 1917.

26. Saenz, *Los México-Americanos,* 13–15.

27. Ibid., 15–16. According to Heras's family members, authorities for some reason dismissed as insufficient proof a baptismal record confirming his true identity. The record is quoted fully in the aforementioned pages.

28. Ibid., 28, 30–31, 44, 57, 160.

29. Ibid., 31, translation mine; Jeanette Keith, "The Politics of Southern Draft Resistance, 1917–1918: Class, Race, and Conscription in the Rural South," *Journal of American History* 87 (March 2001): 1343–44. Keith describes anyone from the former Confederate states—like Texas—as a Southerner. For more on the occupational status of most Mexicans and Mexican Americans in early twentieth-century Texas, see Myron P. Gutmann, W. Parker Frisbie, and K. Stephen Blanchard, "A New Look at the Hispanic Population of the United States in 1910," *Historical Methods* 32 (January 1999): 5–19.

30. Chambers, *To Raise an Army,* 226–29.

31. *Laredo Weekly Times,* November 4, 1917.

32. Britten, *American Indians in World War I,* 123; *Dallas Morning News,* February 14, 1918.

33. *Laredo Weekly Times,* August 19, 1917.

34. On May 9, 1918, Congress rewarded alien servicemen with an amendment to the naturalization laws, making it easier for them to become citizens by eliminating two previous requirements: the minimum of five years' residency in the United States and the filing of the preliminary declaration of intention—the "first papers." The only condition was that an applicant for citizenship needed to produce at least one credible witness to vouch personally for his loyalty. From the time of the passage of the new law until the end of the war, over 150,000 servicemen became American citizens, giving credence to General Crowder's assertion that "the opportunity for naturalization found a hearty response from the

great majority of aliens to whom it was offered." The government never produced a rundown specifying the nationalities of these aliens, but it is not farfetched that many Mexicans were among this group. See, U.S. Provost Marshal General, Second Report to the Secretary of War on the Operations of the Selective Service System (Washington. D.C.: GPO, 1918), 101–2; Ford, *Americans All,* 63–64.

35. Ford, *Americans All,* 44, 66; Britten, *American Indians in World War I,* 63.

36. Interview with Pete Leyva by Oscar J. Martínez, July 22, 1976, Interview No. 312, IOH-UTEP.

37. *San Antonio Express,* February 16, 1918.

38. Chad Louis Williams, "Torchbearers of Democracy: The First World War and the Figure of the African-American Soldier" (Ph.D. diss., Princeton University, 2004), 43–44; Gerard J. De Groot, *The First World War* (Houndmills, England: Palgrave, 2001), 104–5, quote on 105.

39. Saenz, *Los México-Americanos,* 112, original letter composed on August 18, 1918, translation mine.

40. Ibid., 18, original letter composed on February 22, 1918, translation mine.

41. *La Prensa,* June 6, 1917, translation mine. For similar attempts at incorporating ethnic symbols into wartime propaganda, see Phillip Gonzales and Ann Massman, "Loyalty Questioned: Nuevomexicanos in the Great War," *Pacific Historical Review* 75 (November 2006): 636–39.

42. Gov. William P. Hobby to José López, February 8, 1918, Letterpress books, Records of William Pettus Hobby, Texas Office of the Governor, Archives and Information Services Division, Texas State Library and Archives Commission. The actual letter wherein López requests permission from Hobby to join the army is no longer extant, but this reply from the governor reveals why the inmate initiated their correspondence. Hobby referred the matter to the Board of Pardon Advisors, whose decision regarding whether to shorten López's prison term to allow him to enlist is unknown.

43. *La Prensa,* September 21, 1917.

44. *Laredo Weekly Times,* September 23, 1917.

45. *Laredo Weekly Times,* February 24, 1918; *Evolución,* February 24, 1918.

46. Peterson and Fite, *Opponents of War,* 39–40; Chambers, *To Raise an Army,* 214. For more on the Socialist connection to the Green Corn Rebellion, see Garin Burbank, *When Farmers Voted Red: The Gospel of Socialism in the Oklahoma Countryside, 1910–1924* (Westport, Conn.: Greenwood, 1976).

47. *Dallas Morning News,* October 7, 1917.

48. *La Prensa,* December 8, 1917.

49. *Houston Daily Post,* June 22, 1917.

50. *Laredo Weekly Times,* September 30, 1917.

51. Report of P. López, June 5, 1917, #232-1851, r 867, M1085, RG 65, Investigative Records Relating to Mexican Neutrality Violations ("Mexican Files"), Investigative Case Files of the Bureau of Investigation, 1908–22, 1909–21, National Archives and Records Administration [hereafter referred to as Mexican Files].

52. Quoted in Manuel Gamio, *The Mexican Immigrant, His Life Story: Autobiographic Documents Collected by Manuel Gamio* (Chicago: University of Chicago Press, 1931), 71.

53. Chambers, *To Raise an Army,* 211–13.

54. Mark Reisler, *By the Sweat of Their Brow: Mexican Immigrant Labor in the United States, 1900–1940* (Westport, Conn.: Greenwood, 1976), 25; *La Prensa* (San Antonio, Tex.), August 8, 1917, *Evolución* (Laredo, Tex.), June

13, 1917 and June 6, 1918; *Dallas Morning News*, June 6, 1917 and September 11, 1918.

55. Manuel Gamio, *Quantitative Estimate: Sources and Distribution of Mexican Immigration into the United States* (Mexico City: Talleres Gráficos Editorial y "Diario Oficial," 1930), table 1.

56. *Evolución* (Laredo, Tex.), June 5, 1917; *La Prensa* (San Antonio, Tex.), June 7, 1917; E. E. Fischer to J. F. Carl, April 13, 1918, 2J369, Texas War Records Collection, 1916–19, 1940–45, Center for American History, University of Texas, Austin [hereafter referred to as TWRC].

57. Reisler, *By the Sweat of Their Brow*, 25–26.

58. *Laredo Weekly Times*, July 1, 1917. For more on this turbulent era in Mexican history, see Michael C. Meyer, *Huerta: A Political Portrait* (Lincoln: University of Nebraska Press, 1972).

59. *El Demócrata Fronterizo* (Laredo, Tex.), April 28, 1917, in report of P. López, May 10, 1917, #232-1589, r 866, Mexican Files.

60. *Houston Post*, January 4, 1918.

61. Virginia Corn Yeager to William P. Hobby, November 3, 1917, Texas Ranger Correspondence, 1183-16, Archives and Information Services Division, Texas State Library and Archives Commission, quoted in Johnson, *Revolution in Texas*, 152.

62. *La Prensa*, July 3, 1917.

63. Ibid., May 6, 1917; *Evolución*, May 16, 1917.

64. Christian, "Joining the American Mainstream," 571–72; Reisler, *By the Sweat of Their Brow*, 25–27, quote on 26; *Corpus Christi Caller and Daily Herald*, May 29, 1917.

65. Quoted in *Evolución*, June 5, 1917, translation mine.

66. Saenz, *Los México-Americanos*, 277, translation mine. For more on Mexican machismo, see Alfredo Mirandé, *Hombres y Machos: Masculinity and Latino Culture* (Boulder, Colo.: Westview Press, 1997). A classic take on the subject is Octavio Paz, *The Labyrinth of Solitude*, trans. Lysander Kemp (New York: Grove, 1961), especially chaps. 2 and 4.

67. J. C. B. Harkness to J. F. Carl, August 7, 1917, 2J371, TWRC.

68. *San Antonio Express*, May 17, 1917. For a similar case involving the emasculation of African Americans in the cotton belt, see Gerald E. Shenk, "Race, Manhood, and Manpower: Mobilizing Rural Georgia for World War I," *Georgia Historical Quarterly* 81 (Fall 1997): 622–62.

69. See, for example, *San Antonio Express*, June 2 and 4, 1917 and *Evolución*, September 10, 1918.

70. *Corpus Christi Caller*, September 11, 1918; *Houston Daily Post*, September 16, 1918.

71. Reisler, *By the Sweat of Their Brow*, 24–42. See also Otey M. Scruggs, "The First Mexican Farm Labor Program," *Arizona and the West* 2 (Winter 1960): 319–26; and George C. Kiser, "Mexican American Labor before World War II," *Journal of Mexican American History* 2 (Spring 1972): 122–42. For more on the Bracero Program of World War II, see Ernesto Galarza, *Merchants of Labor: The Mexican Bracero Story* (Charlotte, N.C.: McNally and Loftin, 1964); Richard B. Craig, *The Bracero Program: Interest Groups and Foreign Policy* (Austin: University of Texas Press, 1971); and Kitty Calavita, *Inside the State: The Bracero Program, Immigration, and the I.N.S.* (New York: Routledge, 1992).

72. *Houston Post*, July 15, 1917; *La Prensa*, September 13, 14, and 21, 1918.

73. *San Antonio Express*, February 15, 1918.

74. Saenz, *Los México-Americanos*, 23, emphasis and translation mine.

75. *La Prensa,* April 29, 1918 and May 20, 1918.
76. Ibid., April 28, 1918.
77. L. A. Kaufer to W. A. Clampit, September 13, 1918, 2J393, TWRC.
78. *Laredo Weekly Times,* September 15, 1918.
79. *La Prensa,* March 26, 1918.
80. Quoted in ibid., March 25, 1918, translation mine.
81. Saenz, *Los México-Americanos,* 7, translation mine.
82. Chambers, *To Raise an Army,* 211; *Houston Daily Post,* December 21, 1917. For a look at some of these draft dodgers' involvement in Mexican revolutionary politics, see Dan La Botz, "American 'Slackers' in the Mexican Revolution: International Proletarian Politics in the Midst of a National Revolution," *The Americas* 62 (April 2006): 563–90.
83. Morín, *Among the Valiant,* 113–14.

Chapter 3

1. *New York Times,* March 3, 1917.
2. Interestingly, persons of Mexican descent also came under heavy suspicion as potential subversives during the two wars that bookended World War I. For the allegedly pro-Spanish leanings of the Tejano community during the Spanish-American War, see Arnoldo De León, *They Called Them Greasers: Anglo Attitudes toward Mexicans in Texas, 1821–1900* (Austin: University of Texas Press, 1983), 61–62, n. 122, while Mauricio Mazón, *The Zoot-Suit Riots: The Psychology of Symbolic Annihilation* (Austin: University of Texas Press, 1984), 103–6, discusses the equally baseless rumors of Nazi activity among Mexican-origin individuals in Los Angeles and the surrounding areas during World War II.
3. Charles H. Harris III and Louis R. Sadler, "The Witzke Affair: German Intrigue on the Mexican Border, 1917–18," *Military Review* 59 (February 1979): 38; Athan Theoharis, *The FBI and American Democracy: A Brief Critical History* (Lawrence: University Press of Kansas, 2004), 21–22; William E. Leuchtenburg, *The Perils of Prosperity, 1914–32,* 2nd ed. (Chicago: University of Chicago Press, 1993), 28; James and Wells, *America and the Great War,* 12–13, quote on 13.
4. Friedrich Katz, *The Secret War in Mexico: Europe, the United States, and the Mexican Revolution* (Chicago: University of Chicago Press, 1981), 328–67, 411–33, 511–16.
5. Ibid., 433–41.
6. Kornweibel, *"Investigate Everything,"* chap. 1; Texas Adjutant General, Biennial Report of the Adjutant General of Texas from January 1, 1917 to December 31, 1918 (Austin: Von Boeckmann-Jones, 1919), 63–70; Charles H. Harris III and Louis R. Sadler, *The Texas Rangers and the Mexican Revolution,* 396–98. The Bureau of Investigation's reports on Mexican neutrality violations—the so-called Mexican Files—number some eighty thousand pages and are now contained in twenty-four reels of microfilm. See Harris and Sadler, *The Border and the Revolution,* 54.
7. Report of E. T. Needham, May 2, 1917, #232-1646, r 866, M1085, RG 65, Mexican Files.
8. Report of R. Panster, August 17, 1917, #232-1865, r 867, M1085, Mexican Files.
9. Report of R. L. Barnes, 30 April 1917, #232-1541, r 866, M1085, Mexican Files.
10. Kennedy, *Over Here,* 26, 75, quote on 75.
11. Edward M. House diary, entry for February 11, 1918, Edward M. House

Papers, Sterling Library, Yale University, New Haven, Conn., quoted in ibid., 75.

12. Kornweibel, *"Investigate Everything,"* 32–33. Evidence of the Loyalty Rangers' investigations of the mail can be found in W. M. Hanson to James A. Harley, February 15, 1918, Box 401–573, Correspondence, Department Correspondence, Texas Adjutant General's Department, Archives and Information Services Division, Texas State Library and Archives Commission.

13. Kennedy, *Over Here,* 25–26, 65, 77; Kornweibel, *"Investigate Everything,"* 33.

14. Katz, *Secret War in Mexico,* 441–53, 459, quote on 459. On February 24, 1918, *El Demócrata* claimed that almost sixty thousand Mexican citizens had been enlisted in the U.S. military, a figure that was almost certainly inflated to heighten anti-Americanism and fears of the draft. See, Fernando Saúl Alanís Enciso, *El Primer Programa Bracero y el Gobierno de México* (San Luis Potosí: El Colegio de San Luis, 1999), 55.

15. *El Demócrata Fronterizo* (Laredo, Tex.), December 1, 1917.

16. Katz, *Secret War in Mexico,* 453–59.

17. Christian, "Joining the American Mainstream," 569–70. My assertion that no Spanish-language newspapers from Texas were ever labeled disloyal comes from examining every case file on the Tejano press in RG 28, Records Relating to the Espionage Act, World War I, 1917–21, Records of the Post Office Department, National Archives and Records Administration [hereafter referred to as Post Office Records].

18. Report of Seman, April 1, 1917, #232-1784, r 867, M1085, Mexican Files.

19. Report of Charles E. Breniman, April 5, 1917, #232-783, r 865, M1085, Mexican Files.

20. Apparently, the targets of Idar's surveillance during the prewar period were Mexican exiles suspected of plotting revolutionary activities from American soil. See, for example, report of C. N. Idar, August 3, 1916, #232-783, r 865, M1085, Mexican Files and report of C. N. Idar, August 19, 1916, #232-784, M1085, Mexican Files.

21. Quoted in BI report of C. E. Breniman, December 14, 1917, Case File 49490, Box 140, Post Office Records.

22. L. W. Morris to Inspector in Charge, February 18, 1918, Case File 49490, Box 140, Post Office Records.

23. L. W. Morris to Inspector in Charge, February 18, 1918, Case File 50715, Box 188, Post Office Records.

24. W. H. Lamar to Idar Publishing Company, July 12, 1918, Case File 50940, Box 211, Post Office Records.

25. George D. Armistead to the Solicitor Post Office Department, July 16, 1918, Case File 49490, Box 140, Post Office Records.

26. *Evolución* (Laredo, Tex.), September 3, 1918, translation mine. For a critical look at the "Work or Fight" laws, see Gerald E. Shenk, *"Work or Fight!" Race, Gender, and the Draft in World War One* (New York: Palgrave Macmillan, 2005).

27. Memo from the Third Assistant Postmaster General, May 8, 1918, 838.14, Folder 21, r 6, Albert Sidney Burleson Papers, Center for American History, University of Texas, Austin [hereafter referred to as Burleson Papers].

28. James A. Sandos, *Rebellion in the Borderlands: Anarchism and the Plan de San Diego, 1904–1923* (Norman: University of Oklahoma Press, 1982), 167–68.

29. Ygnacio Bonilla to Robert Lansing, June 12, 1918, Case File 51091, Box

223, Post Office Records. My claim that *La República* was the only Tejano periodical to fall victim to the World War I–era's antidissent laws, as with my earlier assertion on the question of disloyalty, comes from examining the Post Office's Espionage Act case files.

30. Newspaper clipping, n.d. [August 1918], Case File 51091, Box 223, Post Office Records.

31. Albert S. Burleson to the Editor and Publisher, October 3, 1917, 838.14, Folder 21, r 6, Burleson Papers.

32. Quoted in untitled statement from Albert S. Burleson, May 31, 1918, 838.14, Folder 21, r 6, Burleson Papers.

33. Upton Sinclair to Woodrow Wilson, October 22, 1917, Woodrow Wilson Papers, Library of Congress, Washington, D.C., quoted in Kennedy, *Over Here,* 76.

34. Kennedy, *Over Here,* 76–78.

35. *Laredo Weekly Times,* November 25 and December 2, 1917; *San Antonio Express* February 25, 1918; PF-38/1, March 22, 1918, r 16, M1474, RG 165, Geographic Index to Correspondence of the Bureau of Investigation, Records of the War Department General and Special Staffs, National Archives and Records Administration [hereafter referred to as GI]. The report on German propaganda in Mexico, like many other personnel files of the Military Intelligence Division that were later termed "useless," was actually destroyed as part of a series of disposal actions undertaken during the late 1920s. The Bureau of Investigation's geographic index, however, contains a short summation of its contents.

36. Kornweibel, *"Investigate Everything,"* 45–46, 49, 54. This book and Ellis, *Race, War, and Surveillance,* are the two best studies on the surveillance of African Americans during World War I. For more on a prewar episode involving the supposed recruitment of African Americans for service in Carranza's army, see James Alexander Garza, "On the Edge of a Storm: Laredo and the Mexican Revolution, 1910–1917" (master's thesis, Texas A&M International University, 1996), 86.

37. F. M. Spencer to Bureau, April 9, 1917, 3057, Old German case file, Investigative Case Files of the Bureau of Investigation, 1908–22, 1909–21, National Archives and Records Administration, quoted in Kornweibel, *"Investigate Everything,"* 45.

38. J. H. Rogers to B. L. Barnes, April 9, 1917, #232-1608, r 866, M1085, Mexican Files.

39. Quoted in report of R. L. Barnes, May 1, 1917, #232-1635, r 866, M1085, Mexican Files.

40. Report of R. L. Barnes, May 3, 1917, #232-1530, r 866, M1085, Mexican Files.

41. Report of F. M. Spencer, April 13, 1917, #232-1546, r 866, M1085, Mexican Files.

42. Report of B. C. Baldwin, April 24, 1917, #232-1597, r 866, M1085, Mexican Files.

43. *Dallas Morning News,* May 10, 1918.

44. Kornweibel, *"Investigate Everything,"* 38, 44–46, 49.

45. Arnold Shankman, "The Image of Mexico and the Mexican-American in the Black Press, 1890–1935," *Journal of Ethnic Studies* 3 (Summer 1975): 43–45.

46. Kornweibel, *"Investigate Everything,"* 272. For more on this aspect of the Red Scare, see idem, *"Seeing Red": Federal Campaigns against Black Militancy, 1919–1925* (Bloomington: Indiana University Press, 1998).

47. *San Antonio Express,* July 11 and 21, 1917.
48. *La Prensa* (San Antonio, Tex.), August 31, 1917.
49. Report of J. J. Lawrence, June 4, 1917, #232-1840, r 867, M1085, Mexican Files.
50. Quoted in *Corpus Christi Caller,* September 8, 1918.
51. Quoted in *San Antonio Express,* September 7, 1918.
52. Ibid., December 16, 1917.
53. Report of E. H. Parker, June 15, 1917, #232–1825, r 867, M1085, Mexican Files.
54. *Laredo Weekly Times,* September 1, 1918.
55. James A. Harley to O. E. Dunlap, September 14, 1918, 2J396, TWRC.
56. *San Antonio Express,* September 7, 1918.
57. Quoted in the *Corpus Christi Caller,* September 8, 1918.
58. Quoted in the *Laredo Weekly Times,* July 15, 1917.
59. James A. Harley to O. E. Dunlap, September 14, 1918, 2J396, TWRC.
60. 10487-1224/1–2, August 22, 1918, r 16, M1474, GI.
61. *Evolución,* September 8, 1918, translation mine.
62. *Dallas Morning News,* June 6, 1917.
63. *Evolución,* June 8, 1917.
64. Report of P. López, May 25, 1917, #232-1959, r 867, M1085, Mexican Files.
65. Report of E. H. Parker, June 25, 1917, #232-1951, r 867, M1085, Mexican Files.
66. Report of P. López, June 7, 1917, #232-1851, r 867, M1085, Mexican Files.
67. Report of Will C. Austin, September 23, 1918, #232-3344, r 871, M1085, Mexican Files.
68. Report of William Nuenhoffer, November 1, 1917, #232-967, r 867, M1085, Mexican Files.
69. J. H. Surles to A. B. Blelaski [*sic*], November 11, 1917, #232-1879, r 867, M1085, Mexican Files.
70. W. E. Girand to W. C. Austin, December 8, 1917, quoted in report of W. C. Austin, December 13, 1917, #232-2403, r 867, M1085, Mexican Files. Unfortunately, the report does not reveal what punishment, if any, Childres received for lying to investigators.
71. Report of [illegible on film] Tinlepaugh, September 27, 1918, #232-1652, r 866, M1085, Mexican Files.
72. Report of Gus T. Jones, January 11, 1919, #232-1652, r 866, M1085, Mexican Files. This report, which officially declares the case closed, does not reveal the fate of the informant.
73. Report of F. S. Smith, June 4, 1918, #232-3105, r 870, M1085, Mexican Files.
74. Quoted in report of Manuel Sorola, May 20, 1917, #232-1539, r 866, M1085, Mexican files; report of B. C. Baldwin, May 1, 1917, #232-1539, r 866, M1085, Mexican files; report of B. C. Baldwin, May 16, 1917, #232-1539, r 866, M1085, Mexican files.
75. Kornweibel, *"Investigate Everything,"* 3–4, 59, 61, 67–68.
76. Paul L. Murphy, *World War I and the Origin of Civil Liberties in the United States* (New York: Norton, 1979), 15, quoted in Kornweibel, *"Investigate Everything,"* 3–4.
77. *La Prensa,* March 6, 1919; *San Antonio Express,* March 2, 1919; *Evolución,* April 29, 1919. For more on convictions for spying under the Espionage

Act, see Norman Polmar and Thomas B. Allen, *Spy Book: The Encyclopedia of Espionage* (New York: Random House, 1997), 195.

78. Harris and Saddler, "The Witzke Affair," 36–50.

79. Report of Manuel Sorola, April 28, 1918, #232-1870, r 867, M1085, Mexican Files; Harris and Sadler, *The Border and the Revolution,* 61–62.

80. Katz, *Secret War in Mexico,* 540–49, 563, quotes on 540. For more on Nazi intrigue in Mexico, see Stanley E. Hilton, *Hitler's Secret War in South America, 1939–1945: German Military Espionage and Allied Counterespionage in Brazil* (Baton Rouge: Louisiana State University Press, 1981), which despite its focus on Brazil—the center of Nazi espionage in the Americas until 1942—nonetheless contains valuable information on Mexico and other Latin American countries.

Chapter 4

1. *La Prensa* (San Antonio, Tex.), April 12, 1917.

2. *Corpus Christi Caller and Daily Herald,* April 6, 1917.

3. *Laredo Weekly Times,* April 15, 1917.

4. Ibid., 15, April 22, 1917.

5. Quoted in Eisenhower and Eisenhower, *Yanks,* 19.

6. William E. Leuchtenburg, *Perils of Prosperity, 1914–32,* 2nd ed. (Chicago: University of Chicago Press, 1993), 34–35; James and Wells, *America and the Great War,* 60–65, 73–74.

7. Kennedy, *Over Here,* 114–17, 286; "List of Members Composing Various County Councils in Texas," 2J392, TWRC; "List of Chairmen of County Councils of Defense of Various Counties in Texas," 2J368, TWRC; Bush, "El Paso County," 38–42; "Women's Committee of Council of Defense—Membership Roll," 2J366, TWRC; Minutes of Woman's Committee, Bexar County, August 5, 1918, 2J366, TWRC. For more on the Texas State Council of Defense, see Oran Elijah Turner, "History of the Texas State Council of Defense" (master's thesis, University of Texas at Austin, 1926). Meanwhile, for more on De Zavala's efforts to preserve the Alamo, see Robert L. Ables, "The Second Battle for the Alamo," *Southwestern Historical Quarterly* 70 (January 1967): 372–413.

8. Kennedy, *Over Here,* 71.

9. Ricardo Romo, "Responses to Mexican Immigration, 1910–1930," *Aztlán* 6 (Summer 1975): 181.

10. *Dallas Morning News,* May 5, 1917.

11. James and Wells, *America and the Great War,* 62–64.

12. Mrs. Joe Walters to Mr. W. A. Clampitt, February 6, 1918, 2J392, TWRC.

13. See, for example, *Evolución* (Laredo, Tex.), January 29, 1918.

14. Christian, "Joining the American Mainstream," 585.

15. Leuchtenburg, *The Perils of Prosperity,* 33–34, quote on 33.

16. Kennedy, *Over Here,* 126–43, quote on 136.

17. Eisenhower and Eisenhower, *Yanks,* 19–21; James and Wells, *America and the Great War,* 73–74.

18. Kennedy, *Over Here,* 61, 105. For more on the Four-Minute Men, see Alfred E. Cornebise, *War as Advertised: The Four Minute Men and America's Crusade, 1917–1918* (Philadelphia: American Philosophical Society, 1984).

19. "Four-Minute Men Insignia Registration: Fort Worth," 2J359, TWRC; "Committee on Public Information List of Four-Minute Speakers, El Paso, Texas," 2J375, TWRC; *Laredo Weekly Times,* August 5, 1917; *Evolución* (Laredo, Tex.), August 16, 1917; Johnson, *Revolution in Texas,* 159

20. William McCormick Blair to Four-Minute Men State Chairmen, memorandum, July 12, 1917, 2J358, TWRC; Memo to the Adjutant General by William S. Graves, July 26, 1918, 2J359, TWRC; "Four Minute Hints," printed card, 2J359, TWRC.
21. Francis J. Lyons to Joseph Hirsch, September 21, 1917, 2J375, TWRC. For more on the Four-Minute Men of New Mexico, see Richard Melzer, "Stage Soldiers of the Southwest: New Mexico's Four Minute Men of World War I," *Military History of the Southwest* 20 (Spring 1990): 23–42.
22. William Gibbs McAdoo, *Crowded Years* (Boston: Houghton Mifflin, 1931), 374–79, quoted in Kennedy, *Over Here,* 105.
23. Kennedy, *Over Here,* 100–107; Bush, "El Paso County," 54–59; James and Wells, *America and the Great War,* 64–65.
24. *Corpus Christi Caller,* October 5, 1918.
25. Quoted in *Evolución,* October 27, 1917, translation mine.
26. Christian, "Joining the American Mainstream," 584–85.
27. *El Demócrata Fronterizo* (Laredo, Tex.), October 12, 1918, translation mine.
28. *Evolución,* June 10, 1917, translation mine.
29. Quoted in Kennedy, *Over Here,* 106.
30. See, for example, *Evolución,* April 19, 1918; Christian, "Joining the American Mainstream," 585.
31. *Laredo Weekly Times,* May 5, 1918.
32. Kennedy, *Over Here,* 106.
33. James and Wells, *America and the Great War,* 72.
34. Ibid., 71–72.
35. *Dallas Morning News,* January 1, 1918; *Corpus Christi Caller and Daily Herald,* July 13, 1917.
36. Rupert N. Richardson, Adrian Anderson, and Ernest Wallace, *Texas: The Lone Star State,* 7th ed. (Upper Saddle River, N.J.: Prentice Hall, 1997), 337–38.
37. *Laredo Weekly Times,* April 7, 1918.
38. C. W. Hellen to J. F. Carl, August 31, 1918, 2J371, TWRC.
39. E. L. Gammage to J. F. Carl, November 24, 1917, 2J370, TWRC; A. B. Bielaski to John J. Keeney, December 20, 1917, 2J373, TWRC; J. F. Carl to John Cravens, January 9, 1918, 2J373, TWRC.
40. *Laredo Weekly Times,* April 15, 1917.
41. Ibid., September 23, 1917.
42. Ibid., April 15, 917.
43. *Corpus Christi Caller and Daily Herald,* April 5, 1917.
44. *Evolución,* April 14, 1917; *Laredo Weekly Times,* May 20, 1917; *Corpus Christi Caller and Daily Herald,* May 18, 1917.
45. *Laredo Weekly Times,* April 15, 1917.
46. Ibid., March 17, 1919.
47. Glenn Justice, *Revolution on the Rio Grande: Mexican Raids and Army Pursuits, 1916–1919* (El Paso: Texas Western Press, 1992), 21–29, 49–51.
48. Ibid., 36–40, 45–47, 52.
49. U.S. Department of State, *Papers Relating to the Foreign Relations of the United States, 1918* (Washington, D.C.: GPO, 1930), 548–76, quote on 572.
50. *Houston Post,* August 28, 1918; *New York Times,* December 26, 1917.
51. *La Prensa,* April 27, 1918.
52. *Corpus Christi Caller,* October 5, 1918.

53. *Houston Post,* October 15, 1918.
54. *La Prensa,* April 28, 1918.
55. *Evolución,* June 13, 1917.
56. *Laredo Weekly Times,* July 7 and 14, 1918; Christian, "Joining the American Mainstream," 584.
57. *Corpus Christi Caller,* September 20, 1918.
58. *La Prensa,* April 27, 1918.
59. Christian, "Joining the American Mainstream," 584 n. 64; *Evolución,* October 17, 1918; *El Demócrata Fronterizo,* October 12 and 19, 1918.
60. *San Antonio Express,* March 27, 1918.
61. *Brownsville Herald,* July 24, 1918.
62. Quoted in the *San Antonio Express,* January 29, 1918.
63. Julie Leininger Pycior, "*La Raza* Organizes: Mexican American Life in San Antonio, 1915–1930, as Reflected in *Mutualista* Activities" (Ph.D. diss., University of Notre Dame, 1979), 123.
64. *La Prensa,* September 3 and September 12 and 18, 1918; *Dallas Morning News,* August 12, 1917; *San Antonio Express,* September 7, 1918.
65. *Brownsville Herald,* December 9, 1918; *Laredo Weekly Times,* May 26, 1918; *Dallas Morning News,* June 5, 1917.
66. *Evolución,* November 20, 1917.
67. Quoted in the *Brownsville Herald,* July 31, 1918.
68. Bush, "El Paso County," 94–95.
69. *Evolución,* June 14, 1918; *Laredo Weekly Times,* March 17, 1918; *San Antonio Express,* July 18, 1918.
70. *La Prensa,* July 13, 1918.
71. Maj. J. S. Upham to Mrs. G. G. López, December 14, 1917, .005, Box 104, RG 120, Decimal File, Headquarters, 36th Division Records, Records of the American Expeditionary Force, National Archives and Records Administration.
72. *La Prensa,* January 15, 1919.
73. *Evolución,* July 19, 1918, translation mine.
74. *Houston Post,* April 7, 1918.
75. *La Prensa,* April 12, 1918, translation mine.
76. *Evolución,* October 5, 1917.
77. Eisenhower and Eisenhower, *Yanks,* 20–21. For more on the music of World War I, see Glenn Watkins, *Proof through the Night: Music and the Great War* (Berkeley: University of California Press, 2003).
78. *Laredo Weekly Times,* February 10, 1918.
79. Quoted in the *Laredo Weekly Times,* July 14, 1918.
80. *Corridos* were also composed in other parts of the Southwest and as tributes to Mexican American veterans of other conflicts, such as the Civil War and the Spanish-American War. See Randall G. Keller, "The Past in the Present: The Literary Continuity of Hispanic Folklore in New Mexico and the Southwest," *Bilingual Review/La Revista Bilingüe* 16 (May–December 1991): 108, 138–40.
81. "Registro de 1918," in *The New Anthology of American Poetry,* vol. 2, *Modernisms 1900–1950,* ed. Stephen Gould Axelrod, Camille Roman, and Thomas Travisano (New Brunswick, N.J.: Rutgers University Press, 2005), 524.
82. "Nuevo Corrido de Laredo," in ibid., 526.

83. Manuel Gamio Papers, Bancroft Library, University of California at Berkeley, quoted in Cynthia Orozco, "The Origins of the League of United Latin American Citizens (LULAC) and the Mexican American Civil Rights Movement in Texas with an Analysis of Women's Political Participation in a Gendered Context, 1910–1929" (Ph.D. diss., University of California at Los Angeles, 1992), 124.
84. *Laredo Weekly Times,* June 2, 1918.
85. Quoted in ibid., June 2, 1918.
86. C. N. Idar to Joe Hirsch, June 10, 1918, 2J376, TWRC. It is unknown what sort of reply Idar received to his appeal on Sánchez's behalf.
87. *La Prensa,* October 11, 1918.
88. *Evolución,* August 11, 1917, translation mine.
89. Christian, "Joining the American Mainstream," 579; *Evolución* (Laredo, Tex.), December 8, 1918, translation mine.
90. *El Imparcial de Texas* (San Antonio, Tex.), July 4, 1918, translation mine.
91. *Evolución,* April 7, 1918, translation mine.
92. *Laredo Weekly Times,* April 21, 1918.

Chapter 5

1. Saenz, *Los México-Americano,* 25, translation mine; Zamora, "Fighting on Two Fronts," 219.
2. Fred Davis Baldwin, "The American Enlisted Man in World War I" (Ph.D. diss., Princeton University, 1964), 95–96; Eisenhower and Eisenhower, *Yanks,* 61–62. The subsequent chapter identifies some of the Tejanos who served in divisions besides the 36th and the 90th.
3. Baldwin, "The American Enlisted Man," 93–94; Eisenhower and Eisenhower, *Yanks,* 298–99.
4. My information on the different camps to which Tejanos were assigned comes from identifying Spanish-surnamed Texans in RG 163, Lists of Men Ordered to Report to Local Boards for Induction, Records of the Selective Service System (World War I), National Archives and Records Administration.
5. Edward M. Coffman, *The War to End All Wars: The American Military Experience in World War I* (New York: Oxford University Press, 1968), 64; Baldwin, "The American Enlisted Man," 94.
6. Coffman, *The War to End All Wars,* 70–71; James and Wells, *America and the Great War,* 78.
7. Christian, "Joining the American Mainstream," 587–88. Only African American servicemen were segregated during the war. For more on the difficulties these men faced in the AEF, see Barbeau and Henri, *Unknown Soldiers.*
8. Quoted in Britten, *American Indians in World War I,* 45.
9. Williams, "Torchbearers of Democracy, 88–90; Kennedy, *Over Here,* 158–60.
10. Coffman, *The War to End All Wars,* 81–84.
11. Ibid., 66, 68.
12. Baldwin, "The American Enlisted Man," 100–101.
13. Coffman, *The War to End All Wars,* 66; Saenz, *Los Mexico-Americanos,* 51–57; Baldwin, "The American Enlisted Man," 104–5.
14. Thomas M. Camfield, "'Will to Win': The U.S. Army Troop Morale Program of World War I," *Military Affairs* 41 (October 1977): 125; Ford, *Americans All,* 10–13, 68–73.

15. Camfield, "Will to Win," 125–28.

16. Ford, *Americans All,* 116–35.

17. Ibid., 117–27.

18. Horgan, memorandum regarding Foreign-Speaking Soldiers, YMCA, and K of C Hut, July 16, 1918, 10565-501G, RG 165, Records of the Military Intelligence Division of the War Department General Staff, National Archives and Records Administration [hereafter referred to as WDGS], quoted in ibid., 117.

19. Ford, *Americans All,* 76–87.

20. Wayne E. Stevens to Director, Military Intelligence Division, November 14, 1918, 10565-564, Box 3533, RG 165, Records of the Military Intelligence Division, Records of the War Department General and Special Staffs, National Archives and Records Administration [hereafter referred to as MID]; Director, Military Intelligence Division to Intelligence Officer, Camp Cody, N.M., October 17, 1918, 10565-564/3, Box 3533, MID; Director, Military Intelligence Division to Intelligence Officer, Camp Bowie, Texas, October 18, 1918, 10565-563, Box 3533, MID; Director, Military Intelligence Division to Intelligence Officer, Camp Travis, Texas, October 18, 1918, 10565-584/1, Box 3533, MID; Ford, *Americans All,* 80–82.

21. Ford, *Americans All,* 67–68, 108–9, quote on 67.

22. Ibid., 108–9.

23. *La Prensa* (San Antonio, Tex.), February 18, 1918.

24. Christina Krysto, "Bringing the World to Our Foreign-Language Soldiers: How a Military Training Camp Is Solving a Seemingly Insurmountable Problem by Using the Geographic," *National Geographic Magazine,* August 1918, 89–90, quoted in Ford, *Americans All,* 109.

25. Anson Phelps Stokes, *Educational Plans for the American Army Abroad* (New York: Association Press, 1918), 21, quoted in Baldwin, "The American Enlisted Man," 119–20; *La Prensa,* December 4, 1918.

26. Anson D. Marston, "Wartime Role for Colleges and Universities," *Military Affairs* 18 (Autumn 1954): 133; Kennedy, *Over Here,* 57; Baldwin, "The American Enlisted Man," 120–21. For examples of Spanish-surnamed students in the SATC, see "Roster of University of Texas Unit Students' Army Training Corps, October 31, 1918," 2J312, TWRC.

27. Mark Gretchen, "World War I Library Service in Texas Military Training Camps," *Texas Libraries* 48 (Fall 1987): 73–77. For more on the efforts of the ALA during the war, see Arthur P. Young, *Books for Sammies: The American Library Association and World War I* (Pittsburgh: Beta Phi Mu, 1981).

28. Mr. Frank L. Tolman, camp librarian at Camp Upton, New York, to Perkins and Horgan, August 12, 1918, 10565-531/12, WDGS, quoted in Ford, *Americans All,* 106.

29. *La Prensa,* October 4 and 14, 1918, translation mine.

30. Ford, *Americans All,* 90–91.

31. Donald Smythe, "Venereal Disease: The AEF's Experience," *Prologue* 9 (Summer 1977): 66; quoted in Ford, *Americans All,* 91.

32. John Dickinson, *The Building of an Army: A Detailed Account of Legislation, Administration, and Opinion in the United States, 1915–1920* (New York: Century, 1922), 205–6; quoted in Nancy K. Bristow, *Making Men Moral: Social Engineering during the Great War* (New York: New York University Press, 1998), 101.

33. Quoted in David C. Frederick, *Rugged Justice: The Ninth Circuit Court of Appeals and the American West, 1891–1941* (Berkeley: University of California Press, 1994), 144.

34. Bristow, *Making Men Moral,* 102–7.

35. Coffman, *The War to End All Wars,* 132–34, quote on 132; Baldwin, "The American Enlisted Man," 112.

36. Bristow, *Making Men Moral,* 22–34, quotes on 22.

37. Quoted in Kennedy, *Over Here,* 186.

38. Ford, *Americans All,* 100–101, quote on 100.

39. Baldwin, "The American Enlisted Man," 125, 128, quote on 125.

40. Ibid., 130–32, quote on 131; Saenz, *Los México-Americanos,* 46.

41. Marshall Bartholomew, secretary, National War Work Council of the YMCA, to other secretaries, May 6, 1918, file Birchard, C.C.B., Box 3, entry 399, RG 165, Records of the Military Intelligence Division, National Archives and Records Administration, quoted in Bristow, *Making Men Moral,* 42.

42. Bristow, *Making Men Moral,* 42–43, 221–23.

43. Baldwin, "The American Enlisted Man," 125–27.

44. Bristow, *Making Men Moral,* 38–40, quote on 38. For more on the anxieties among American males that led to boxing's popularity, see John F. Kasson, *Houdini, Tarzan, and the Perfect Man: The White Male Body and the Challenge of Modernity in America* (New York: Hill and Wang, 2001), 10–19.

45. *San Antonio Express,* March 11 and 15, 1918; August 9 and 13, 1918; December 25, 1918; and February 23, 1919.

46. Quoted in ibid., December 5, 1918.

47. *Evolución* (Laredo, Tex.), October 28, 1917, translation mine.

48. Ford, *Americans All,* 95–6; *La Prensa,* May 28, 1918.

49. Bristow, *Making Men Moral,* 205–6.

50. Baldwin, "The American Enlisted Man," 134–35.

51. Saenz, *Los México-Americanos,* 26, original letter composed on February 26, 1918, translation mine.

52. James and Wells, *America and the Great War,* 49–53, quote on 50; Kennedy, *Over Here,* 189.

53. Saenz, *Los México-Americanos,* 59; Harris and Sadler, "The Plan of San Diego," 391 n. 33; Jim Coffey, "Will Wright: Rangers and Prohibition," *Texas Ranger Dispatch* 20 (Summer 2006). Journal online. Available at http://www.texasranger.org/dispatch/ 20/ Will%20Wright/ Wright.htm. Accessed October 28, 2006.

54. Maury Maverick, *A Maverick American* (New York: Covici Friede, 1937), 115–20, quote on 116.

55. Baldwin, "The American Enlisted Man," 135–36; Coffman, *The War to End All Wars,* 65.

56. Chris Emmett, *Give 'Way to the Right: Serving with the AEF in France, during the World War* (San Antonio: Naylor, 1934), 9.

57. "Years of Segregation Are Recalled," *Corpus Christi Times,* January 23, 1970, Vertical Files, Corpus Christi Public Library, quoted in Orozco, "Origins," 125–26.

58. E. B. Johns, comp., *Camp Travis and Its Part in the World War* (New York: by the compiler, 1919), 27; quoted in Baldwin, "The American Enlisted Man," 141.

59. *San Antonio Express,* October 14, 1917 and February 24, 1918.

60. Saenz, *Los México-Americanos,* 43, 64, translation mine. The conclusions presented here are based on my research in its entirety, but particularly

on the insights found in Saenz's writings, as the former schoolteacher was extremely sensitive to racial and ethnic injustice and never shy about recording any evidence of it for posterity.

61. Ibid., 51–60.

62. *Evolución,* November 30, 1917, translation mine; *Laredo Weekly Times,* June 2, 1918.

Chapter 6

1. Baldwin, "The American Enlisted Man," 143–60.

2. Mead, *Doughboys,* 210–13; Randal Gray and Christopher Argyle, *Chronicle of the First World War,* vol. 2 (New York: Facts on File, 1991), 133.

3. Christian, "Joining the American Mainstream," 578; Saenz, *Los México-Americanos,* 239. The list of Tejano casualties comes from an examination of the war service cards at the Texas Military Forces Museum in Austin, Texas. Florencio Heras appears as "Florencio Erras" in official military records.

4. Saenz, *Los México-Americanos,* 81–90, 248, original letter dated April 11, 1919, quote on 248, translation mine.

5. Quoted in the *Brownsville Herald,* December 9, 1918.

6. Bernice B. Maxfield, comp., *Camp Bowie, Fort Worth, 1917–1918: An Illustrated History of the 36th Division in the First World War* (Fort Worth, Tex.: by the compiler, 1975), 80; James and Anne Sharp Wells, *America and the Great War,* 53–55.

7. In Colonial Mexico, according to Edgar F. Love, the "Spanish considered persons of African blood to be . . . of *mala raza* (bad race)." Consequently, they "relegate[d] the Negro to the lowest rung of the social ladder." See Edgar F. Love, "Negro Resistance to Spanish Rule in Colonial Mexico," *Journal of Negro History* 52 (April 1967): 90. For more on how this aspect of Mexican history might be impairing black-brown relations in the United States today, see Tanya Katerí Hernández, "Latino Anti-Black Violence in Los Angeles: Not 'Made in the USA,'" *Harvard Journal of African American Public Policy* 13 (May 2007): 37–40.

8. Quoted in *Brownsville Herald,* December 9, 1918.

9. Saenz, *Los México-Americanos,* 262, 264, quote on 264, translation mine.

10. Baldwin, "The American Enlisted Man," 169–77.

11. John Eisenhower and Eisenhower, *Yanks,* 59–60, quote on 60.

12. Quoted in John Keegan, *The First World War* (New York: Vintage, 1998), 372.

13. Eisenhower and Eisenhower, *Yanks,* 55–56; James and Wells, *America and the Great War,* 39.

14. Gamio, *The Mexican Immigrant,* 280; *La Prensa* (San Antonio, Tex.), June 2, 1919.

15. *La Prensa,* October 21, 1918 and January 15, 1919, quotes on the latter issue, translation mine.

16. U.S. Department of War, *American Decorations: A List of the Congressional Medal of Honor, the Distinguished-Service Cross, and the Distinguished-Service Medal Awarded under Authority of the Congress of the United States, 1862–1926* (Washington, D.C.: GPO, 1927), 136.

17. Keegan, *The First World War,* 409–12, quote on 412.

18. John J. Pershing, *My Experiences in the World War,* vol. 2 (New York: Fredcrick A. Stokes, 1931), 272–73, quoted in Mead, *Doughboys,* 297.

19. Saenz, *Los México-Americanos,* 128–29.

20. U.S. Department of Defense, *Hispanics in America's Defense* (Washington, D.C.: The Pentagon, 1982), 35–36; *La Prensa* (San Antonio, Tex.), June 15, 1919. I also obtained information on Serna's exploits from a booklet published in 1982 by the Marcos B. Armijo VFW Post No. 2753 in El Paso—which boasted the war hero as a lifelong member—to commemorate its fiftieth anniversary. I would like to thank Antonio Acosta, its current post commander, for providing me with a copy of this "Golden Anniversary Program."
21. Saenz, *Los México-Americanos,* 127–28.
22. Ibid., 133, 151, 153, 156, 158, 168, 174. "Dog tag" is the military identification tag worn by soldiers on a chain around their necks.
23. Ibid., 128, 155; Keegan, *The First World War,* 197–99; De Groot, *The First World War,* 172.
24. *Evolución* (Laredo, Tex.), October 26, 1918.
25. Saenz, *Los México-Americanos,* 175, 199.
26. Ibid., 122, 166.
27. Ibid., 164–66, 284.
28. Ibid., 130–31.
29. Ibid., 147, 149.
30. Quoted in the *Brownsville Herald,* December 9, 1918.
31. Saenz, *Los México-Americanos,* 174–75, quote on 174, translation mine.
32. Ibid., 169–70, translation mine.
33. *Evolución,* November 27, 1918; *Laredo Weekly Times,* June 29, 1919.
34. War Department, *American Decorations,* 298, 483.
35. Heller, "On the Front Lines," 36; "Texan Who Concealed His Origin Is 38th Hispanic Medal of Honor Recipient," 25; Phelon, "The Hero Who Hid His Heritage," 6–7, 14–19; War Department, *American Decorations,* 4.
36. Eisenhower and Eisenhower, *Yanks,* 284–86.
37. Niall Ferguson, *Pity of War: Explaining World War I* (New York: Basic Books, 1999), 295; Keegan, *The First World War,* 422–23.
38. The figures for American casualties come from Eisenhower and Eisenhower, *Yanks,* 288, while those for the state of Texas—excluding those for the Spanish surnamed—come from Seymour V. Connor, *Texas: A History* (New York: Crowell, 1971), 314. I obtained the numbers for Spanish-surnamed casualties from "Alphabetical List of the Army, Navy, and Marine Corps, and Army Nurse Corps from Texas Who Lost Their Lives during the World War," 2J207, Texas War Records Collection, 1916–19, 1940–45, Center for American History, University of Texas, Austin.
39. Saenz, *Los México-Americanos,* 165.
40. *Evolución,* September 12 and October 23, 1918, quote on the latter issue, translation mine.
41. Quoted in *La Prensa,* November 3, 1918, translation mine.
42. Quoted in the *Brownsville Herald,* December 9, 1918.
43. Quoted in the *San Antonio Express,* May 15, 1918.
44. Quoted in the *Corpus Christi Caller,* October 3, 1918.
45. *San Antonio Express,* May 25, 1919.
46. Quoted in *La Prensa,* September 29, 1918, translation mine.
47. Ibid., November 3, 1918, translation mine.
48. This information was obtained from Sosa's war service card at the Texas Military Forces Museum in Austin, Texas.

49. Britten, *American Indians in World War I,* 82, 99, 116–20; Barbeau and Henri, *Unknown Soldiers,* chap. 6.

50. De León, *They Called Them Greasers,* 64–66, 72.

51. Walter Prescott Webb, *The Texas Rangers: A Century of Frontier Defense* (Austin: University of Texas Press, 1935), 13–14.

52. *Houston Daily Post,* August 25, 1918.

53. Quoted in *La Prensa,* September 5, 1929, newspaper clipping in Folder 14, O. D. Weeks Papers, LULAC Collection, Benson Latin American Collection, University of Texas, Austin, translation mine.

54. Quoted in ibid., January 5, 1919, translation mine.

55. Despite appearing as "David B. Barkeley" in official army records, David Cantú Barkley is included among the Spanish surnamed in this count of total number of medals for bravery. I found the other twelve individuals by checking for Spanish surnames in War Department, *American Decorations.*

56. Bush, "El Paso County," 97, 126, 171; Christian, "Joining the American Mainstream," 582; Lonnie J. White, *Panthers to Arrowheads: The 36th (Texas-Oklahoma) Division in World War I* (Austin: Presidial Press, 1984), 43.

57. Christian, "Joining the American Mainstream," 581; *La Prensa,* January 13, 1919.

58. Interview with Pete Leyva by Oscar J. Martínez, July 22, 1976, Interview No. 312, Institute of Oral History, University of Texas at El Paso.

59. U.S. Bureau of Naval Personnel, *Officers and Enlisted Men of the United States Navy, Who Lost Their Lives during the World War, from April 6, 1917, to November 11, 1918* (Washington, D.C.: GPO, 1920), 296. For more on the disappearance of the *Cyclops* and other marine accidents, see Kit Bonner and Carolyn Bonner, *Great Naval Disasters* (Osceola, Wis.: MBI, 1998).

60. Eisenhower and Eisenhower, *Yanks,* 287.

61. Saenz, *Los México-Americanos,* 242.

62. Headquarters Ninetieth Division, Memos, February 2 and 4; March 12, 18, and 22; and April 19, 1919, 353.8, Box 70, RG 120, Decimal File, Headquarters, 90th Division Records, Records of the American Expeditionary Force, National Archives and Records Administration; Saenz, *Los México-Americanos,* 239.

63. Coffman, *The War to End All Wars,* 358; Saenz, *Los México-Americanos,* 219.

64. Quoted in Gamio, *The Mexican Immigrant,* 280.

65. Saenz, *Los México-Americanos,* 268–77, quote on 277, translation mine.

Chapter 7

1. Eisenhower and Eisenhower, *Yanks,* 289.

2. *San Antonio Light,* June 15, 1919, quoted in Lonnie J. White, *The 90th Division in World War I: The Texas-Oklahoma Draft Division in the Great War* (Manhattan, Kans.: Sunflower University Press, 1996), 204.

3. Saenz, *Los México-Americanos,* 279, translation mine.

4. Ibid., 279–80; White, *90th Division,* 205.

5. *Corpus Christi Caller,* June 9, 1919.

6. Ibid., April 10, 1919.

7. *Laredo Weekly Times,* June 8, 1919.

8. *Dallas Morning News,* June 1, 1919.

9. *El Imparcial de Texas* (San Antonio, Tex.), June 5, 1919, translation mine.
10. *Dallas Morning News,* June 15, 1919.
11. *San Antonio Express,* June 18, 1919.
12. Ibid.
13. White, *90th Division,* 208.
14. *Corpus Christi Caller,* June 15, 1919.
15. *Laredo Weekly Times,* June 29 and July 6, 1919.
16. *Corpus Christi Caller,* June 5, 1919.
17. *La Prensa* (San Antonio, Tex.), April 4 and June 27, 1919.
18. Saenz, *Los México-Americanos,* 286, translation mine.
19. *Corpus Christi Caller,* June 19, 1919.
20. *Evolución* (Laredo, Tex.), June 24, 1919, translation mine.
21. *El Imparcial de Texas,* June 26, 1919, translation mine.
22. Coffman, *The War to End All Wars,* 357–58; Saenz, *Los México-Americanos,* 287.
23. Interview with Pete Leyva by Oscar J. Martínez, July 22, 1976, Interview No. 312, IOH-UTEP.
24. Ibid; Christian, "Joining the American Mainstream," 592 n. 80.
25. *La Prensa,* February 18, 1919; *San Antonio Express,* February 20, 1919; Phelon, "The Hero Who Hid His Heritage," 15–16; John H. Hatcher, "Camp Barkeley, Abilene, Texas," *Texas Military History* 3 (Winter 1963): 221–22.
26. Interview with Antonio Acosta, Post Commander, VFW Post No. 2753, by author, June 8, 2004, El Paso, Texas.
27. Scholars disagree about when the Mexican Revolution came to an end, with some arguing that it continued well past the end of its armed conflict stage. See, for example, Donald C. Hodges and Ross Gandy, *Mexico: The End of the Revolution* (Westport, Conn.: Praeger, 2002).
28. Interview with Salvador Peña by Rolando Peña, April 10, 1987, ABY 2865, No. 707, Oral History Collection, Lower Rio Grande Valley Historical Collection, University of Texas–Pan American.
29. Interview with Severiano Torres Ortiz by Severiano Torres Jr., December 2, 1976, Interview No. 254, IOH-UTEP, translation mine.
30. For more on the immediate postwar era, see Burl Noggle, *Into the Twenties: The United States from Armistice to Normalcy* (Urbana: University of Illinois Press, 1974); Dixon Wecter, *When Johnny Comes Marching Home* (Boston: Houghton Mifflin, 1944); and Wesley M. Bagby, *The Road to Normalcy: The Presidential Campaign and Election of 1920* (Baltimore: Johns Hopkins Press, 1962).
31. Ezra Pound, *Personae: The Collected Poems of Ezra Pound* (New York: New Directions, 1926), 187–88. For an analysis of the literature of this period, see Frederick John Hoffman, *The Twenties: American Writing in the Postwar Decade* (New York: Viking, 1955).
32. Britten, *American Indians in World War I,* 162–65.
33. Willis Brown Goodwin, Virginia War History Commission Questionnaire, The Library of Virginia, quoted in Williams, "Torchbearers of Democracy," 251–52.
34. Moises Sandoval, *Our Legacy: The First Fifty Years* (Washington, D.C.: League of United Latin American Citizens—LULAC, 1979), 6.
35. Manuel C. Gonzales, "Preface," Folder 2, Manuel C. Gonzales Papers, LULAC Collection, Benson Latin American Collection, University of Texas, Austin.

36. Sandoval, *Our Legacy,* 5–6, quote on 6.
37. William D. Carrigan and Clive Webb, "The Lynching of Persons of Mexican Origin or Descent in the United States, 1848–1928," *Journal of Social History* 37 (Winter 2003): 412–13, 423.
38. Quoted in Paul S. Taylor, *An American-Mexican Frontier* (Chapel Hill: University of North Carolina Press, 1934), 245.
39. J. Luz Saenz, "Racial Discrimination," in *Are We Good Neighbors?* ed. Alonso S. Perales (San Antonio: Artes Gráficas, 1948), 33.
40. M. C. Gonzales, "Echoes of the Kingsville Convention," *LULAC News,* September 1931, 8, Paul S. Taylor Papers, Bancroft Library, University of California at Berkeley, quoted in Orozco, "Origins," 129.
41. Jovita González, "Social Life in Cameron, Starr and Zapata Counties" (master's thesis, University of Texas at Austin, 1930), 108–9, quote on 109.
42. Pycior, "*La Raza* Organizes," 98.
43. *La Prensa,* September 5, 1929.
44. Saenz, *Los México-Americanos,* unpaginated epilogue, translation mine.
45. For more on the civil rights activities of African American veterans, see Williams, "Torchbearers of Democracy," chap. 6.
46. James and Wells, *America and the Great War,* 55.
47. Quoted in Britten, *American Indians in World War I,* 173.
48. From *The Crusader,* quoted in Williams, "Torchbearers of Democracy," 264.
49. Judge Goodwin, Virginia War History Commission Questionnaire, The Library of Virginia, quoted in Williams, "Torchbearers of Democracy," 252.
50. Saenz, *Los Mexico-Americanos,* 277, translation mine.
51. Edwin Larry Dickens, "The Political Role of Mexican Americans in San Antonio, Texas" (Ph.D. diss., Texas Tech University, 1969), 134–35.
52. George J. Garza, "The Founding and History of LULAC," *LULAC News,* February 1954, 21–25; Orozco, "Origins," 175–78, 200–201; "A History of LULAC—Part 1," *LULAC News,* June 1974, 10–13; Sandoval, *Our Legacy,* 8–10; Christian, "Joining the American Mainstream," 589–91; Pycior, "*La Raza* Organizes," 174–75.
53. Dickens, "The Political Role of Mexican Americans," 134; Pycior, "*La Raza* Organizes," 175; Christian, "Joining the American Mainstream," 589; Sandoval, *Our Legacy,* 9–10.
54. Quoted in Pycior, "*La Raza* Organizes," 174–75.
55. Johnson, *Revolution in Texas,* 182.
56. Pycior, "*La Raza* Organizes," 177–83.
57. Quoted in *El Paladín* (Corpus Christi, Tex.), February 22, 1929, newspaper clipping in Folder 10, O. D. Weeks Papers, LULAC Collection, Benson Latin American Collection, University of Texas, Austin, [hereafter referred to as Weeks Collection].
58. Orozco, "Origins," 272–76.
59. Garza, "The Founding and History of LULAC," 22.
60. Quoted in Alonso S. Perales, "The Unification of the Mexican-Americans," Folder 3; Weeks Collection.
61. Garza, "The Founding and History of LULAC," 22.
62. Sandoval, *Our Legacy,* 20–21.
63. Ibid., 78–86; Christian, "Joining the American Mainstream," 591.

64. For more on LULAC, see Benjamin Márquez, *LULAC: The Evolution of a Mexican American Political Organization* (Austin: University of Texas Press, 1993) and Craig A. Kaplowitz, *LULAC, Mexican Americans, and National Policy* (College Station: Texas A&M University Press, 2005).

65. The best analysis of the legal fight against discrimination against Mexicans in Texas schools is Guadalupe San Miguel Jr., *"Let All of Them Take Heed": Mexican Americans and the Campaign for Educational Equality in Texas, 1910–1981* (Austin: University of Texas Press, 1987).

66. García, *Rise of the Mexican American Middle Class,* 114–15. A good source for the repatriation drives in Texas is R. Reynolds McKay, "Texas Mexican Repatriation during the Great Depression" (Ph.D. diss., University of Oklahoma, 1982).

67. Quoted in Morín, *Among the Valiant,* 15.

68. Ibid., 24.

69. Chávez, *Lost Land,* 117; Juan Gómez-Quiñones, *Chicano Politics: Reality and Promise, 1940–1990* (Albuquerque: University of New Mexico Press, 1990), 34; Michele A. Heller, "On the Front Lines," 34–40.

70. For more on the American G.I. Forum, see Carl Allsup, *The American G.I. Forum: Origins and Evolution* (Austin: University of Texas, Center for Mexican American Studies, 1982). For the Félix Longoria affair, see Patrick J. Carroll, *Félix Longoria's Wake: Bereavement, Racism, and the Rise of Mexican American Activism* (Austin: University of Texas Press, 2003).

71. Jerry D. Thompson, *Laredo: A Pictorial History* (Norfolk: Donning, 1986), 173.

72. Antonio Acosta interview; Salvador Peña interview; Zamora, "Fighting on Two Fronts," 220 n. 22; Saenz, "Racial Discrimination," 33.

Conclusion

1. Quoted in Phelon, "The Hero Who Hid His Heritage," 16; "Texan Who Concealed His Origin Is 38th Hispanic Medal of Honor Recipient," 25.

2. Telephone interview with Richard K. Chamberlain Jr., Commander, Military Order of the Purple Heart David Barkley Cantú Chapter No. 766, by author, August 5, 2008; *Laredo Morning Times,* September 22, 2002, May 11, 2003, July 5, 2004, and November 10, 2006.

3. For the impact of World War II on Mexican American history, see Maggie Rivas-Rodríguez, ed., *Mexican Americans and World War II* (Austin: University of Texas Press, 2005); Morín, *Among the Valiant;* Mario T. García, "Americans All: The Mexican American Generation and the Politics of Wartime Los Angeles, 1941–45," *Social Science Quarterly* 65 (June 1984): 278–89; and Chávez, *Lost Land,* 106, 113, 116.

4. Rivas-Rodríguez, *Mexican Americans and World War II,* xvii–xviii.

5. The defining work on the Mexican-American Generation is Mario T. García, *Mexican Americans: Leadership, Ideology, and Identity, 1930–1960* (New Haven, Conn.: Yale University Press, 1989).

6. Johnson, *Revolution in Texas.*

7. Virgil Fernández, *Hispanic Military Heroes* (Austin: VFG, 2006), chap. 3; Heller, "On the Front Lines," 36, 38. The estimate of ethnic Mexican World War II servicemen comes from Rivas-Rodríguez, *Mexican Americans and World War II.*

8. *Washington Post,* March 1, 2003.

9. Quoted in ibid.

10. Telephone interview with Emilio Zamora by author, July 13, 2008.

11. Zamora interview; Zamora, "Fighting on Two Fronts," 217, 229.

Bibliography

ARCHIVAL AND MANUSCRIPT COLLECTIONS

Burleson, Albert Sidney. Papers. Center for American History, University of Texas, Austin.

Gonzales, Manuel C. Papers. LULAC Collection. Benson Latin American Collection, University of Texas at Austin.

Hobby, William Pettus. Papers. Archives and Information Services Division, Texas State Library and Archives Commission, Austin.

Investigative Case Files of the Bureau of Investigation, 1908–22, 1909–21. Record Group 65. National Archives and Record Administration, College Park, Maryland.

Records of the American Expeditionary Force. Record Group 120. National Archives and Records Administration, College Park, Maryland.

Records of the Post Office Department. Record Group 28. National Archives and Records Administration, Washington, D.C.

Records of the Selective Service System (World War I). Record Group 163. National Archives and Records Administration, Fort Worth, Texas, and Laguna Niguel, California.

Records of the Texas Adjutant General's Department. Archives and Information Services Division, Texas State Library and Archives Commission, Austin.

Records of the War Department General and Special Staffs. Record Group 165. National Archives and Records Administration, College Park, Maryland.

Texas War Records Collection, 1916–19, 1940–45. Center for American History, University of Texas at Austin.

War Service Card Records. Texas Military Forces Museum, Austin, Texas.

Weeks, O. D. Papers. LULAC Collection. Benson Latin American Collection, University of Texas at Austin.

Wilson, Woodrow. Papers. Library of Congress, Washington, D.C.

GOVERNMENT PUBLICATIONS

Texas Adjutant General. *Biennial Report of the Adjutant General of Texas from January 1, 1917 to December 31, 1918*. Austin: Von Boeckmann-Jones, 1919.

Texas Congress. House. *Journal of the House of Representatives of the First Session of the Thirty-Fourth Legislature: Convened April 29, 1915 and Adjourned May 28, 1915*. Austin: Von Boeckmann-Jones, 1915.

U.S. Bureau of Naval Personnel. *Officers and Enlisted Men of the United*

States Navy, Who Lost Their Lives during the World War, from April 6, 1917, to November 11, 1918. Washington, D.C.: GPO, 1920.

U.S. Congress. Senate. Committee on Foreign Relations. *Investigation of Mexican Affairs*, 2 vols. 66th Cong., 2nd sess. Sen. Doc. 285. Washington, D.C.: GPO, 1920.

U.S. Department of Defense. *Hispanics in America's Defense.* Washington, D.C.: The Pentagon, 1982.

U.S. Department of State. *Papers Relating to the Foreign Relations of the United States, 1916.* Washington, D.C.: GPO, 1925.

———. *Papers Relating to the Foreign Relations of the United States, 1918.* Washington, D.C.: GPO, 1930.

U.S. Department of War. *American Decorations: A List of the Congressional Medal of Honor, the Distinguished-Service Cross, and the Distinguished-Service Medal Awarded under Authority of the Congress of the United States, 1862–1926.* Washington, D.C.: GPO, 1927.

U.S. Provost Marshal General. *Second Report to the Secretary of War on the Operations of the Selective Service System.* Washington, D.C.: GPO, 1918.

NEWSPAPERS

Brownsville Herald

Corpus Christi Caller

Corpus Christi Caller and Daily Herald

Dallas Morning News

El Demócrata Fronterizo (Laredo, Tex.)

Evolución (Laredo, Tex.)

Houston Daily Post

Houston Post

El Imparcial de Texas (San Antonio, Tex.)

Laredo Morning Times

Laredo Weekly Times

LULAC *News*

New York Times

El Paladín (Corpus Christi, Tex.)

La Prensa (San Antonio, Tex.)

San Antonio Express

Washington Post

INTERVIEWS

Acosta, Antonio. Interview by author, June 8, 2004, El Paso, Texas.

Chamberlain, Richard K., Jr. Telephone interview by author, August 5, 2008.

Leyva, Pete. Interview by Oscar J. Martínez, July 22, 1976. Interview No. 312. Institute of Oral History, University of Texas at El Paso.

Mendoza, Conrado. Interview by Mike Acosta, December 4, 1976. Interview No. 252. Institute of Oral History, University of Texas at El Paso.

Peña, Salvador. Interview by Rolando Peña, April 10, 1987. ABY 2865, No. 707. Oral History Collection, Lower Rio Grande Valley Historical Collection, University of Texas Pan American, Edinburg.

Torres Ortiz, Severiano. Interview by Severiano Torres Jr., December 2, 1976. Interview No. 254, Institute of Oral History, University of Texas at El Paso.

Varela, Luis O. Interview by Daniel Varela, November 18, 1976. Interview No. 274. Institute of Oral History, University of Texas at El Paso.

Zamora, Emilio. Telephone interview by author, July 13, 2008.

ARTICLES FROM JOURNALS AND MAGAZINES

Ables, Robert L. "The Second Battle for the Alamo." *Southwestern Historical Quarterly* 70 (January 1967): 372–413.

Camfield, Thomas M. "'Will to Win': The U.S. Army Troop Morale Program of World War I." *Military Affairs* 41 (October 1977): 125–28.

Carrigan, William D., and Clive Webb. "The Lynching of Persons of Mexican Origin in the United States, 1848–1928." *Journal of Social History* 37 (Winter 2003): 411–38.

Christian, Carole E. "Joining the American Mainstream: Texas's Mexican Americans during World War I." *Southwestern Historical Quarterly* 92 (April 1989): 559–95.

Coffey, Jim. "Will Wright: Rangers and Prohibition." *Texas Ranger Dispatch* 20 (Summer 2006). Journal online. Available at http://www.texasranger.org/dispatch/20/Will%20Wright/Wright.htm. Accessed October 28, 2006.

Coffman, Edward M. "The Course of Military History in the United States since World War II." *Journal of Military History* 61 (October 1997): 761–75.

———. "The New American Military History." *Military Affairs* 48 (January 1984): 1–5.

Cox, Patrick L. "'An Enemy Closer to Us Than Any European Power': The Impact of Mexico on Texan Public Opinion before World War I." *Southwestern Historical Quarterly* 105 (July 2001): 40–80.

Di Stefano, Onofre. "'Venimos a luchar': A Brief History of *La Prensa's* Founding." *Aztlán* 16 (Spring–Fall 1985): 95–118.

García, Mario T. "Americans All: The Mexican American Generation and the Politics of Wartime Los Angeles, 1941–45." *Social Science Quarterly* 65 (June 1984): 278–89.

Gonzales, Juan. "Forgotten Pages: Spanish-Language Newspapers in the Southwest." *Journalism History* 4 (Summer 1977): 50–51.

Gonzales, Phillip, and Ann Massman. "Loyalty Questioned: Nuevomexicanos in the Great War." *Pacific Historical Review* 75 (November 2006): 629–66.

Gratton, Brian, and Myron P. Gutmann. "Hispanics in the United States, 1850–1990: Estimates of Population Size and National Origin." *Historical Methods* 33 (Spring 2000): 137–53.

Gretchen, Mark. "World War I Library Service in Texas Military Training Camps." *Texas Libraries* 48 (Fall 1987): 73–78.

Griswold del Castillo, Richard. "The Mexican Revolution in the Spanish-Language Press in the Borderlands." *Journalism History* 4 (Summer 1977): 42–47.

Gutiérrez, David G. "Significant to Whom? Mexican Americans and the History of the American West." *Western Historical Quarterly* 24 (November 1993): 519–39.

Gutmann, Myron P., W. Parker Frisbie, and K. Stephen Blanchard. "A New Look at the Hispanic Population of the United States in 1910." *Historical Methods* 32 (January 1999): 5–19.

Harris, Charles H., III, and Louis R. Sadler. "The 1911 Reyes Conspiracy: The Texas Side." *Southwestern Historical Quarterly* 82 (April 1980): 325–48.

———. "The Plan of San Diego and the Mexican-United States Crisis of 1916: A Reexamination." *Hispanic American Historical Review* 58 (August 1978): 381–408.

———. "The Witzke Affair: German Intrigue on the Mexican Border, 1917–18." *Military Review* 59 (February 1979): 36–50.

Hatcher, John H. "Camp Barkeley, Abilene, Texas." *Texas Military History* 3 (Winter 1963): 219–27.

Heller, Michele A. "On the Front Lines." *Hispanic,* August 1993, 36.

Hernández, Tanya Katerí. "Latino Anti-Black Violence in Los Angeles: Not 'Made in the USA.'" *Harvard Journal of African American Public Policy* 13 (May 2007): 37–40.

Karsten, Peter. "The 'New' American Military History: A Map of the Territory Explored and Unexplored." *American Quarterly* 36 (1984): 389–418.

Katz, Friedrich. "Pancho Villa and the Attack on Columbus, New Mexico." *American Historical Review* 83 (February 1978): 101–30.

Keith, Jeanette. "The Politics of Southern Draft Resistance, 1917–1918: Race, Class, and Conscription in the Rural South." *Journal of American History* 87 (March 2001): 1335–61.

Keller, Randall G. "The Past in the Present: The Literary Continuity of Hispanic Folklore in New Mexico and the Southwest." *Bilingual Review/La Revista Bilingüe* 16 (May–December 1991): 99–158.

Kennedy, Paul. "The Rise and Fall of Military History." *MHQ: The Quarterly Journal of Military History* 3 (Winter 1991): 9–12.

Kiser, George C. "Mexican American Labor before World War II." *Journal of Mexican American History* 2 (Spring 1972): 122–42.

Kohn, Richard R. "The Social History of the American Soldier: A Review and Prospectus for Research." *American Historical Review* 86 (June 1981): 533–67.

La Botz, Dan. "American 'Slackers' in the Mexican Revolution: International Proletarian Politics in the Midst of a National Revolution." *The Americas* 62 (April 2006): 563–90.

Leonard, William. "Where Both Bullets and Ballots Are Dangerous." *Survey,* October 28, 1916, 86–87.

Love, Edgar F. "Negro Resistance to Spanish Rule in Colonial Mexico." *Journal of Negro History* 52 (April 1967): 87–103.

Marston, Anson D. "Wartime Role for Colleges and Universities." *Military Affairs* 18 (Autumn 1954): 131–44.

Melzer, Richard. "Stage Soldiers of the Southwest: New Mexico's Four Minute Men of World War I." *Military History of the Southwest* 20 (Spring 1990): 23–42.

Millet, Allan R. "The Study of American Military History in the United States." *Military Affairs* 41 (April 1977): 58–61.

Myers, Sandra L. "Frontier Historians, Women, and the 'New' Military History." *Military History of the Southwest* 19 (Spring 1989): 27–37.

Paret, Peter. "The New Military History." *Parameters: The Journal of the Army War College* 21 (Autumn 1991): 10–18.

Phelon, Craig. "The Hero Who Hid His Heritage." *San Antonio Express-News Sunday Magazine,* May 21, 1989, 6–7, 14–19.

Romo, Ricardo. "Responses to Mexican Immigration, 1910–1930." *Aztlán* 6 (Summer 1975): 173–94.

Sandos, James A. "German Involvement in Northern Mexico, 1915–1916: A New Look at the Columbus Raid." *Hispanic American Historical Review* 50 (February 1970): 70–88.

———. "Pancho Villa and American Security: Woodrow Wilson's Mexican Diplomacy Reconsidered." *Journal of Latin American Studies* 13 (November 1981): 293–311.

Saragoza, Alex M. "Recent Chicano Historiography: An Interpretive Essay." *Aztlán* 19 (Spring 1988): 1–77.

Scruggs, Otey M. "The First Mexican Farm Labor Program." *Arizona and the West* 2 (Winter 1960): 319–26.

Shankman, Arnold. "The Image of Mexico and the Mexican-American in the Black Press, 1890–1935." *Journal of Ethnic Studies* 3 (Summer 1975): 43–56.

Shenk, Gerald E. "Race, Manhood, and Manpower: Mobilizing Rural Georgia for World War I." *Georgia Historical Quarterly* 81 (Fall 1997): 622–62.

Showalter, Dennis. "The United States in the Great War: A Historiography." *OAH Magazine of History,* October 2002, 5–13.

Skop, Emily, Brian Gratton, and Myron P. Guttman. "*La Frontera* and Beyond: Geography and Demography in Mexican American History." *Professional Geographer* 58 (February 2006): 78–98.

Smythe, Donald. "Venereal Disease: The AEF's Experience." *Prologue* 9 (Summer 1977): 65–74.

"Texan Who Concealed His Origin Is 38th Hispanic Medal of Honor Recipient." *Vista,* 4 January 1992, 25.

Weeks, O. Douglas. "The Texas-Mexican and the Politics of South Texas." *American Political Science Review* 24 (August 1930): 606–27.

Zecker, Robert. "The Activities of Czech and Slovak Immigrants during World War I." *Ethnic Forum* 15 (Spring–Fall 1995): 35–54.

BOOKS

Allsup, Carl. *The American G.I. Forum: Origins and Evolution.* Austin: University of Texas, Center for Mexican American Studies, 1982.

Alvarez, Everett, Jr., and Anthony S. Pitch. *Chained Eagle: The Heroic*

Story of the First American Shot Down over North Vietnam. Washington, D.C.: Potomac Books, 2005.

Bagby, Wesley M. *The Road to Normalcy: The Presidential Campaign and Election of 1920.* Baltimore: Johns Hopkins Press, 1962.

Barbeau, Arthur E., and Florette Henri. *The Unknown Soldiers: African American Troops in World War I.* New York: Da Capo Press, 1996.

Benavídez, Roy P., and John R. Craig. *Medal of Honor: One Man's Journey from Poverty and Prejudice.* Washington, D.C.: Potomac Books, 2005.

Billac, Pete. *The Last Medal of Honor.* New York: Swan, 1990.

Bonner, Kit, and Carolyn Bonner. *Great Naval Disasters.* Osceola, Wis.: MBI, 1998.

Britten, Thomas E. *American Indians in World War I: At War and at Home.* Albuquerque: University of New Mexico Press, 1997.

Bristow, Nancy K. *Making Men Moral: Social Engineering during the Great War.* New York: New York University Press, 1998.

Burbank, Garin. *When Farmers Voted Red: The Gospel of Socialism in the Oklahoma Countryside, 1910–1924.* Westport, Conn.: Greenwood, 1976.

Calavita, Kitty. *Inside the State: The Bracero Program, Immigration, and the I.N.S.* New York: Routledge, 1992.

Calvert, Robert A., Arnoldo De León, and Gregg Cantrell. *The History of Texas,* 4th ed. Wheeling, Ill.: Harlan Davidson, 2007.

Cardoso, Lawrence A. *Mexican Emigration to the United States, 1897–1931.* Tucson: University of Arizona Press, 1980.

Carroll, Patrick J. *Felix Longoria's Wake: Bereavement, Racism, and the Rise of Mexican American Activism.* Austin: University of Texas Press, 2003.

Chambers, John W., II. *To Raise an Army: The Draft Comes to Modern America.* New York: Free Press, 1987.

Chávez, John R. *The Lost Land: The Chicano Image of the Southwest.* Albuquerque: University of New Mexico Press, 1984.

Coerver, Don M., and Linda B. Hall. *Texas and the Mexican Revolution: A Study in State and National Border Policy, 1910–1920.* San Antonio: Trinity University Press, 1984.

Coffman, Edward M. *The War to End All Wars: The American Military Experience in World War I.* New York: Oxford University Press, 1968.

Connor, Seymour V. *Texas: A History.* New York: Crowell, 1971.

Cornebise, Alfred E. *War as Advertised: The Four Minute Men and America's Crusade, 1917–1918.* Philadelphia: American Philosophical Society, 1984.

Corwin, Arthur F., ed. *Immigrants—and Immigrants: Perspectives on Mexican Labor Migration to the United States.* Westport, Conn.: Greenwood Press, 1978.

Craig, Richard B. *The Bracero Program: Interest Groups and Foreign Policy.* Austin: University of Texas Press, 1971.

Crowder, Enoch. *The Spirit of Selective Service.* New York: Century, 1920.

De Groot, Gerard J. *The First World War.* Houndmills, England: Palgrave, 2001.

De León, Arnoldo. *They Called Them Greasers: Anglo Attitudes toward Mexicans in Texas, 1821–1900.* Austin: University of Texas Press, 1983.

Dickinson, John. *The Building of an Army: A Detailed Account of Legislation, Administration, and Opinion in the United States, 1915–1920.* New York: Century, 1922.

Eisenhower, John S. D., and Joanne T. Eisenhower. *Yanks: The Epic Story of the American Army in World War I.* New York: Free Press, 2001.

Ellis, Mark. *Race, War, and Surveillance: African Americans and the United States Government during World War I.* Bloomington: Indiana University Press, 2001.

Emmett, Chris. *Give 'Way to the Right: Serving with the AEF in France, during the World War.* San Antonio: Naylor, 1934.

Ferguson, Niall. *The Pity of War: Explaining World War I.* New York: Basic Books, 1999.

Fernández, Virgil. *Hispanic Military Heroes.* Austin: VFG, 2006.

Ford, Nancy Gentile. *Americans All! Foreign-Born Soldiers in World War I.* College Station: Texas A&M University Press, 2001.

Frederick, David C. *Rugged Justice: The Ninth Circuit Court of Appeals and the American West, 1891–1941.* Berkeley: University of California Press, 1994.

Galarza, Ernesto. *Merchants of Labor: The Mexican Bracero Story.* Charlotte, N.C.: McNally and Loftin, 1964.

Gamio, Manuel. *The Mexican Immigrant, His Life Story: Autobiographical Documents Collected by Manuel Gamio.* Chicago: University of Chicago Press, 1931.

———. *Quantitative Estimate: Sources and Distribution of Mexican Immigration into the United States.* Mexico City: Talleres Gráficos Editorial y "Diario Oficial," 1930.

García, Mario T. *Desert Immigrants: The Mexicans of El Paso, 1880–1920.* New Haven, Conn.: Yale University Press, 1981.

———. *Mexican Americans: Leadership, Ideology, and Identity, 1930–1960.* New Haven, Conn.: Yale University Press, 1989.

García, Richard A. *Rise of the Mexican American Middle Class: San Antonio, 1929–1941.* College Station: Texas A&M University Press, 1991.

Garner, Paul. *Porfirio Díaz.* Harlow, England: Longman, 2001.

Gavin, Lettie. *American Women in World War I: They Also Served.* Niwot: University of Colorado Press, 1997.

Gómez-Quiñones, Juan. *Chicano Politics: Reality and Promise, 1940–1990.* Albuquerque: University of New Mexico Press, 1990.

González, Gilbert G., and Raul A. Fernández. *A Century of Chicano History: Empire, Nations, and Migration.* New York and London: Routledge, 2003.

Gray, Randal, and Christopher Argyle. *Chronicle of the First World War,* vol. 2. Oxford and New York: Facts on File, 1991.

Greenwald, Maurine Weiner. *Women, War, and Work: The Impact of World War I on Women Workers in the United States.* Westport, Conn.: Greenwood Press, 1980.

Hall, Linda B., and Don M. Coerver. *Revolution on the Border: The United*

States and Mexico, 1910–1920. Albuquerque: University of New Mexico Press, 1988.

Hallas, James H., ed. *Doughboy War: The American Expeditionary Force in World War I.* Boulder, Colo.: Lynne Rienner, 2000.

Harris, Charles H., III, and Louis R. Sadler. *The Border and the Revolution: Clandestine Activities of the Mexican Revolution, 1910–1920.* Silver City, N.Mex.: High-Lonesome Books, 1988.

———. *The Texas Rangers and the Mexican Revolution: The Bloodiest Decade, 1910–1920.* Albuquerque: University of New Mexico Press, 2004.

Hilton, Stanley E. *Hitler's Secret War in South America, 1939–1945: German Military Espionage and Allied Counterespionage in Brazil.* Baton Rouge: Louisiana State University Press, 1981.

Hodges, Donald C., and Ross Gandy. *Mexico: The End of the Revolution.* Westport, Conn.: Praeger, 2002.

Hoffman, Frederick John. *The Twenties: American Writing in the Postwar Decade.* New York: Viking, 1955.

James, D. Clayton, and Anne Sharp Wells. *America and the Great War, 1914–1920.* Wheeling, Ill.: Harlan Davidson, 1998.

Johns, E. B., comp. *Camp Travis and Its Part in the World War.* New York: by the compiler, 1919.

Johnson, Benjamin Heber. *Revolution in Texas: How a Forgotten Rebellion and Its Bloody Suppression Turned Mexicans into Americans.* New Haven, Conn.: Yale University Press, 2003.

Justice, Glenn. *Revolution on the Rio Grande: Mexican Raids and Army Pursuits, 1916–1919.* El Paso: Texas Western Press, 1992.

Kaplowitz, Craig A. *LULAC, Mexican Americans, and National Policy.* College Station: Texas A&M University Press, 2005.

Kasson, John F. *Houdini, Tarzan, and the Perfect Man: The White Male Body and the Challenge of Modernity in America.* New York: Hill and Wang, 2001.

Katz, Friedrich. *The Secret War in Mexico: Europe, the United States, and the Mexican Revolution.* Chicago: University of Chicago Press, 1981.

Keegan, John. *The First World War.* New York: Vintage, 1998.

Kennedy, David M. *Over Here: The First World War and American Society.* New York: Oxford University Press, 1980.

Knight, Alan. *The Mexican Revolution.* 2 vols. Cambridge: Cambridge University Press, 1986.

Knock, Thomas J. *To End All Wars: Woodrow Wilson and the Quest for a New World Order.* Princeton, N.J.: Princeton University Press, 1992.

Kornweibel, Theodore, Jr. *"Investigate Everything": Federal Efforts to Compel Black Loyalty during World War I.* Bloomington: Indiana University Press, 2002.

———. *"Seeing Red": Federal Campaigns against Black Militancy, 1919–1925.* Bloomington: Indiana University Press, 1998.

Leuchtenburg, William E. *The Perils of Prosperity, 1914–32,* 2nd ed. Chicago: University of Chicago Press, 1993.

Link, Arthur S. *Woodrow Wilson and the Progressive Era, 1910–1917.* New York: Harper and Row, 1954.

Márquez, Benjamin. *LULAC: The Evolution of a Mexican American Political Organization.* Austin: University of Texas Press, 1993.

Maverick, Maury. *A Maverick American.* New York: Covici Friede, 1937.

Maxfield, Bernice B., comp. *Camp Bowie, Fort Worth, 1917–1918: An Illustrated History of the 36th Division in the First World War.* Fort Worth, Tex.: by the compiler, 1975.

Mazón, Mauricio. *The Zoot-Suit Riots: The Psychology of Symbolic Annihilation.* Austin: University of Texas Press, 1984.

McAdoo, William Gibbs. *Crowded Years.* Boston: Houghton Mifflin, 1931.

Mead, Gary. *The Doughboys: America and the First World War.* New York: Overlook, 2000.

Meigs, Mark. *Optimism at Armageddon: Voices of American Participants in the First World War.* London: Macmillan, 1997.

Meyer, Michael C. *Huerta: A Political Portrait.* Lincoln: University of Nebraska Press, 1972.

Meyer, Michael C., and William L. Sherman. *The Course of Mexican History,* 5th ed. New York and Oxford: Oxford University Press, 1995.

Mirandé, Alfredo. *Hombres y Machos: Masculinity and Latino Culture.* Boulder, Colo.: Westview Press, 1997.

Montejano, David. *Anglos and Mexicans in the Making of Texas, 1836–1986.* Austin: University of Texas Press, 1987.

Morín, Raúl. *Among the Valiant: Mexican Americans in World War II and Korea.* Los Angeles: Borden, 1963.

Murphy, Paul L. *World War I and the Origin of Civil Liberties in the United States.* New York: Norton, 1979.

Noggle, Burl. *Into the Twenties: The United States from Armistice to Normalcy.* Urbana: University of Illinois Press, 1974.

Paz, Octavio. *The Labyrinth of Solitude.* Translated by Lysander Kemp. New York: Grove, 1961.

Pershing, John J. *My Experiences in the World War.* Vol. 2. New York: Frederick A. Stokes, 1931.

Peterson, H. C., and Gilbert C. Fite. *Opponents of War, 1917–1918.* Seattle: University of Washington Press, 1957.

Polmar, Norman, and Thomas B. Allen. *Spy Book: The Encyclopedia of Espionage.* New York: Random House, 1997.

Pound, Ezra. *Personae: The Collected Poems of Ezra Pound.* New York: New Directions, 1926.

Quirk, Robert E. *An Affair of Honor: Woodrow Wilson and the Occupation of Vera Cruz.* New York: McGraw-Hill, 1964.

Reisler, Mark. *By the Sweat of Their Brow: Mexican Immigrant Labor in the United States, 1900–1940.* Westport, Conn.: Greenwood, 1976.

Rivas-Rodríguez, Maggie, ed. *Mexican Americans and World War II.* Austin: University of Texas Press, 2005.

Saenz, José de la Luz. *Los México-Americanos en la Gran Guerra: Y Su Contingente en Pro de la Democracia, la Humanidad, y la Justicia.* San Antonio: Artes Gráficas, 1933.

Sandos, James A. *Rebellion in the Borderlands: Anarchism and the Plan de San Diego, 1904–1923.* Norman: University of Oklahoma Press, 1992.

Sandoval, Moises. *Our Legacy: The First Fifty Years.* Washington, D.C.: League of United Latin American Citizens—LULAC, 1979.

San Miguel, Guadalupe, Jr. *"Let All of Them Take Heed": Mexican Americans and the Campaign for Educational Equality in Texas, 1910–1981.* Austin: University of Texas Press, 1987.

Shenk, Gerald E. *"Work or Fight!" Race, Gender, and the Draft in World War One.* New York: Palgrave Macmillan, 2005.

Steinson, Barbara Jean. *American Women's Activities in World War I.* New York: Garland, 1982.

Stokes, Anson Phelps. *Educational Plans for the American Army Abroad.* New York: Association Press, 1918.

Taylor, Paul S. *An American-Mexican Frontier.* Chapel Hill: University of North Carolina Press, 1934.

Theoharis, Athan. *The FBI and American Democracy: A Brief Critical History.* Lawrence: University Press of Kansas, 2004.

Thompson, Jerry D. *Laredo: A Pictorial History.* Norfolk: Donning, 1986.

———. *Mexican Texans in the Union Army.* El Paso: Texas Western Press, 1986.

———. *Vaqueros in Blue and Gray: Mexican Texans in the Civil War.* Austin: Presidial Press, 1976. Reprint, Austin: State House Press, 2000.

———. *Warm Weather and Bad Whiskey: The 1886 Laredo Election Riot.* El Paso: Texas Western Press, 1991.

Trujillo, Charley. *Chicanos in Viet Nam.* San Jose, Calif.: Chusma House Publications, 1990.

Tuchman, Barbara W. *The Zimmermann Telegram,* Trade ed. New York: Ballantine Books, 1985.

Watkins, Glenn. *Proof through the Night: Music and the Great War.* Berkeley: University of California Press, 2003.

Webb, Walter Prescott. *The Texas Rangers: A Century of Frontier Defense.* Austin: University of Texas Press, 1935.

Wecter, Dixon. *When Johnny Comes Marching Home.* Boston: Houghton Mifflin, 1944.

White, Lonnie J. *The 90th Division in World War I: The Texas-Oklahoma Draft Division in the Great War.* Manhattan, Kans.: Sunflower University Press, 1996.

———. *Panthers to Arrowheads: The 36th (Texas-Oklahoma) Division in World War I.* Austin: Presidial Press, 1984.

Ybarra, Lea. *Vietnam Veteranos: Chicanos Recall the War.* Foreword by Edward James Olmos. Austin: University of Texas Press, 2004.

Young, Arthur P. *Books for Sammies: The American Library Association and World War I.* Pittsburgh: Beta Phi Mu, 1981.

Zeiger, Susan. *In Uncle Sam's Service: Women Workers with the American Expeditionary Force, 1917–1919.* Ithaca, N.Y.: Cornell University Press, 1999).

SELECTIONS FROM COLLECTED WORKS

Kanellos, Nicolás. "A Socio-Historic Study of Hispanic Newspapers in the United States." In *Recovering the U.S. Hispanic Literary Heri-*

tage, ed. Ramón Gutiérrez and Genaro Padilla, 110–17. Houston, Tex: Arte Público Press, 1993.

Millett, Allan R. "American Military History: Over the Top." In *The State of American History,* ed. Herbert J. Bass, 157–82. Chicago: Quadrangle Press, 1970.

"Nuevo Corrido de Laredo." In *The New Anthology of American Poetry.* Vol. 2, *Modernisms 1900–1950,* ed. Stephen Gould Axelrod, Camille Roman, and Thomas Travisano, 526. New Brunswick, N.J.: Rutgers University Press, 2005.

"Registro de 1918." In *The New Anthology of American Poetry.* Vol. 2, *Modernisms 1900–1950,* ed. Stephen Gould Axelrod, Camille Roman, and Thomas Travisano, 524. New Brunswick, N.J.: Rutgers University Press, 2005.

Romo, Ricardo. "The Urbanization of Southwestern Chicanos in the Early Twentieth Century." In *New Directions in Chicano Scholarship,* ed. Ricardo Romo and Raymond A. Paredes, 183–207. La Jolla, Calif.: University of California at San Diego, 1978.

Saenz, J. Luz. "Racial Discrimination." In *Are We Good Neighbors?* ed. Alonso S. Perales. San Antonio: Artes Gráficas, 1948.

"Los Sediciosos." In *Major Problems in Mexican American History,* ed. Zaragosa Vargas, *Major Problems in American History,* 214–15. Boston and New York: Houghton Mifflin, 1999.

Zamora, Emilio. "Fighting on Two Fronts: José de la Luz Saenz and the Language of the Mexican-American Civil Rights Movement." In *Recovering the U.S. Hispanic Literary Heritage,* vol. 4, ed. José F. Aranda, Jr., and Silvio Torres-Saillant, 214–39. Houston: Arte Público, 2002.

THESES AND DISSERTATIONS

Baldwin, Fred Davis. "The American Enlisted Man in World War I." Ph.D. diss., Princeton University, 1964.

Bush, Mary Elizabeth. "El Paso County, Texas, in the First World War." Master's thesis, University of Texas at Austin, 1950.

Dickens, Edwin Larry. "The Political Role of Mexican Americans in San Antonio, Texas." Ph.D. diss., Texas Tech University, 1969.

Downing de De Juana, Ana Cristina. "Intermarriage in Hidalgo County, 1860 to 1900." Master's thesis, University of Texas–Pan American, 1998.

Garza, James Alexander. "On the Edge of a Storm: Laredo and the Mexican Revolution, 1910–1917." Master's thesis, Texas A&M International University, 1996.

González, Jovita. "Social Life in Cameron, Starr and Zapata Counties." Master's thesis, University of Texas at Austin, 1930.

McKay, R. Reynolds. "Texas Mexican Repatriation during the Great Depression." Ph.D. diss., University of Oklahoma, 1982.

Milner, Elmer Ray. "An Agonizing Evolution: A History of the Texas National Guard, 1900–1945." Ph.D. diss., North Texas State University, 1979.

Orozco, Cynthia. "The Origins of the League of United Latin American Citizens (LULAC) and the Mexican American Civil Rights Movement in Texas with an Analysis of Women's Political Participation in a Gendered Context, 1910–1929." Ph.D. diss., University of California at Los Angeles, 1992.

Pycior, Julie Leininger. "*La Raza* Organizes: Mexican American Life in San Antonio, 1915–1930, as Reflected in *Mutualista* Activities." Ph.D. diss., University of Notre Dame, 1979.

Turner, Oran Elijah. "History of the Texas State Council of Defense." Master's thesis, University of Texas at Austin, 1926.

Williams, Chad Louis. "Torchbearers of Democracy: The First World War and the Figure of the African-American Soldier." Ph.D. diss., Princeton University, 2004.

Index

ISBN-13: 978-1-60344-136-0
ISBN-10: 1-60344-136-0
52995
9 781603 441360